Drawing Proper
Drawing Improper

Kevin Hirth

AXIOMATIC
EDITIONS

Proper / Improper

Architects work through drawing. This statement carries no intended polemic, nor is there a clear definition of what drawing means. The act of resolving a three-dimensional object into a two-dimensional one is simply what we do. The distinction between correct and incorrect ways of doing this is becoming increasingly muddy and meaningless. My old copy of Ramsey & Sleeper's *Architectural Graphic Standards* is not necessarily anathema. It can coexist with a wide array of other two-dimensional approaches. Ultimately, the ways we work are designed to convey a spatial or formal impression, emerging from a process of translation that aims to generate something imbued with greater complexity. To me, that is essentially the point. Some ways of working serve a specific goal, while others are pursued for their exploratory value. This does not imply that one approach has greater autonomy or value over another—that a particular method is more proper or improper than another. If anything, architectural drawing defies such boundaries in pursuit of a greater cause: to communicate and interpret.

I suppose the audience of any given drawing becomes important. Are you presenting your drawing to someone who needs to derive utility from it? Is it an implementable contract, essentially an instruction manual for assembly? Is it

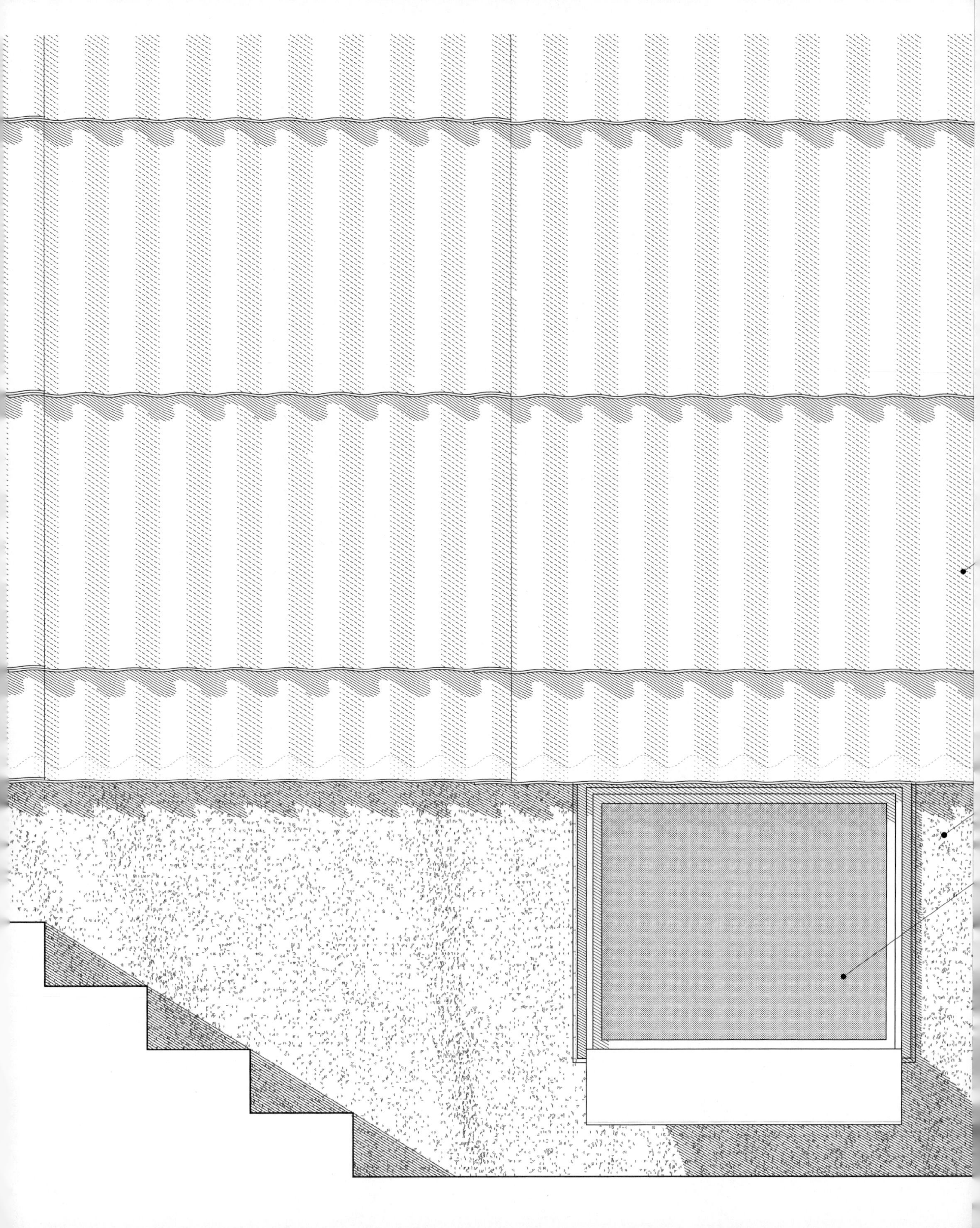

approaches to how architects communicate. I state this directly so that, as you browse the works, you make no mistake in interpretation. Numerous disciplinary discussions focus on how different the practice is today, emphasizing that architects no longer operate around a collective set of methods or stylistic leanings. This collection is a conversation on the valor and grandeur of things, both empty and full. It is an open celebration of architecture as a practice that allows for obsessive individuation in the pursuit of a unique voice. In short, it offers both a proper and an improper look at architectural drawing as something that can and should exist within and outside the exercises of pragmatics. This is a catalog of some things dutiful and some things mischievous. The works and prompt were originally displayed in a gallery exhibit at the University of Colorado Denver. Anca Matyiku, my collaborator and partner in the exhibit, initiated conversations around pragmatism and the value of frivolousness in our profession, prompting this collection of work. The exhibit, installed in a gallery with only eleven feet of blank wall space, necessitated the creation of a room within a room, with walls clad in black bituminous roofing paper. Up for only six days, the show closed on March 6, 2020, along with the building that housed it. This book honors the work and serves as a record and meditation on the significance and idiosyncrasies of drawing in our time.

–KH

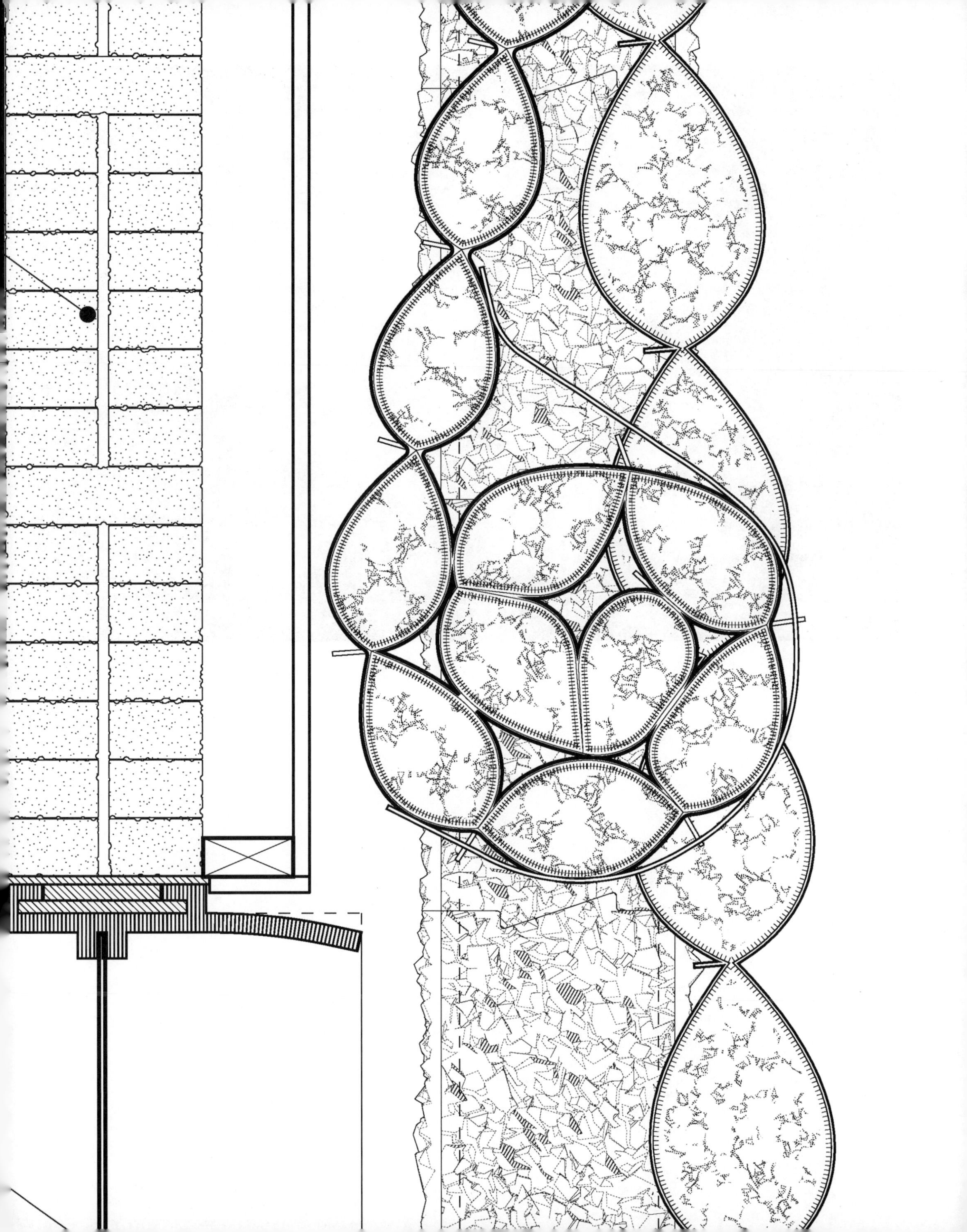

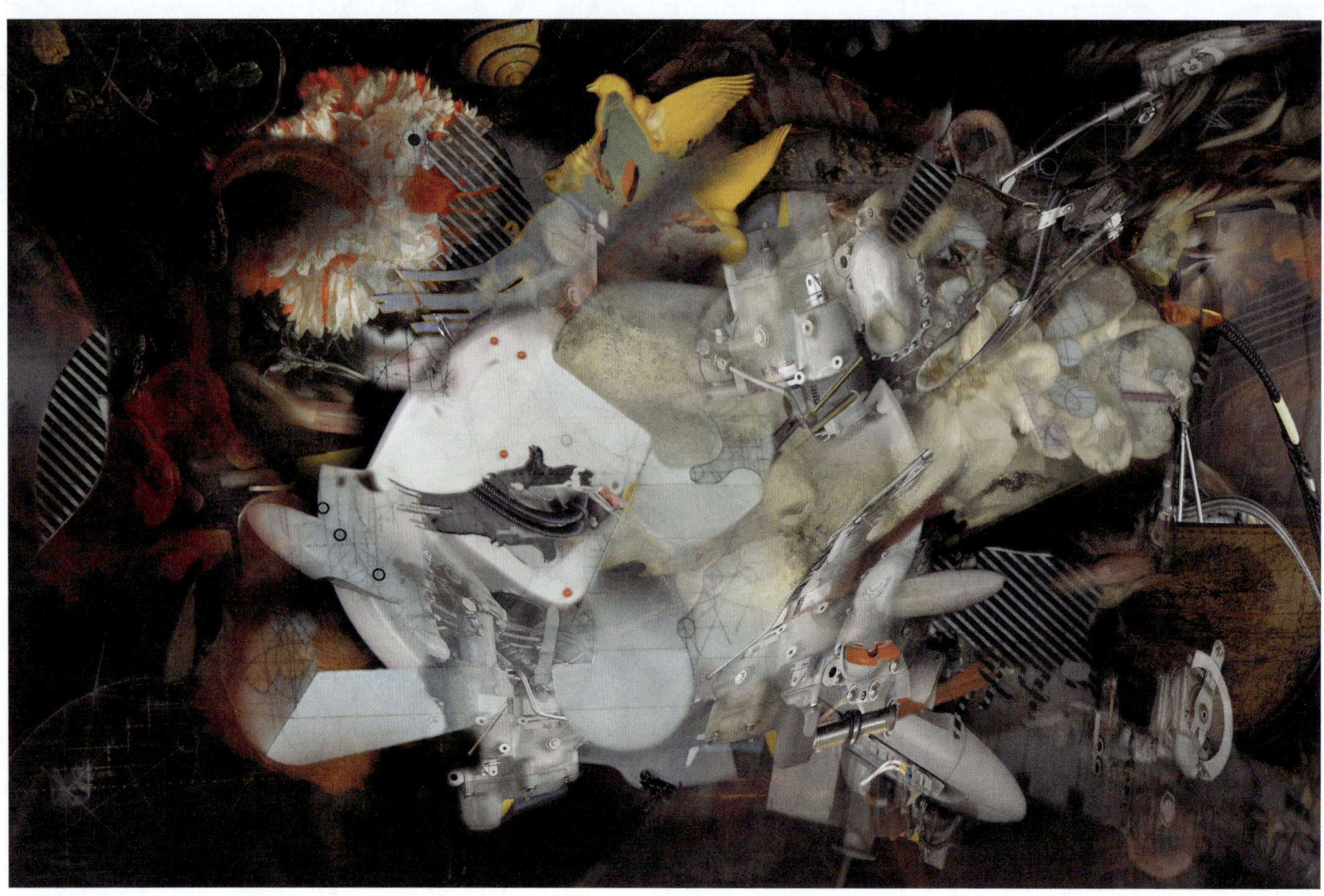

The image presents a composite scene featuring blended figures of wildly different and ambiguous origins. It reveals compositional cues that extend the architectural into the realms of the biological and mechanical. The lighter center contains distorted objects resembling arcane machinery, which bleed into opalescent, egg-like surfaces. This center gradually fades into a dark background filled with overlapping objects and textures, blending seemingly lifelike figures. Joyful contradictions emerge as a bird's head transforms into a target encircled by flower petals, and previously legible objects are revealed as vaguely baroque fabric patterns. The use of texture mapping compresses the image's depth, creating a deliberately flattened visual field.

Drawing in collaboration with Mark West.

Perry Kulper

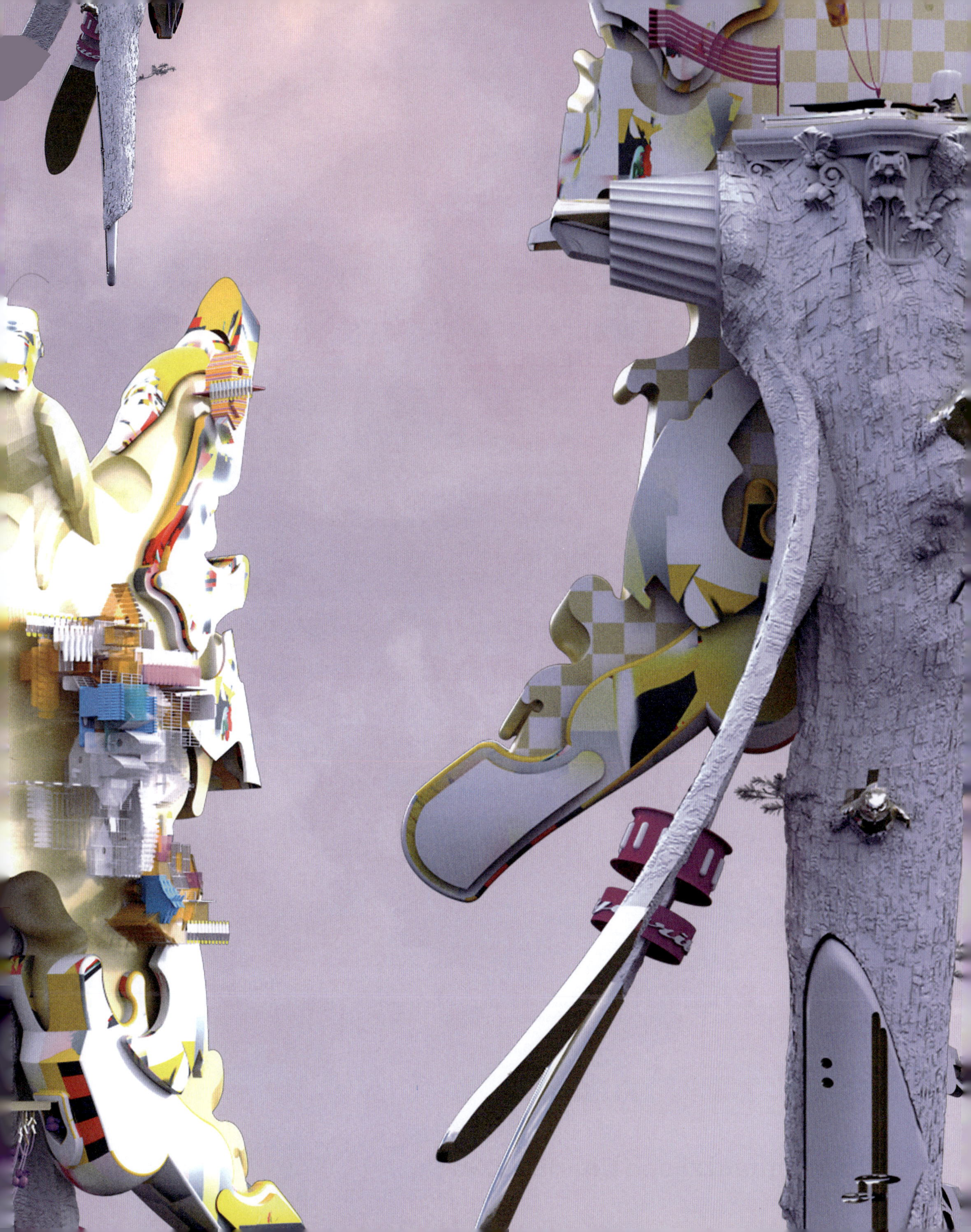

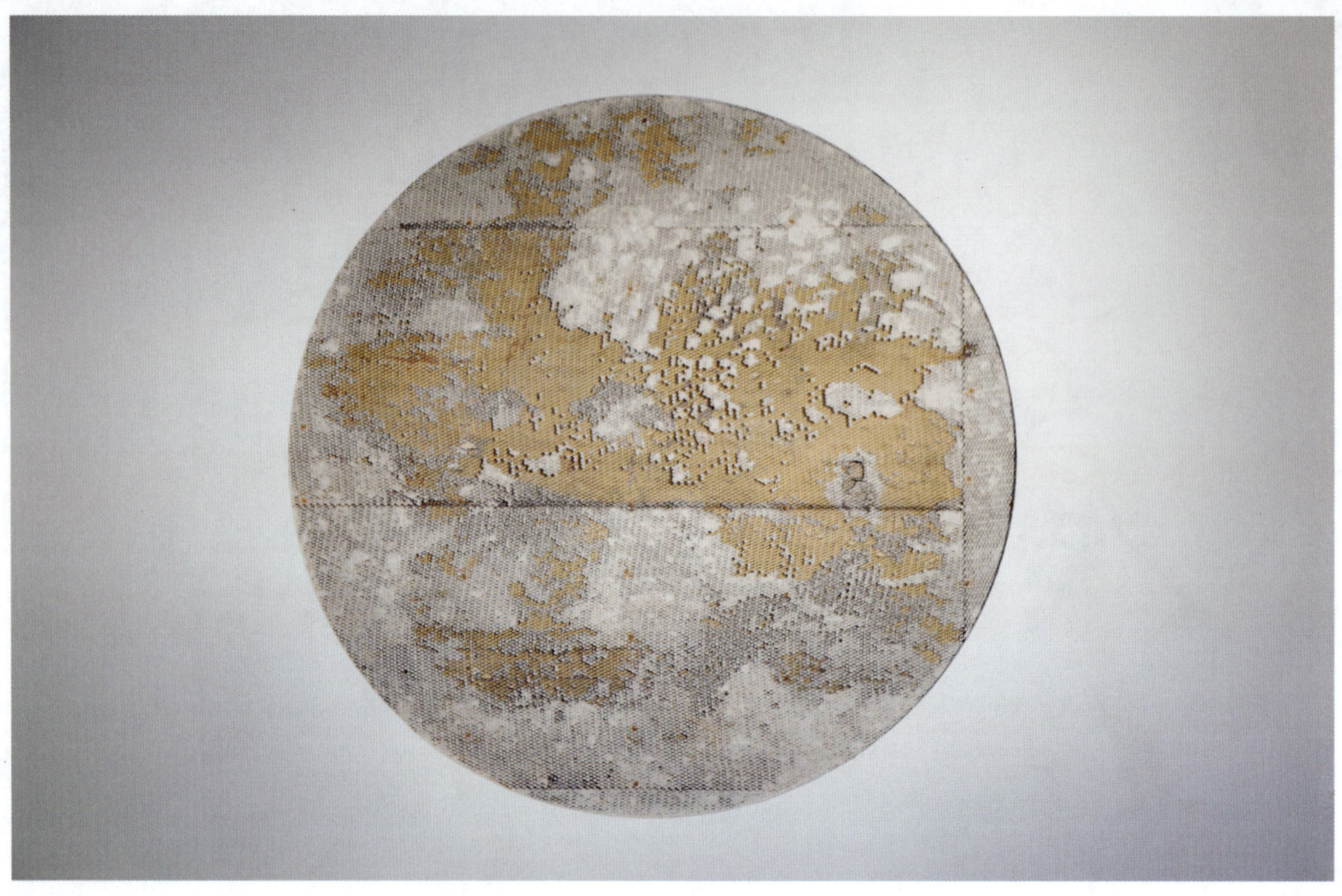

The image, depicting a textured circle inscribed on a vignetted grey expanse, might initially read as an imagined lunar projection or a pixelated meteorological diagram. Closer inspection reveals this to be a photograph of a wall with plaster removed, exposing a subsurface of fine metal mesh over wood planking. What appeared to be a lunar surface or clouds above a planet is in fact the remnants of plaster pulling away from the underlying structure. The image has an unresolved, ambiguous quality, simultaneously appearing sharply focused and detailed, while also blurred, as if caught in a moment of uncertain motion.

Photographs by Travis Roozée.

Frank Fantauzzi and Charlie O'Geen

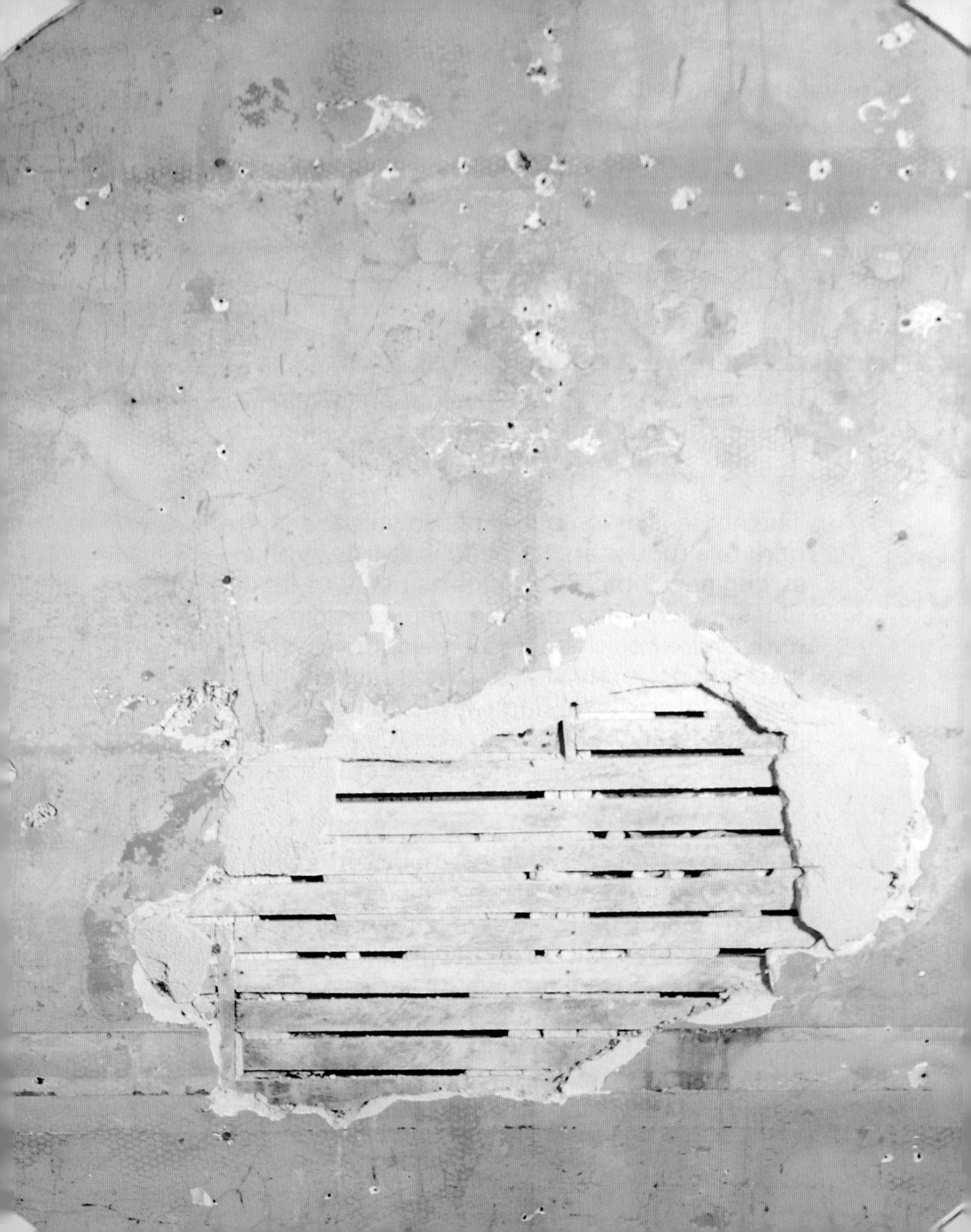

The valor of empty things

According to legend, Eero Saarinen would ask applicants seeking jobs in his Michigan office to draw a horse during their interview. Apparently, Saarinen could determine the quality of the applicant within the first few lines. Setting aside the obvious issues with this prompt and the privileges implied in its origin, consider for a moment the image of a horse in your mind:

The horse is a rich blend of brown shades, from dark to a ruddy tan. Its build is sturdy, with a strong neck holding a mane as black as its deep, glossy eyes, which are seemingly fixed on you. Its hooves are positioned as if it's about to move, yet it stands perfectly still, with its tail flicking at regular intervals. A single large white spot marks its back haunch. Standing about five feet tall, its long head is turned in your direction, looming yet graceful.

The horse cannot be fully visually represented while preserving both the precision of its definition and the clarity of the effects of its qualities that defy measurement. In short, my medium is limited in its power to translate what I see in my mind. Neither objective nor precise, my words fall short of whatever real or imagined thing to which they refer. Similarly, my drawings, representational or otherwise, are incapable of capturing the horse.

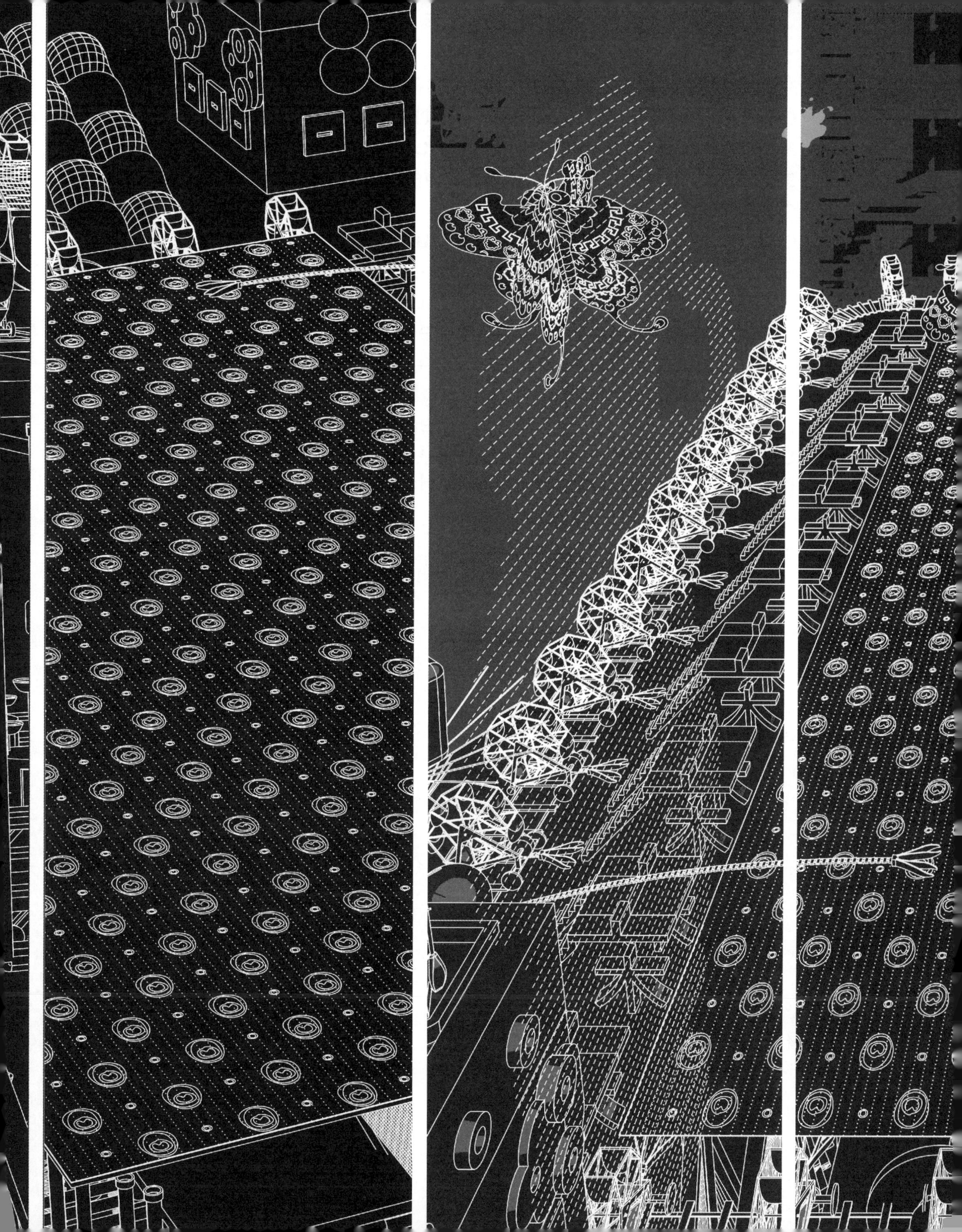

Allowing for mischief in ideas enables the pursuit of interpretation and translation rather than a finite, often disappointing, completeness. After all, no matter how dutifully we work to describe our intents, there will always be an exception: a corner under-labeled, a texture ambiguously applied, a value under-exposed. By setting aside the pragmatics of representation and allowing for interpretative mischief, we deepen our work rather than foreshorten it. Architecture has always been beholden to the pragmatics of its translation in the field; however, it has never been defined by those expectations. In the end, the value is the thing itself—be it a drawing, a building, or a horse.

–KH

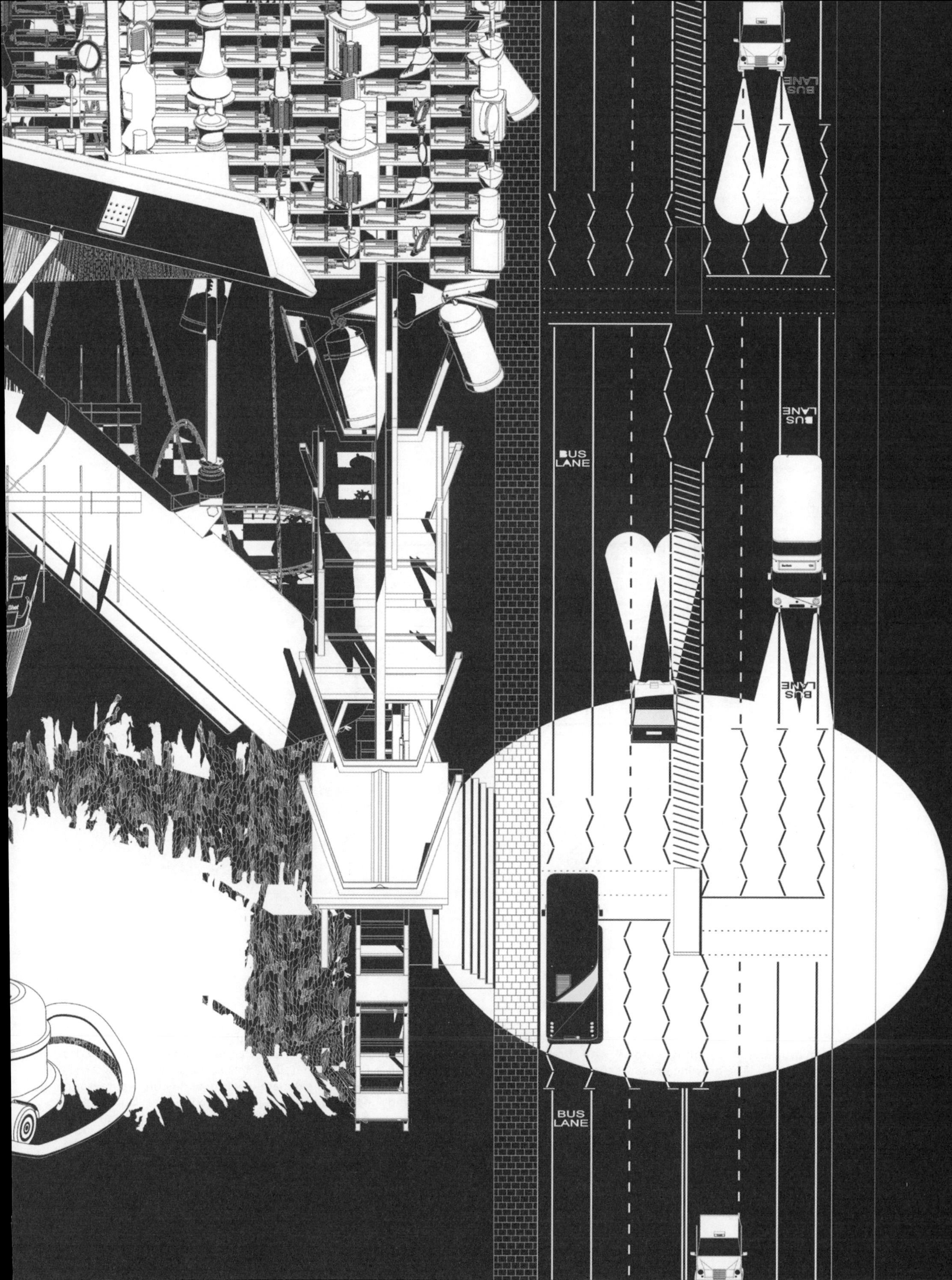
BUS
LANE
BUS
LANE

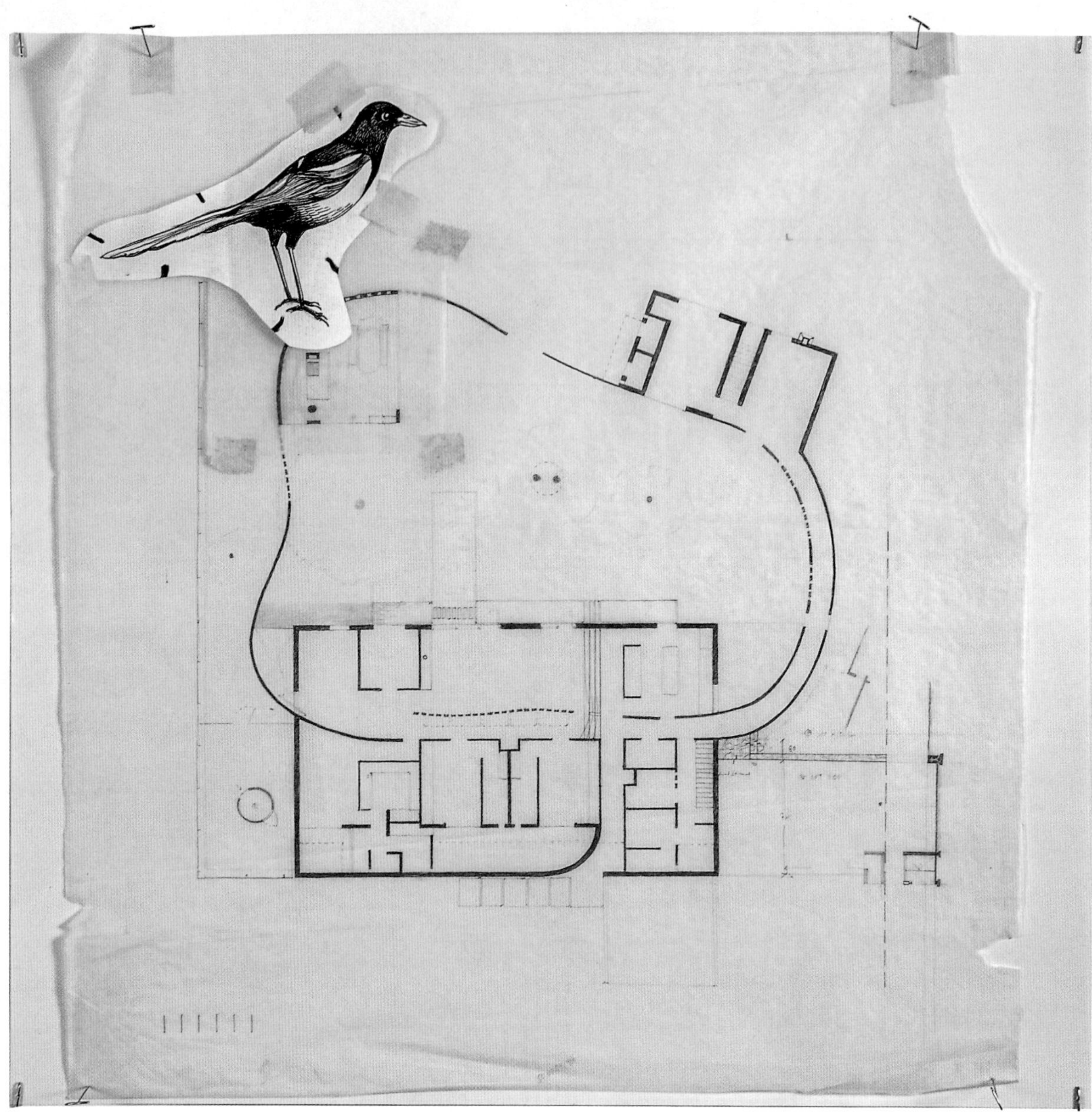

This floor plan, hand-drawn in graphite on trace paper, bears the marks of the design process—it is slightly rumpled, with a fragment of another plan taped into it. The drawing presents three distinct enclosures linked by a meandering wall. The home at the bottom is orderly and rectilinear but pierced by the irregular curve of the wall, forming an unconventional threshold between exterior and interior. The second structure is pushed to the outer boundary of the wall, while the third, more tentative in its drawing, mischievously features the cutout of a bird. This playful intrusion contrasts with the clean, untouched, and precise semi-circular enclosure in the paired drawing. Imbued both with a living vitality and a static architectural form, the drawing encapsulates the dynamic nature of design, where fragments and interventions build toward a final, evolving idea. This sketch's layered complexity replaces the clarity and order of the paired drawing, reflecting two different approaches to design.

LANZA Atelier

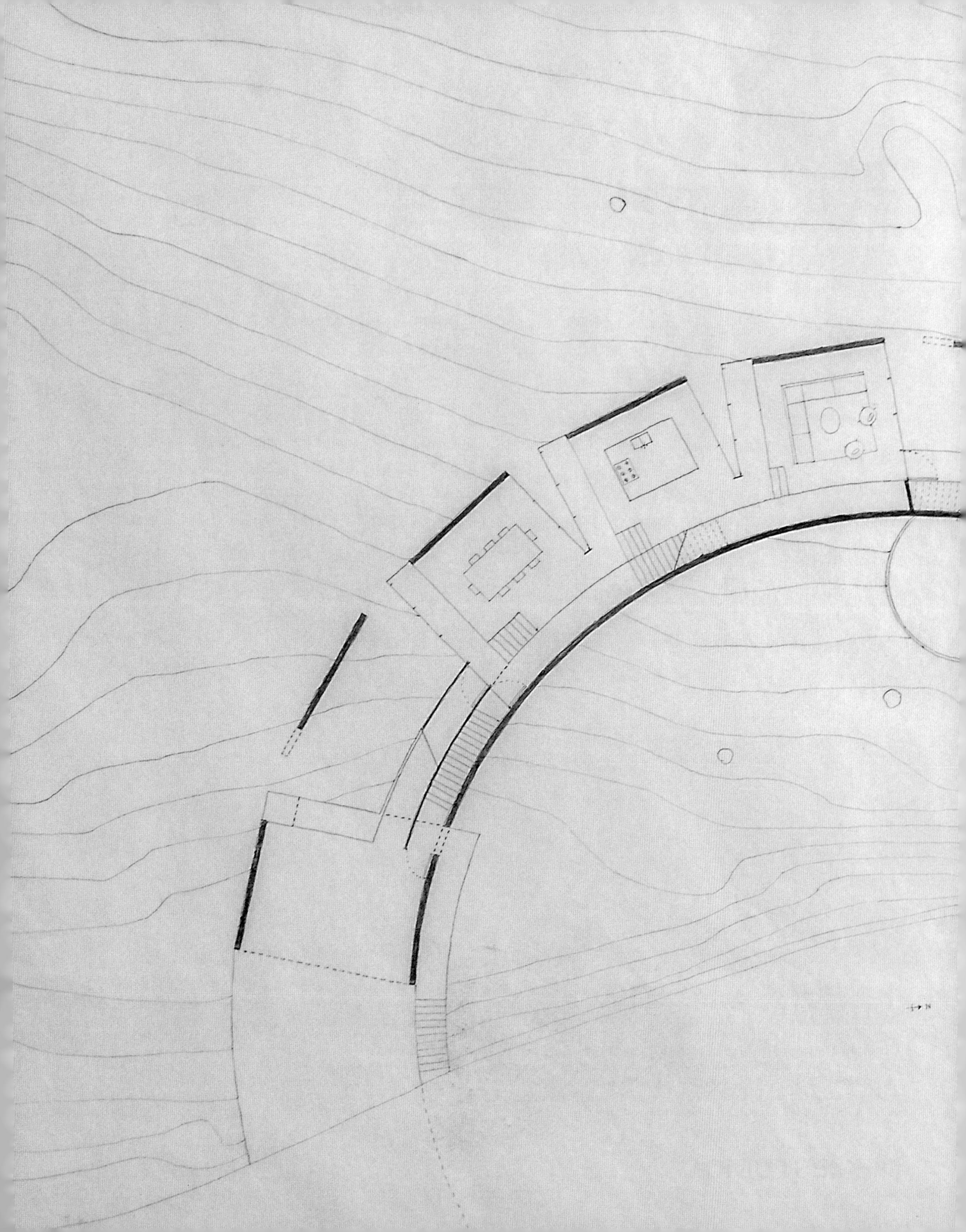

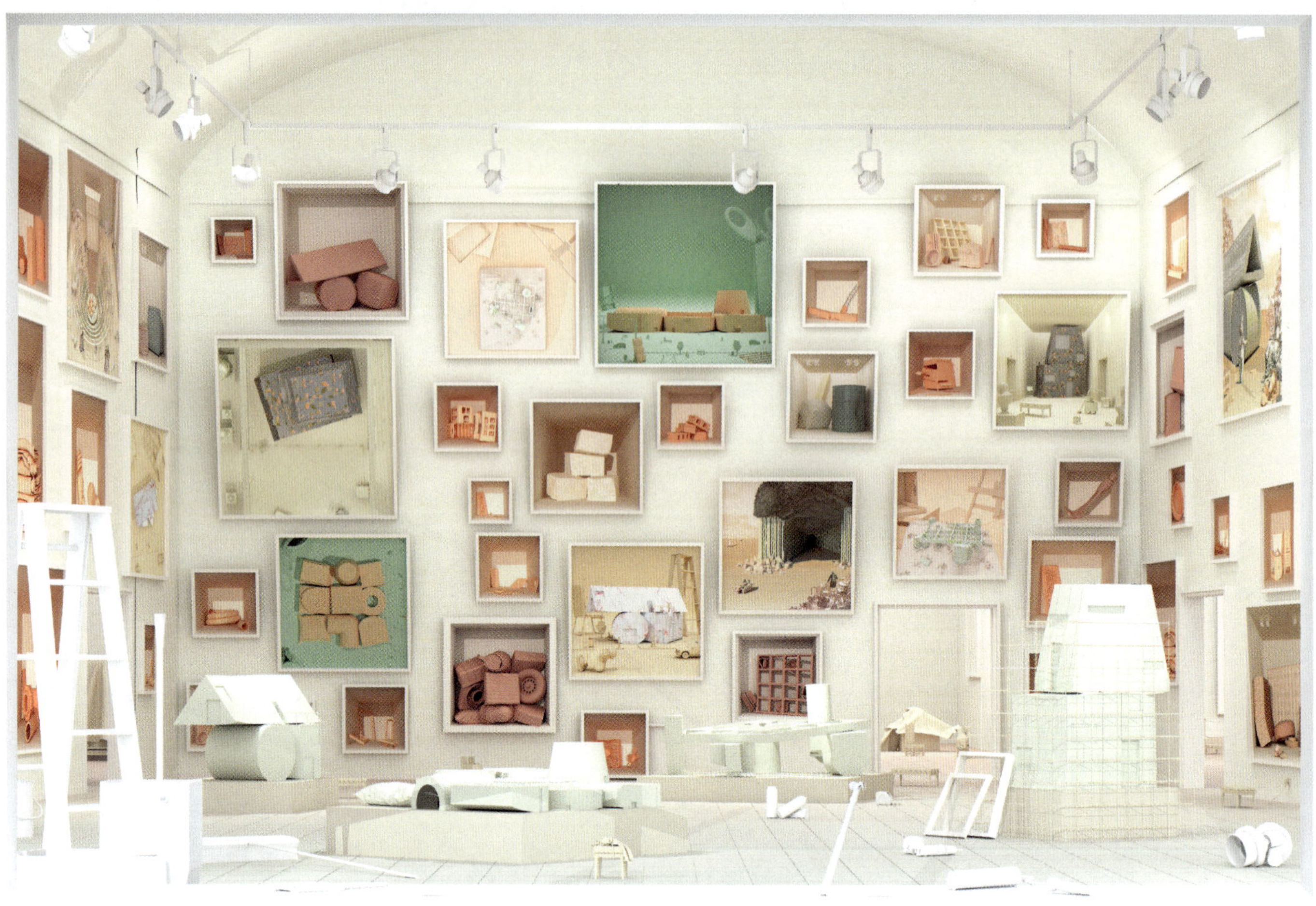

A rendering of a room is scattered with objects: models, furniture, fixtures, and a ladder. Surrounding this seemingly haphazard assortment are three walls covered with frames. But things are not so straightforward—while some picture frames hang on the wall, others are penetrations, breaking the plane and creating spaces filled with more objects—bricks, tools, a box fan. The overall effect is one of coexisting contrast—verisimilitude and artificiality, order and informality, flatness and depth, the intentional and the accidental.

This is a complicated choreography of objects, a curated collection carefully composed on a stage, designed to play with our expectations of the familiar and the strange. The sense that the image is delivered unaltered as a rendering adds to the impression of completeness. There is an authenticity at play in the image that denies a complex multi-platform software workflow in its production.

NEMESTUDIO

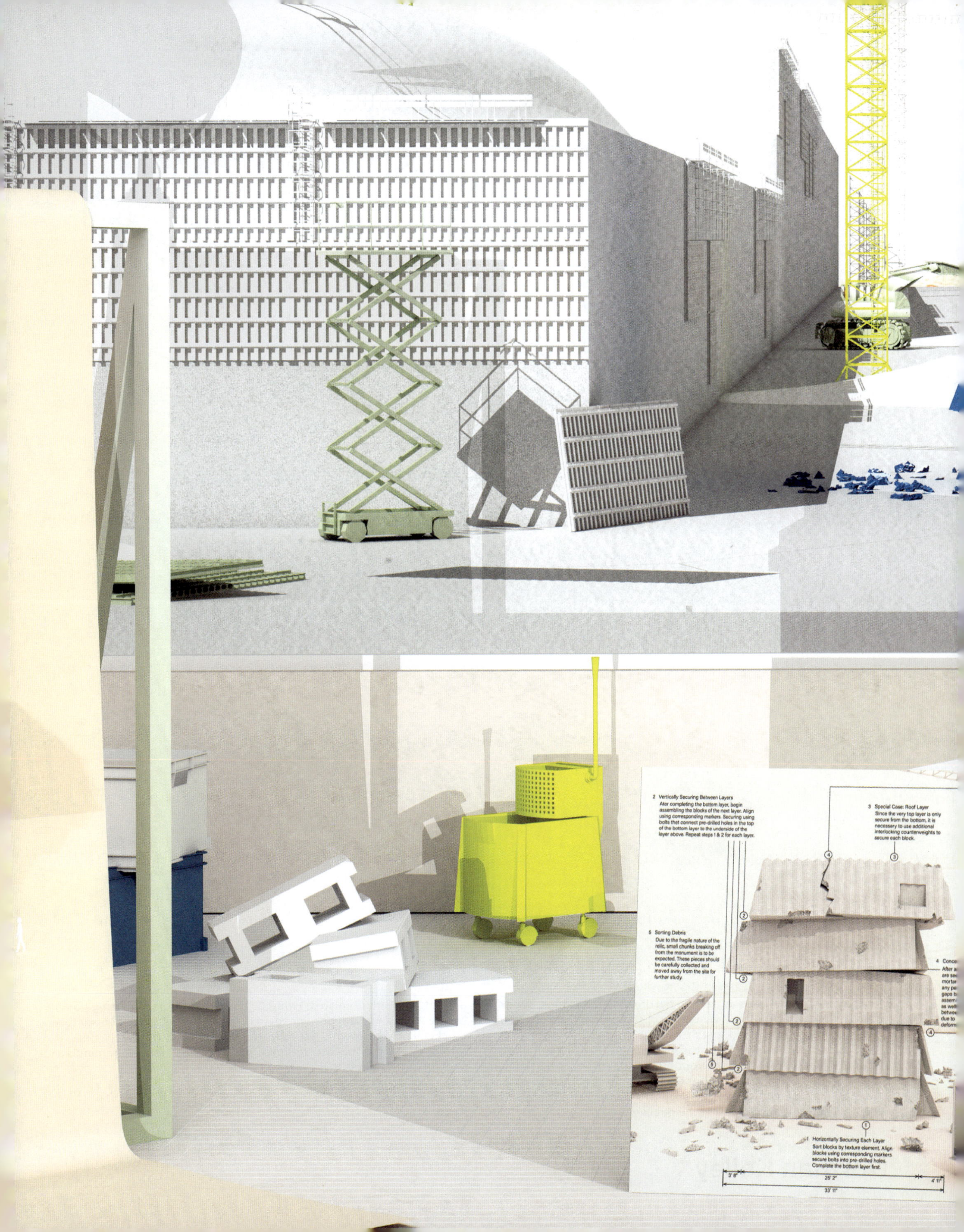
2 Vertically Securing Between Layers
Ater completing the bottom layer, begin assembling the blocks of the next layer. Align using corresponding markers. Securing using bolts that connect pre-drilled holes in the top of the bottom layer to the underside of the layer above. Repeat steps 1 & 2 for each layer.
3 Special Case: Roof Layer
Since the very top layer is only secure from the bottom, it is necessary to use additional interlocking counterweights to secure each block.
5 Sorting Debris
Due to the fragile nature of the relic, small chunks breaking off from the monument is to be expected. These pieces should be carefully collected and moved away from the site for further study.
1 Horizontally Securing Each Layer
Sort blocks by texture element. Align blocks using corresponding markers secure bolts into pre-drilled holes. Complete the bottom layer first.
3' 8"
25' 2"
4' 11"
33' 11"

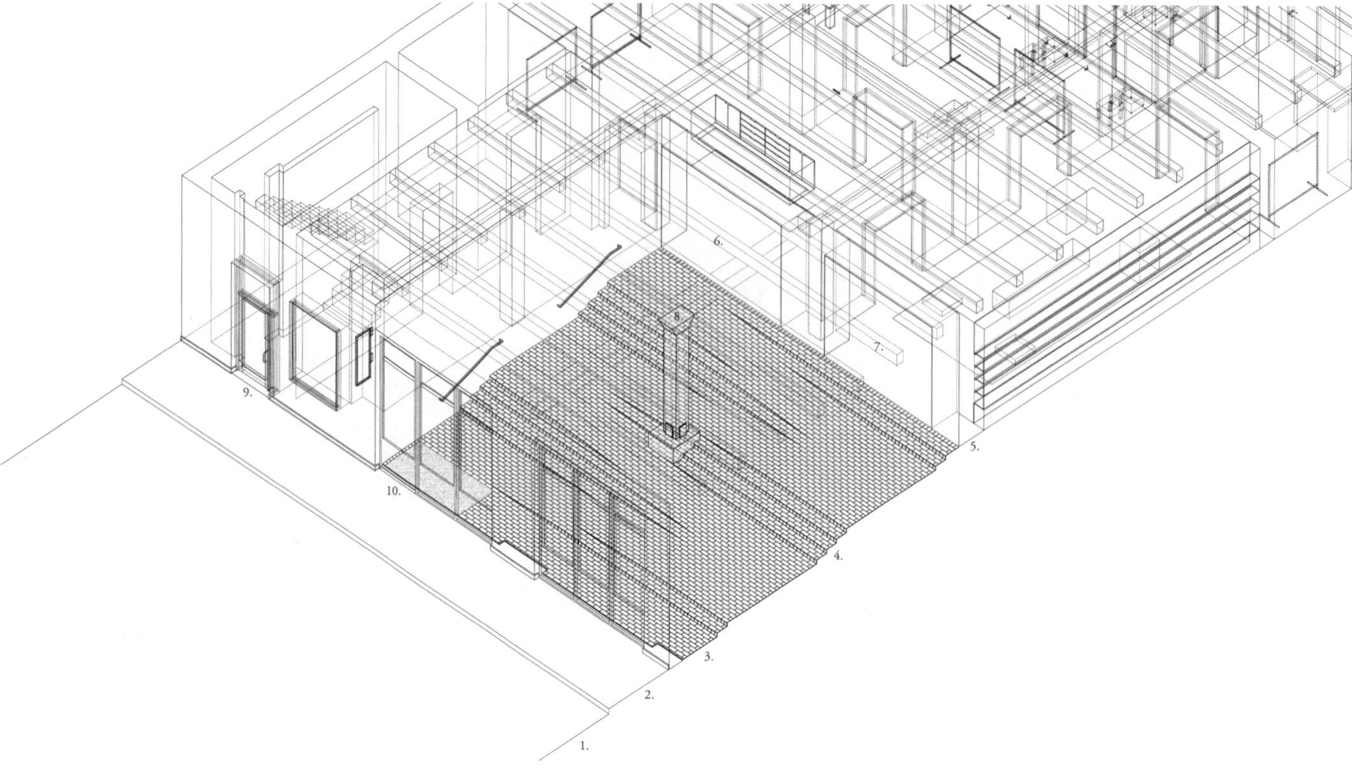

1. Street (0'-0")
2. Sidewalk (+0'-6")
3. Vestibule (+0'-7")
4. Stair-Ramp (1:20 Inclines)
5. Merchandise Level (+3'-7")
6. Interior Storefront (Left)
7. Interior Storefront (Right)
8. Existing Column
9. Existing Private Building Entry
10. Main Store Entry

This isometric view reads as a technical drawing for a store, superimposing lines that articulate a vast array of components across a series of rooms. In the foreground, a stair-ramp is drawn with obsessive attention to detail, emphasizing the viewer's intimate awareness of brickwork. Peculiarly, the brick continues beneath the central column, literally undermining it and further elevating the significance of the stair-ramp. A clear connection emerges between the craft of building with highly articulated brick and the necessity of communicating that craft through precise drawing. In some ways, this rendering obviates the need for a conventional plan or section, as it could convey to a skilled mason the full extent of the brick plane. Ultimately, one wonders if the true attraction of this store lies in the merchandise for sale or the space itself.

Norman Kelley

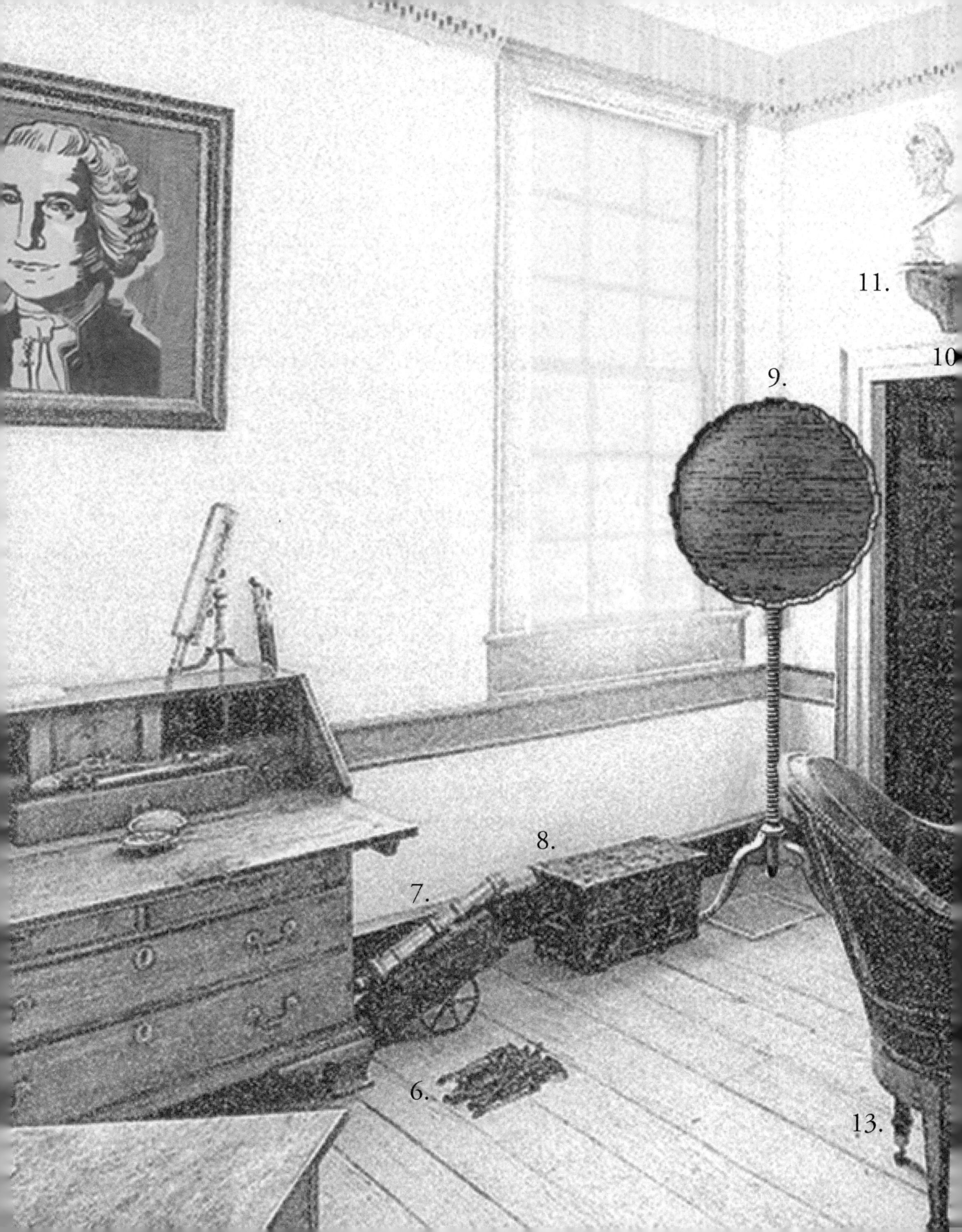
11.
10
9.
8.
7.
6.
13.

We are all romantics and that is fine

Let's take a moment to parse some subtleties of definition. So far, the content you have encountered has intentionally situated all forms of architectural production under the specific category of drawing. The intent is to give equal significance to architecture's diverse modes of production. However, it would be misleading not to draw out the specific idiosyncrasies within the subset of image generation. The image, understood broadly, can be further categorized into various pursuits, many of which carry forward legacies of visual information that sit outside or parallel to the discipline itself.

After all, the image of our present is a stone-cold, inanimate, non-existent, fizzing thing. It is perfectly suited to a life of duplicity. Nowadays, the image appears much more comfortable flitting across a screen than fixed in a frame and hung from a nail in a museum. Better to live fast and die young than suffer the indignity of stasis, only to watch the world move on without you. At its core, the image of today increasingly relies on the subjectivity of the observer. This inherent distortion invites multiple readings based on the ambiguity of the creator's intent.

Over the past fifteen years, the role of the image has transformed remarkably, evolving from a record of the past to one that is seemingly fluid and atemporal. Images are shared and distributed virtually,

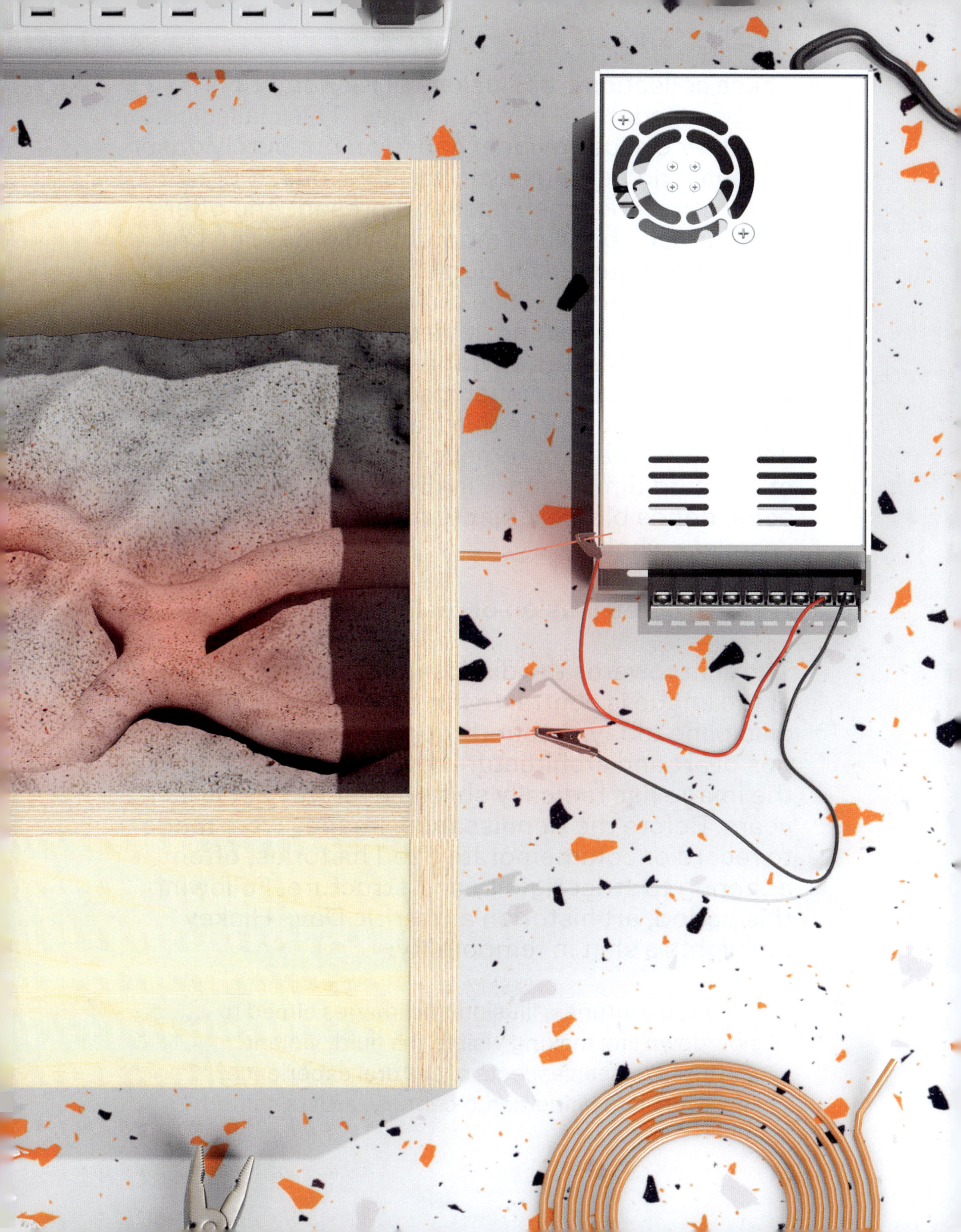

These collections, or illusions of reorientation, can be categorized into four types. This classification is neither exclusive nor exhaustive, but purely observational and perhaps even mischievous. It draws connections between past and present and offers comparisons between moments in time. The first type, a constructed illusion of realism, is pervasive in contemporary practice but is waning as it becomes exhausted. The second, a manufactured context of structure, creates an impression of a conceptual whole, creating relationships between seemingly unrelated objects. The third, an illusion of space, flattens the image to remove the clear registration of the third dimension. Finally, a camouflage of coincidence blends objects together, creating a seamless whole.

A constructed illusion of realism.

The shift towards the disposability and malleability of the image is central to the challenges facing our discipline today. A tour through the past five centuries of art and architecture reveals how the role of the image has radically shifted over the last fifteen years. Before the Renaissance, images were made to record or commemorate fixed histories, often adhering to strict rigidity and structure. Following this period, art historian and critic Dave Hickey highlights a shift in temporality:

> For three centuries, illusionistic images aimed to slow down life, making visible the fluid, violent, and often unseen aspects of cultural experience. However, in the nineteenth century, artists shifted

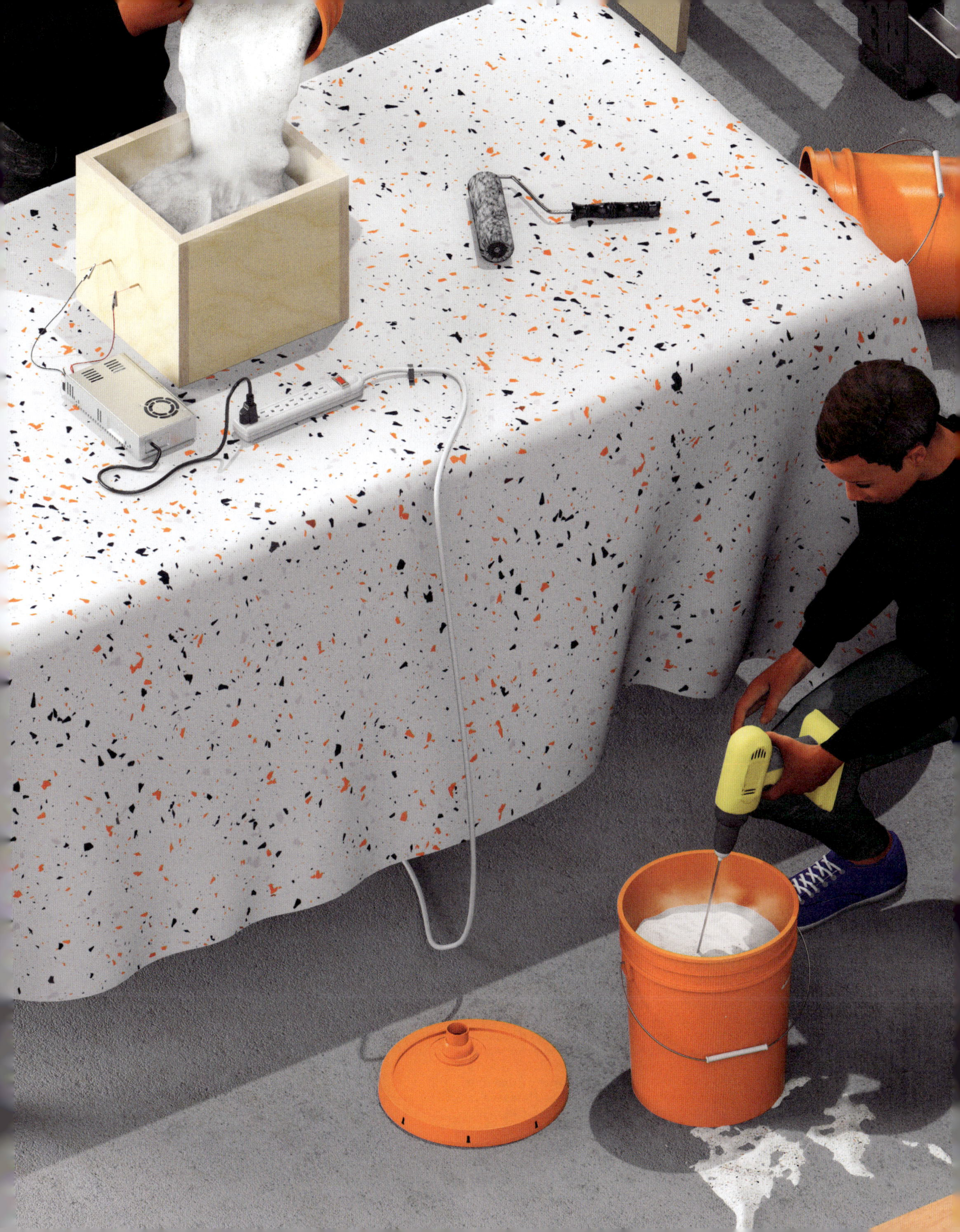

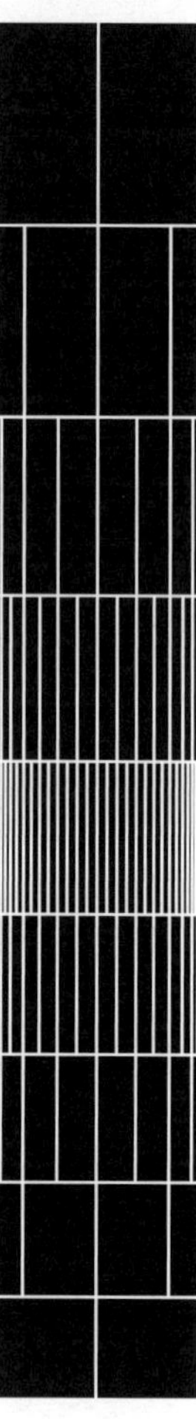

This vector drawing presents an array of black rectangular fills against a white background, lacking a clear orientation or singular, coherent form and encouraging interpretive flexibility. The diminishing scale of these fills along the horizontal axis suggests a subtle convexity, which could imply the image of a column or simply a collection of figures on a static plane. The abstraction within the vector format opens a dialogue about resolution, image, and interpretation across media. Here, the resolution of the depicted object aligns directly with the resolution of the drawing itself, creating an infinitely discrete yet paradoxically scaleless image. This invites viewers to question whether they see an object of specific scale or merely a field of compositional elements that refuses fixed interpretation.

WOJR

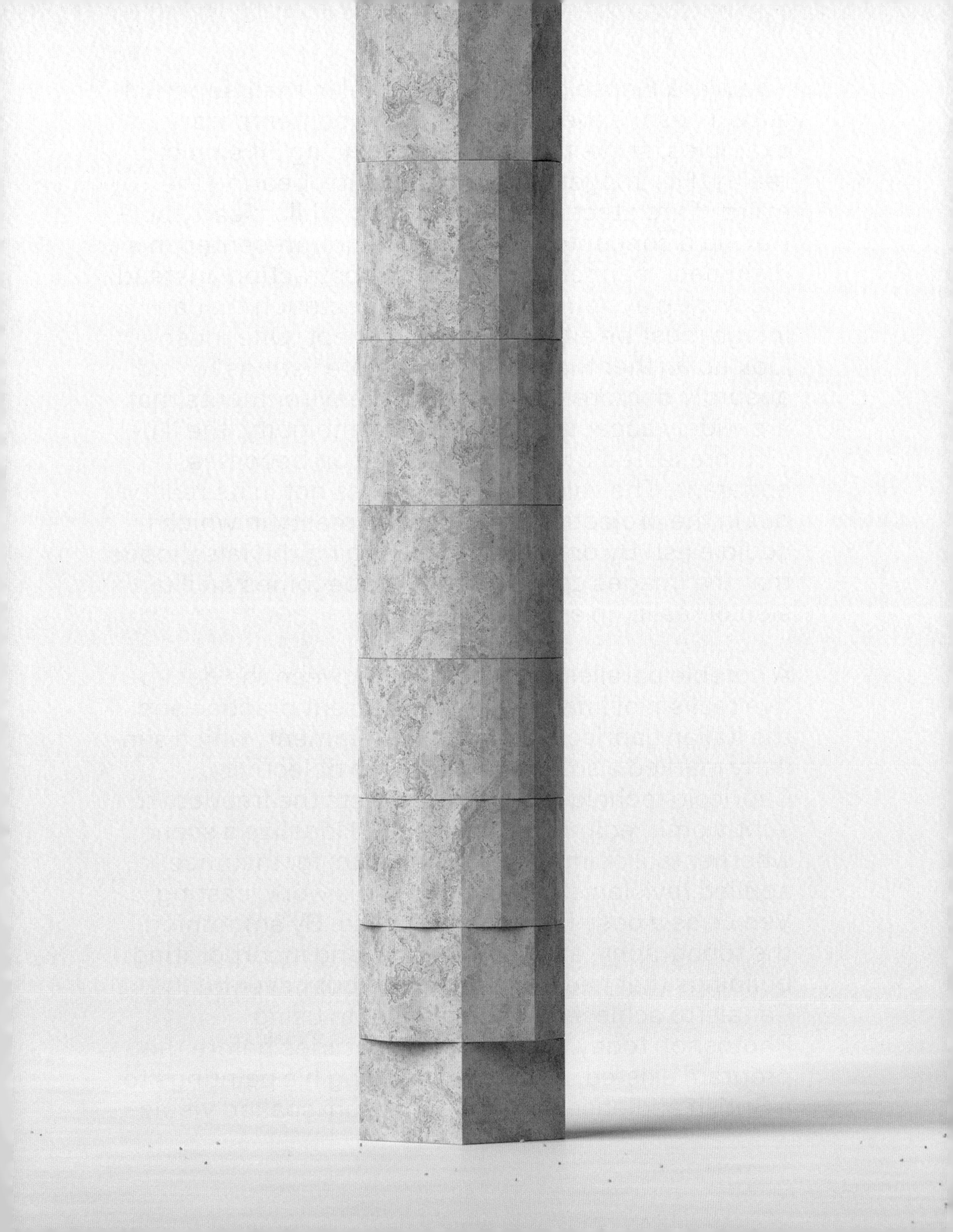

The Mask House, which are playful in their superficiality. These renderings, like many contemporary examples, strive to create a convincing illusion of reality. His images display virtuosity, bearing the traits of architectural photography while clearly portraying a conceptual project. It is not presented in a dishonest manner that hides its abstraction. Instead, the work plays on our current expectation that an image must be either authentic or not. One must look no further than local real estate listings to find absurdly doctored photos of real environments that are widely accepted. Due to this ambiguity, the illusion presented by William O'Brien Jr. becomes apparent. The value of the work lies not in its reality, but in the projection of a possible reality in which it could exist. By openly acknowledging the falsehoods that the images convey, the work becomes an illusion of reality in a state of flux.

A notable parallel can be drawn between the deceptive realism of images found in current practice and the Italian capriccio of the Enlightenment, which similarly marked a soft departure from objectivity. Capriccio techniques granted artists the freedom to subtly omit, edit, reconstitute, and idealize a scene, whether real or imagined. Canaletto, for instance, applied revisionist techniques in his work, casting Venice as a post-Palladian paradise. By smoothing the topography, altering facades, and incorporating buildings that had been designed but never built, Canaletto achieved effects similar to using Photoshop today, nearly three centuries before the program existed, all the while selling his paintings to a British audience hungry for his sun-soaked vistas

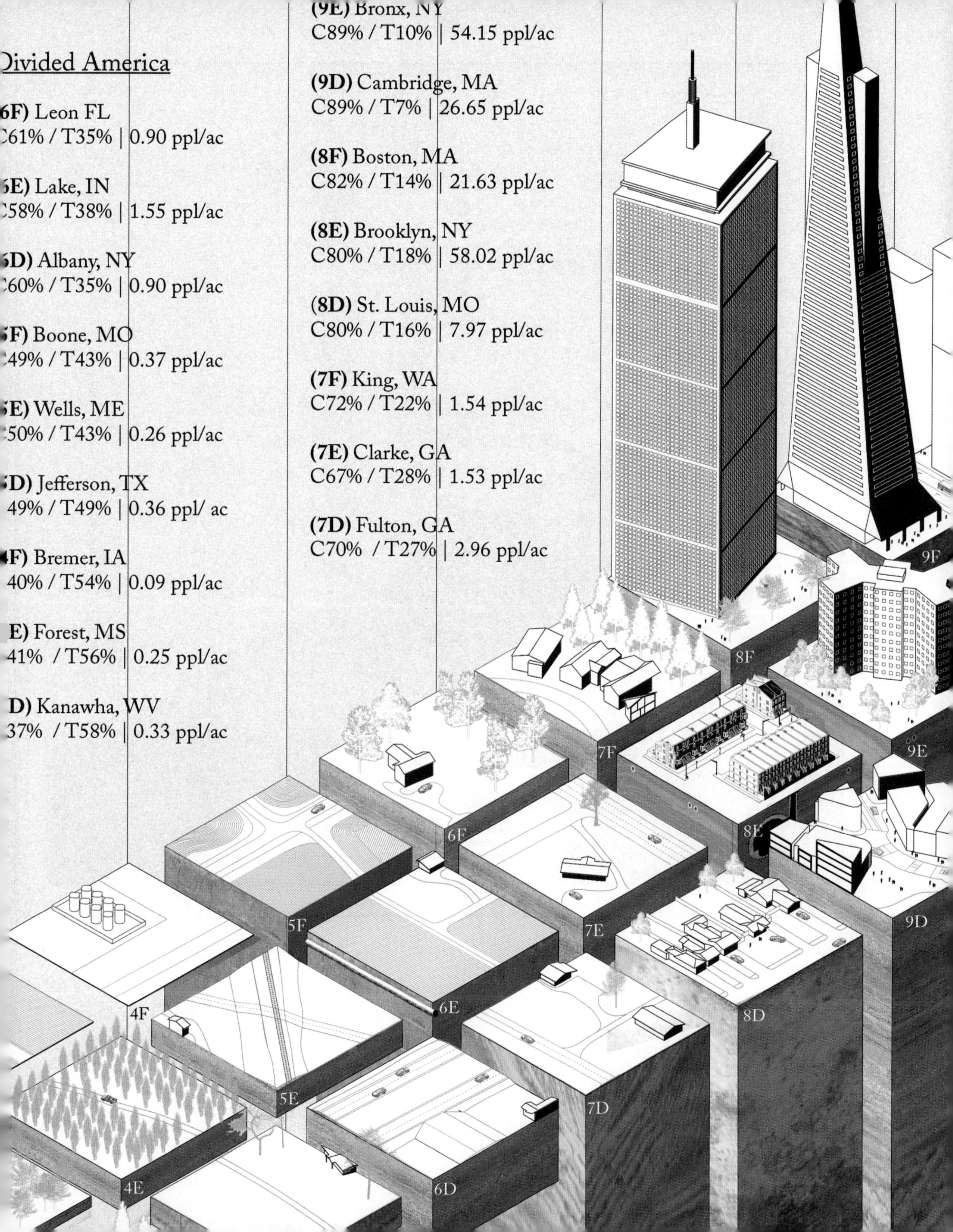

ivided America
6F) Leon FL
61% / T35% | 0.90 ppl/ac
E) Lake, IN
58% / T38% | 1.55 ppl/ac
D) Albany, NY
60% / T35% | 0.90 ppl/ac
F) Boone, MO
49% / T43% | 0.37 ppl/ac
E) Wells, ME
50% / T43% | 0.26 ppl/ac
D) Jefferson, TX
49% / T49% | 0.36 ppl/ ac
F) Bremer, IA
40% / T54% | 0.09 ppl/ac
E) Forest, MS
41% / T56% | 0.25 ppl/ac
D) Kanawha, WV
37% / T58% | 0.33 ppl/ac
(9E) Bronx, NY
C89% / T10% | 54.15 ppl/ac
(9D) Cambridge, MA
C89% / T7% | 26.65 ppl/ac
(8F) Boston, MA
C82% / T14% | 21.63 ppl/ac
(8E) Brooklyn, NY
C80% / T18% | 58.02 ppl/ac
(8D) St. Louis, MO
C80% / T16% | 7.97 ppl/ac
(7F) King, WA
C72% / T22% | 1.54 ppl/ac
(7E) Clarke, GA
C67% / T28% | 1.53 ppl/ac
(7D) Fulton, GA
C70% / T27% | 2.96 ppl/ac
9F
8F
9E
7F
8E
6F
9D
7E
5F
8D
4F
6E
5E
7D
4E
6D

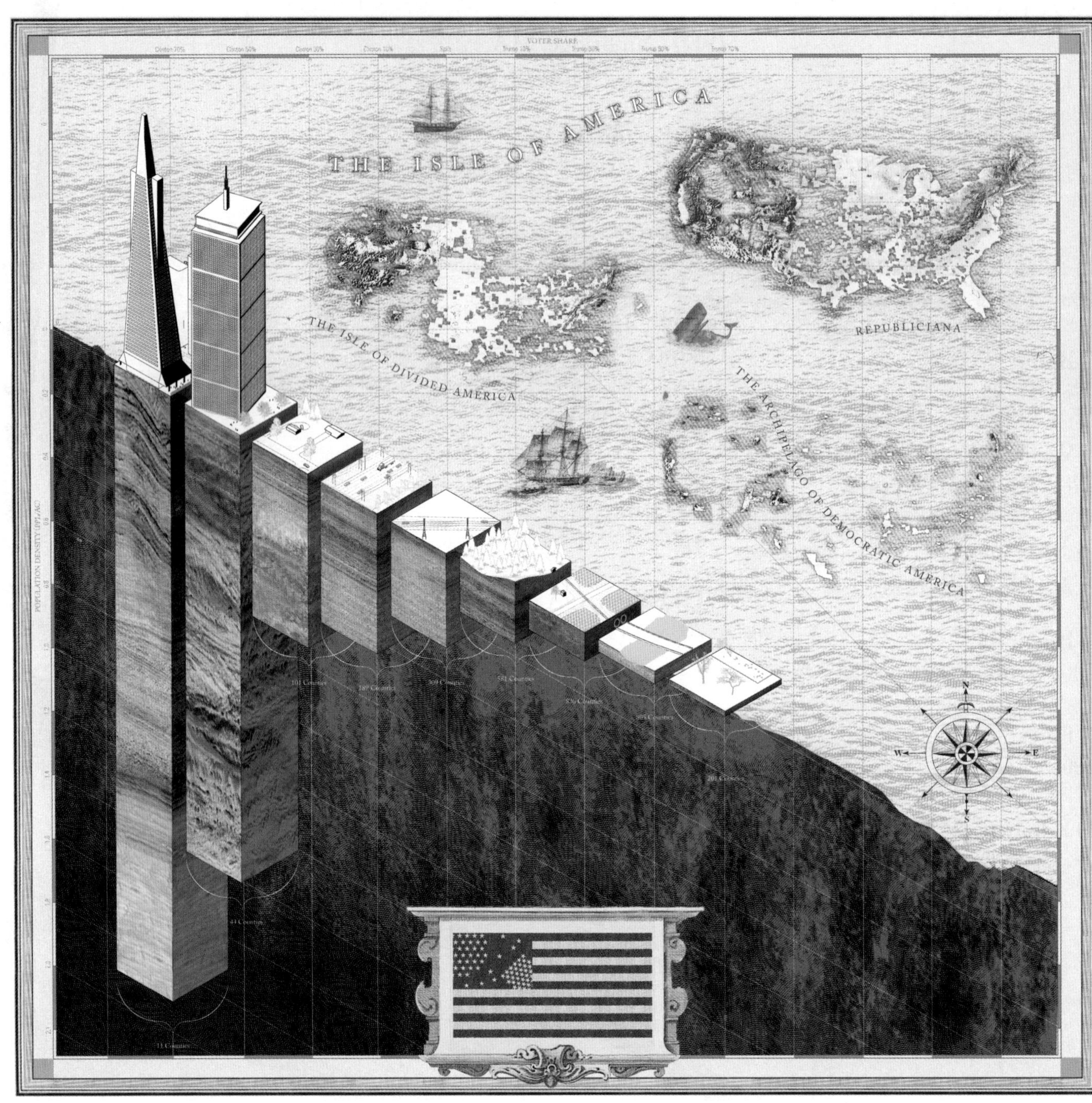
VOTER SHARE
Clinton 70%
Clinton 50%
Clinton 30%
Clinton 10%
Split
Trump 10%
Trump 30%
Trump 50%
Trump 70%
POPULATION DENSITY (PPL/AC)
THE ISLE OF AMERICA
THE ISLE OF DIVIDED AMERICA
REPUBLICIANA
THE ARCHIPELAGO OF DEMOCRATIC AMERICA
N
W
E
S

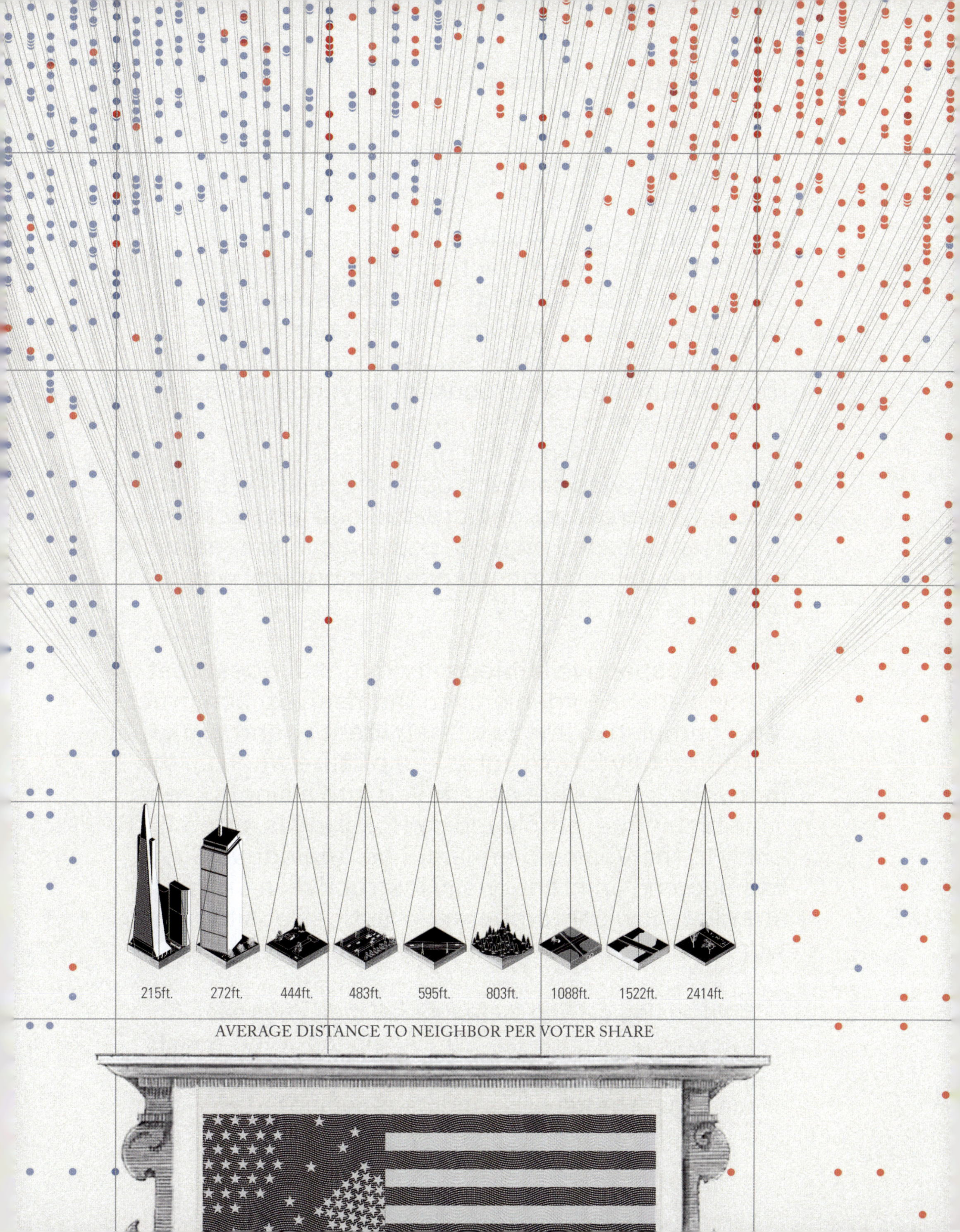
215ft.
272ft.
444ft.
483ft.
595ft.
803ft.
1088ft.
1522ft.
2414ft.
AVERAGE DISTANCE TO NEIGHBOR PER VOTER SHARE

A manufactured context of structure

While Canaletto smoothed the rougher lines of Venice into a more attractive whole, several centuries later, Aldo Rossi adopted the technique of *capriccio* as a conceptual armature for a different type of formal appropriation. Rossi used a methodology rooted in an internally focused, psychoanalytical structuralism. He looked inward to his own personal context rather than to the particularities of the specific work he was carrying out. The buildings that he studied, referenced, and created ceased to carry importance based on their existence in the real world but rather gained significance as a body of work within his own memory.

This introspective subjectivity might suggest that authors are beholden only to themselves, constructing a cumulative image of their identity and work that will ultimately form a complete picture when all the individual pieces are assembled into a single scene. This technique, employed by Rossi in his noted 1976 entry to the Venice Biennale, *The Analogous City*, has become unintentionally instructive in understanding how contemporary practices position their work. As Pierluigi Nicolin once succinctly put it:

> Both analogical and metaphorical meanings can, in this way, be ascribed to "The Analogous City" panel. That is to say, the work is open to a pair of double readings. The panel is a montage composed of

Such associative methods have become commonplace in contemporary practice, as architects now surround themselves with a wide array of precedents to imbue their work with meaning. Today's architecture is often created in a vacuum, disconnected from unified coherent cultural association, prompting practitioners to return to history and the arts for grounding their work.

As practices become increasingly isolated, it is appropriate that they spend so much time looking inward rather than engaging through colloquium. In the quest for a coherent movement or disciplinary milieu, many are increasingly reaching for the support of the evidence of things outside of the present moment. Like dumpster divers of the digital age, contemporary practitioners demand that one seek and find the bespoke detritus that fell through the cracks. This approach is evident in Johnston Marklee's installation for the 2015–16 Chicago Architecture Biennial, *House is a House is a House is a House is a House*, which exemplifies this search for meaning. Johnston Marklee has established itself as an architectural firm engaged with contemporary art practices, drawing on the work of artists, graphic designers, writers, and photographers to broaden the scope of its research. In the early phases of a project, collage serves as a method for quickly and freely drawing on diverse historical precedents, and for selecting key elements from the lineage of existing architecture for the project to engage.[3]

Rossi and his collaborators were foundational to this approach. The scope of the analogical project required

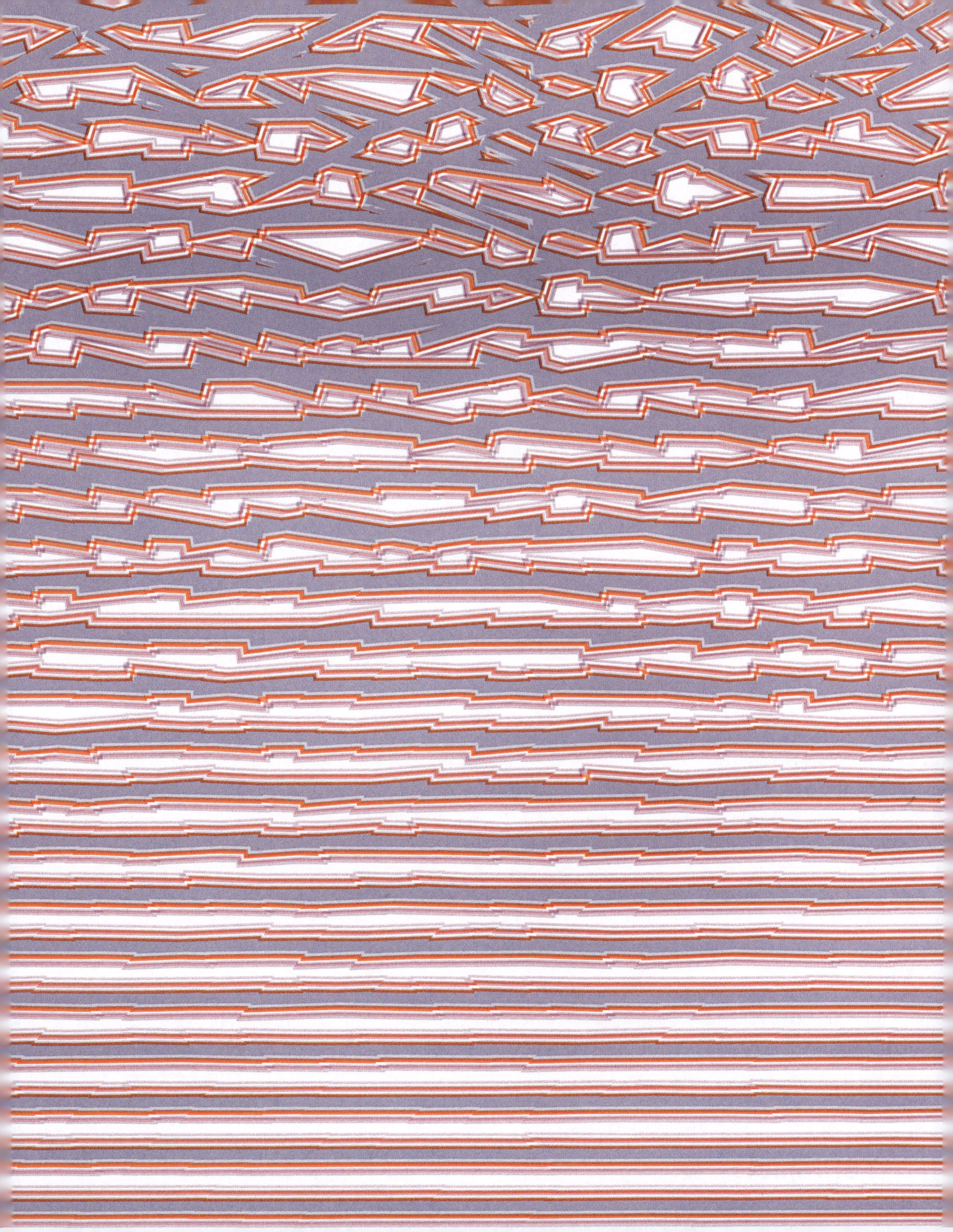

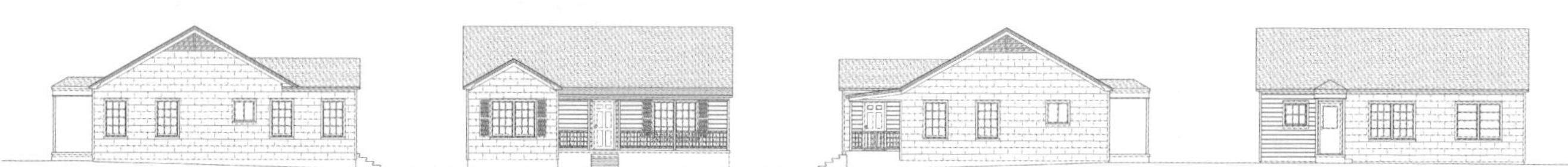

This set of four architectural elevation drawings illustrates the existing conditions of a home. Their technical precision allows for a direct understanding of the building's current state. While architectural elevations are often flat and prone to misinterpretation, the careful rendition showcases a pure form of architectural documentation that can stand alongside more elaborate visualizations. The precision and technical acumen evident here elevate these drawings beyond their functional purpose, making them an important visual record of a possibly mundane existing condition.

T8Projects

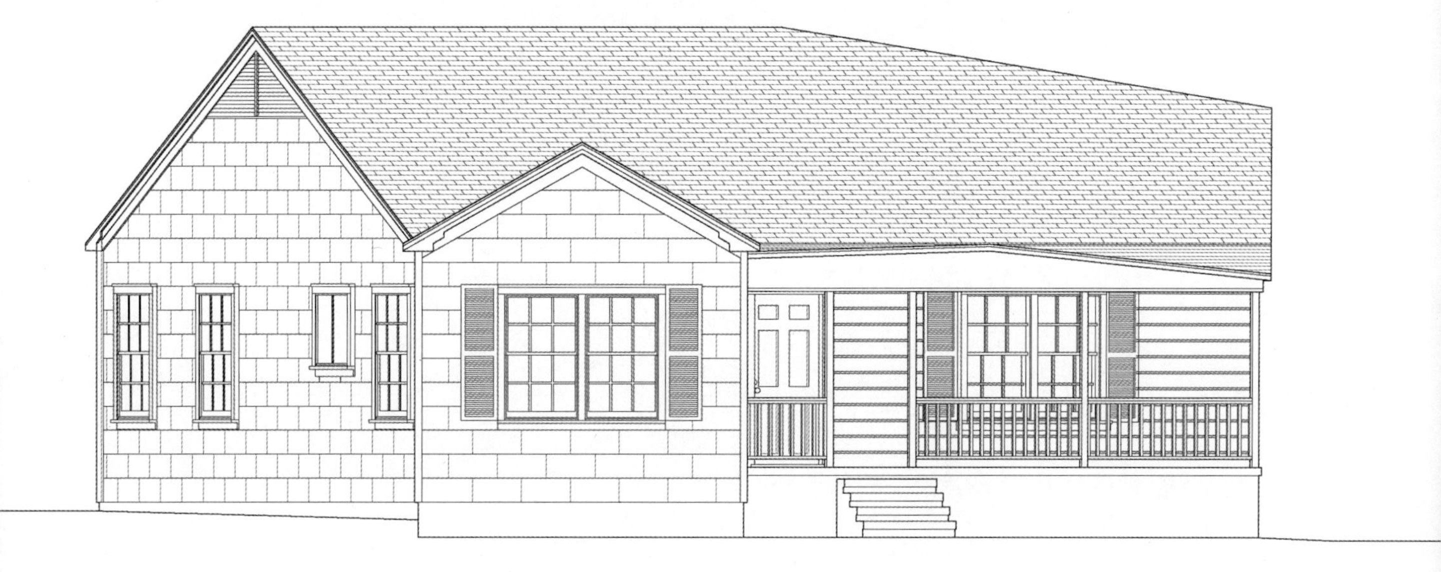

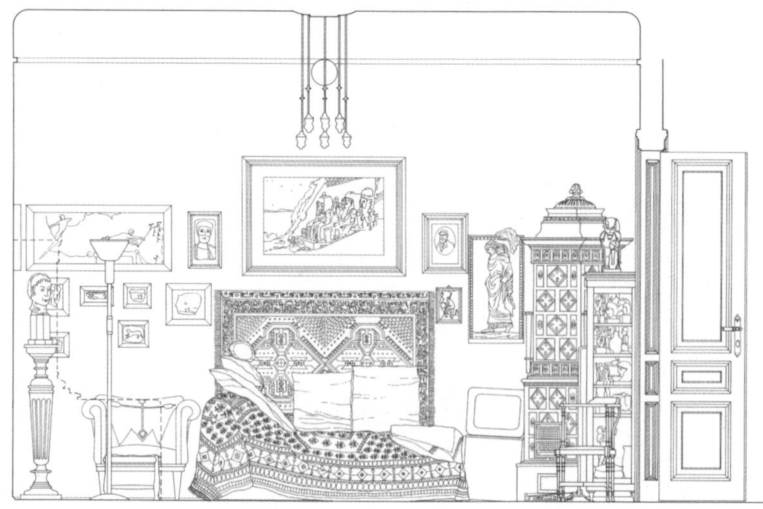

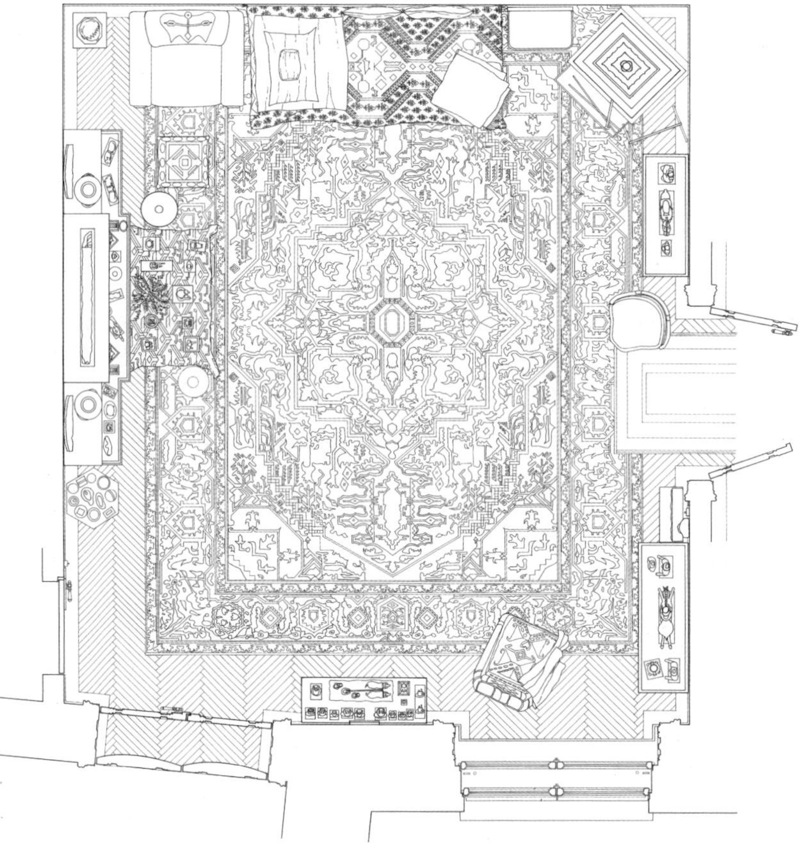

This first drawing, a hand-drawn documentary record of Sigmund Freud's home and office, captures the space as it exists in its preserved, museum-like state, frozen in time yet teeming with objects. The level of care and craftsmanship is remarkable, showcasing meticulous attention to detail. The drawings depict a domestic scene layered with a vast array of objects, all oriented towards a relatively empty center, which enhances the sense of presence through absence. It feels as though Freud has only just left the room, leaving behind an "impossible moment" of stillness. This drawing parallels LANZA Atelier's trace sketches seen earlier in the book, but here the medium is employed in a distinct way. The control and near-obsessive precision in this work highlight an extraordinary level of technical skill, imbuing the scene with a subtle yet powerful tension.

Nada Subotincic

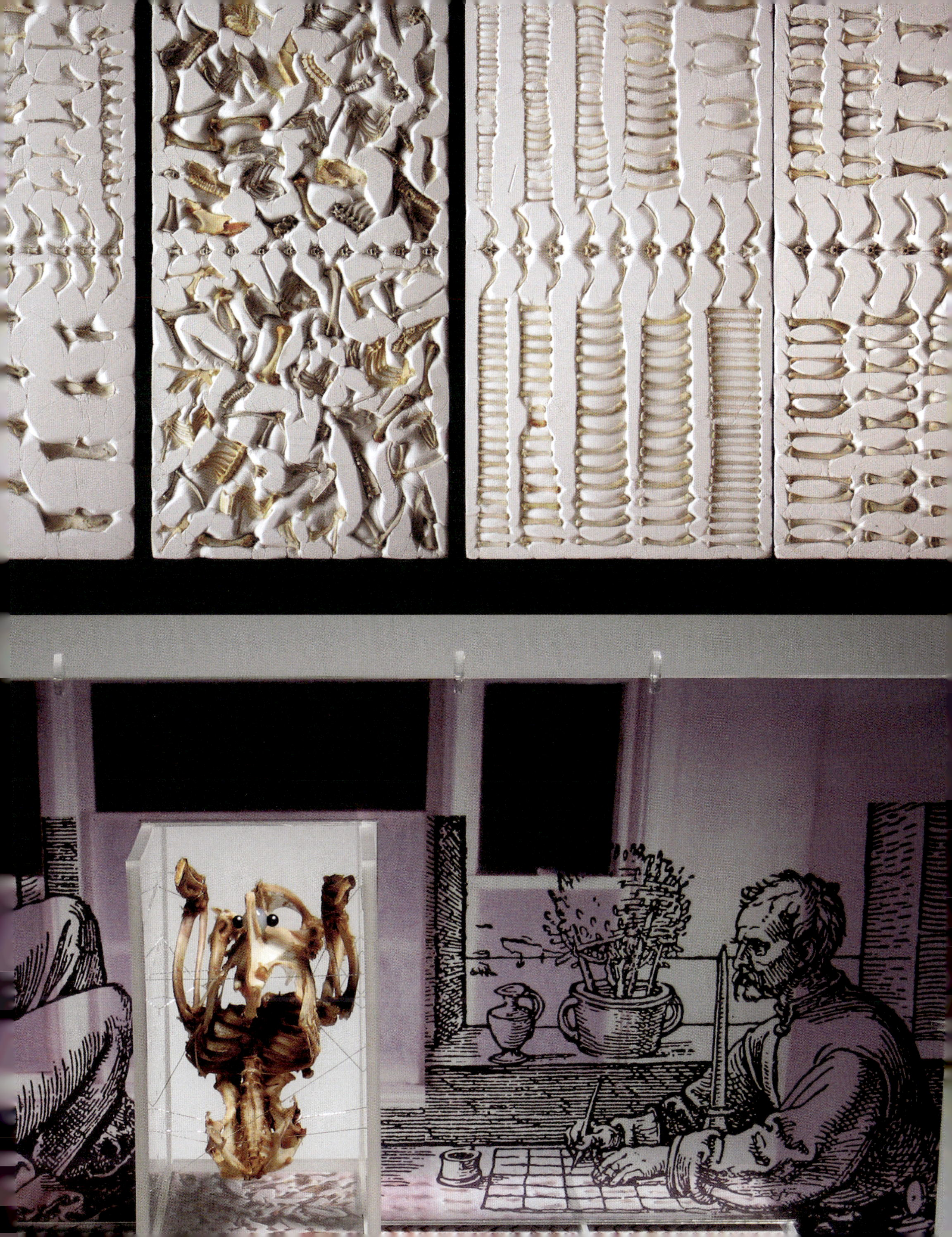

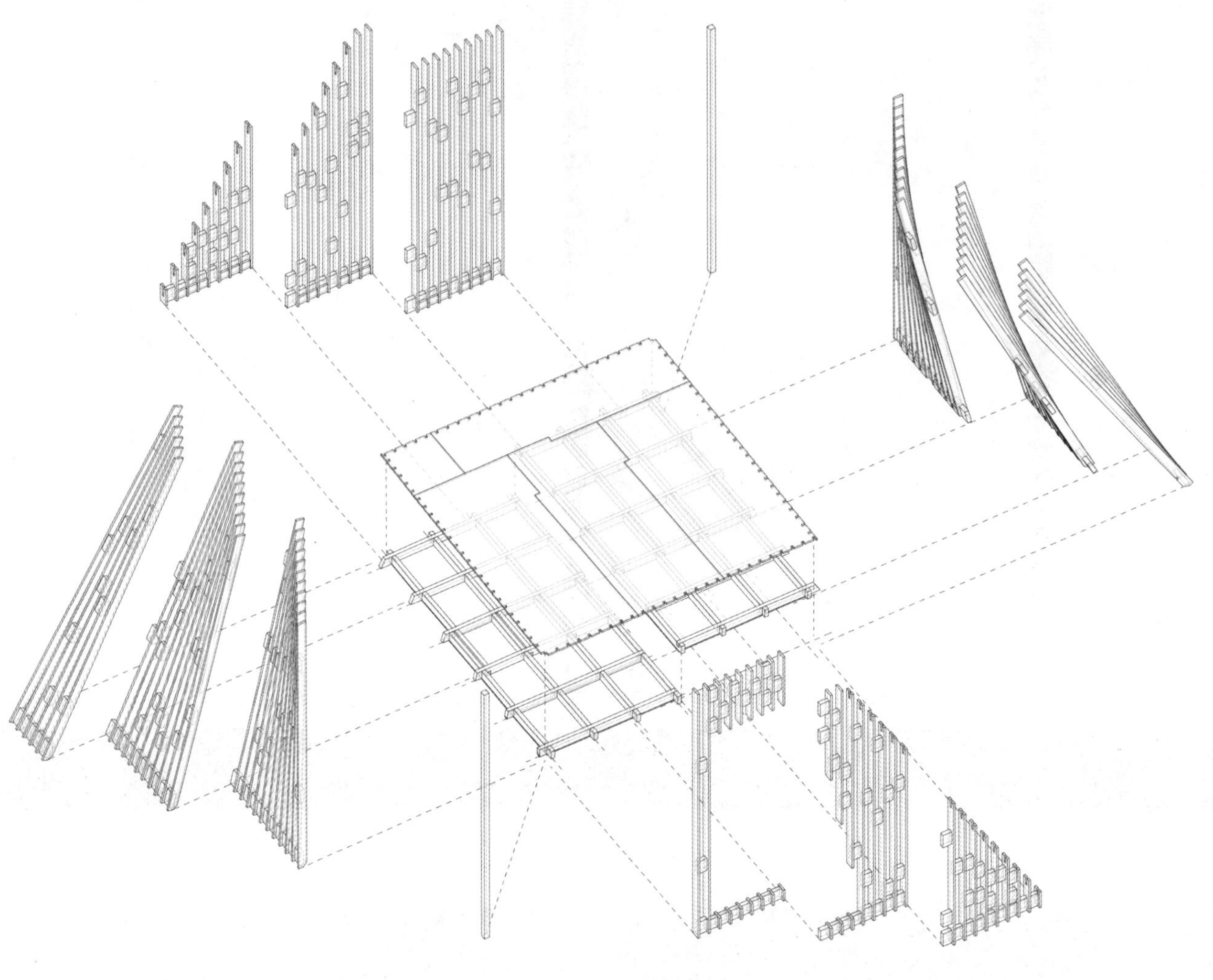

This exploded axonometric drawing illustrates a precise assembly of components for constructing a small pavilion, functioning as both a formal proposition and an instruction manual. The structure reflects a hybrid design, blending off-the-shelf dimensional elements with detailed tooling and custom fabrication. While the construction showcases precision, it also introduces a sense of informal variability. Notably, a series of spacers, depicted with exact precision in the drawing, are implied to be installed at random, adding an element of unpredictability to the otherwise minimal shelter. The drawing's clear straightforward style resembles the do-it-yourself graphics commonl seen in modern construction drawings, particularly those involving complex, hybrid components. It highlights the growing intersection between accessible, prefabricated materials and the increasingly sophisticated custom designs seen in contemporary architecture.

Sort Studio

A dutiful drawing and a mischievous drawing

imagine a world where architecture and artifact are as restless as verbs

moments of resistance become what they need to, by seizing tangents serendipitously lying in wait within their proximity[1]

descriptions follow an entirely reasonable and logical thread that culminate in wildly messy and stunningly beautiful random events[2]

spectacular musings generously parade about like speeding airwaves through one's spatial imagination, scattering the seeds of possibilities known, unknown and discoverable[3]

how do you grasp the agency of the place in which the man who contextualised the psyche of others formed his ideas?[4]

well I consider it my duty to be mischievous, so that leaves me with a problem[5]

Anca Matyiku with Nat Chard, Perry Kulper, Natalija Subottincic,

on the mischievous and dutiful aspects of one another's drawings, or in the practice more broadly.[10] This group also participated in the *In Drawing* symposium and *Drawing Conversations* exhibition at UQAM School of Design in Montreal.[11] Together with *Im/proper* contributor CJ Lim, they were engaged in the "Drawing Architecture" research project and the related publication, *Drawing Architecture: Conversations on Contemporary Practice*.[12] I leverage this overlap between the *Drawing Im/proper* project to point to a constellation of ongoing dialogues surrounding contemporary drawing practices.

Notes

1. Nada Subotincic on the drawings of Perry Kulper.
2. Mark West on the work of Nat Chard.
3. Perry Kulper on the dutiful and mischievous of Mark West.
4. Nat Chard on the drawings of Nada Subotincic.
5. Mark West in conversation with the author.
6. Douglas Darden, *Condemned Building: An Architect's Pre-Text* (New York: Princeton Architectural Press, 1993), 9.
7. Lois Ellen Nesbitt, Alexander Brodsky, and Ilya Utkin, *Brodsky & Utkin: The Complete Works,* 2nd ed. (New York: Princeton Architectural Press, 2003).
8. Igor Marjanović and Jan Howard, *Drawing Ambience: Alvin Boyarsky and the Architectural Association* (St. Louis: Mildred Lane Kemper Art Museum, 2015) accompanied the exhibition at the Kemper Art Museum, Washington University in St. Louis, 12 September 2014–4 January 2015.
9. Peter Cook, *Drawing: The Motive Force of Architecture*, 2nd ed, AD Primers (Chichester, West Sussex, England: Wiley, 2014) offers an expansive collection of speculative drawing practices.
10. The drawings these architects shared for the *Drawing Im/proper* exhibition are included in this publication.
11. The -*In Drawing* symposium and *Drawing Conversations* exhibition took place in September 2022 at the UQAM School of Design in Montreal, Canada. Both were organized and curated by Carole Lévesque and Thomas-Bernard Kenniff, together with Design Center Director Louise Pelletier.
12. Mark Dorrian, Riet Eeckhout and Arnaud Hendrickx, eds., *Drawing Architecture: Conversations on Contemporary Practice* (London: Lund Humphries, 2022). This research collective also includes Peter Cook, Micheal Webb, Neil Spiller, Reit Eeckhout, Shaun Murray, Mark Smout and Laura Allen, Michael Young, Bryan Cantley, Mark Dorrian, and Adrian Hawker.

Dutiful Shenanigans: the other ‘both-and’. . .

Speaking dutifully about Mark West’s drawings is the representational corollary to crimes against humanity. Rather, evocatively pithy, ticklishly provocative, and confoundingly puzzling, Mark’s ever evolving opus is a kind of Joycean odyssey, promiscuously bred with the hallucinatory promise of ‘home sweet home’. He is an innovative juggernaut who tickles a tensional play between exemplary duty and ‘off-leash’ shenanigans. His visual cosmologies are metaphorical looking glasses, nourishing our starved optical appetites, and collective desires, all the while satiating curious observers with his unique, and toxically beautiful imagination acting as tour guide.

A cross between a mild-mannered draftsman, alchemist, Hieronymus Bosch, and madman, his erudite mark making seduces hungry eyes and deprived imaginations—the mesmeric visual puzzles are kinds of optical Venus flytraps, innovatively conjured through apparitional figures, emerging ghosts and worlds nested in others. Undoubtedly, he is akin to a mischievous Harry Houdini, picking the pockets of optical legibility, with a quixotic wink of the figurative eye. His drawings, metaphorical birds in flight with a dash of magic up their sleeves, are naughty forms of release—spectacular musings that generously parade about like speeding airwaves through one’s spatial imagination, scattering the seeds of possibilities known, unknown and discoverable. . . maybe. Alice would be proud. Real proud. . .

— Perry Kulper

Nat Chard's drawings are simultaneously, and inherently, dutiful and mischievous. Looking at the paint-flinging machines we are confronted by a highly programmatic, seriously technical construction (are they part of the U.S. space program?) whose purpose in life is to luxuriously spew colored goo. Chard's descriptions of this work follow an entirely reasonable and logical thread that culminate in wildly messy and stunningly beautiful random events. These are taken very seriously and dutifully recorded and analyzed with the kind of urgent precision we don't usually expect when things get this messy. Well before the arrival of chaos theory, Gregory Bateson reminded us that the world displays both convergent and divergent phenomena: convergent events, like the action of the balls on a billiard table, are predictable over time; divergent events, like the weather, are inherently unpredictable over time. Chard's non-Newtonian drawing machines swallow both classes of events whole, eating its own logic in a delicious and contradictory meal that generates colored standing-waves in the brain.

— Mark West

An illusion of space

To further reflect on Canaletto's continuing influence on successive architects, we turn to Britain, where his work was widely purchased and circulated. Canaletto relocated to London in 1746 to stay close to his largest market during an embargo between Britain and Venice. His presence and his art swept through the city as Romanticism began to take root. By 1833, Sir John Soane had officially handed over his home to Parliament to establish it as a museum. Upon his demise, Soane's disciples applied his collector's methodology to shape their own visions of hegemonic Western classical architecture. This period marked a moment in which Soane's "architecture as a collection" merged with Canaletto's "architecture as fantasy." A new generation of architects appropriated the language of history and Canaletto's capriccio techniques, blurring the boundaries between the past and present, as well as reality and illusion.

Take C.R. Cockerell's *The Professor's Dream* (1848). Following in Soane's footsteps, both at the Royal Academy and as a surveyor for the Royal Bank of England, Cockerell embraced the tradition of the Grand Tour, returning to England having experienced a wealth of architectural precedents. In "The Professor's Dream" he presents a perspectival elevation of an array of buildings, both real and imagined, that ascend and recede into the distance, increasing

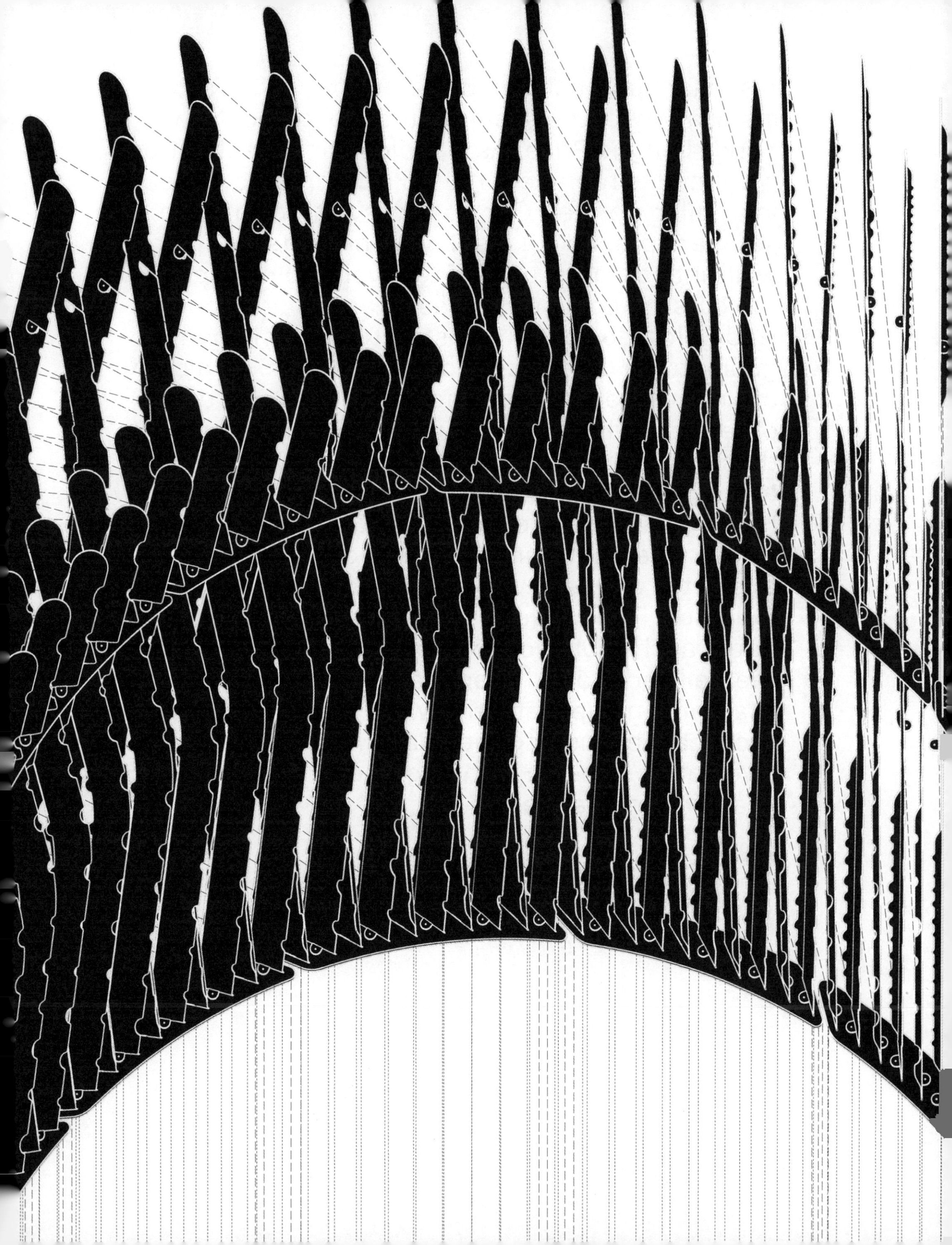

A similar approach can be seen in my office's 2017 installation for the Architectural League of New York's League Prize. As is typical for the exhibition, we aimed to represent multiple completed projects in a gallery format. Our goal was to translate the standard practice of displaying projects on adjacent walls into a single, unfolding, overlapping scene. The projects are collaged representations of a fictionalized Colorado context, abstracted into elemental geometry in unexpected configurations. As a body of work viewed in total, each project supports the others, creating a greater whole. Scattered among these projects are a series of blank figures, placed to suggest anticipated future work. Unambiguously typological in nature, the projects use uncomplicated primary geometry in unexpected configurations to exist in concert with the grandiose context of Colorado. The models, constructed from the same paper as the collage, appear to have been torn from the wall and draped over a table. Presented without scale and in duplicate, this work was meant to be provocative, pushing the image into new territory as a vehicle for illusion, echoing Cockerell's approach in a different manner.

Note

1. Watkin, David. *The Life and Work of C.R. Cockerell*. London: A. Zwimmer Ltd., 1974, 132.

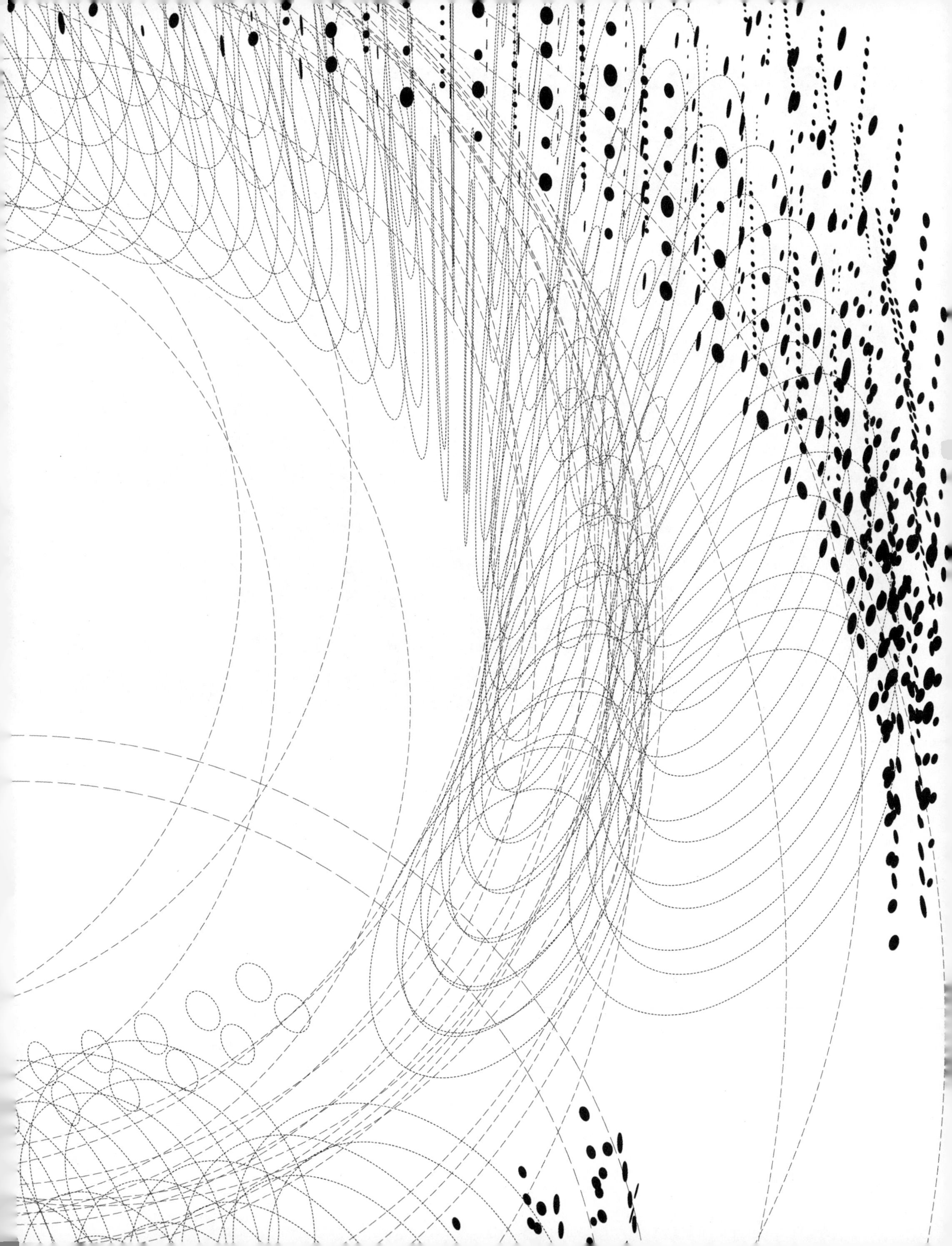

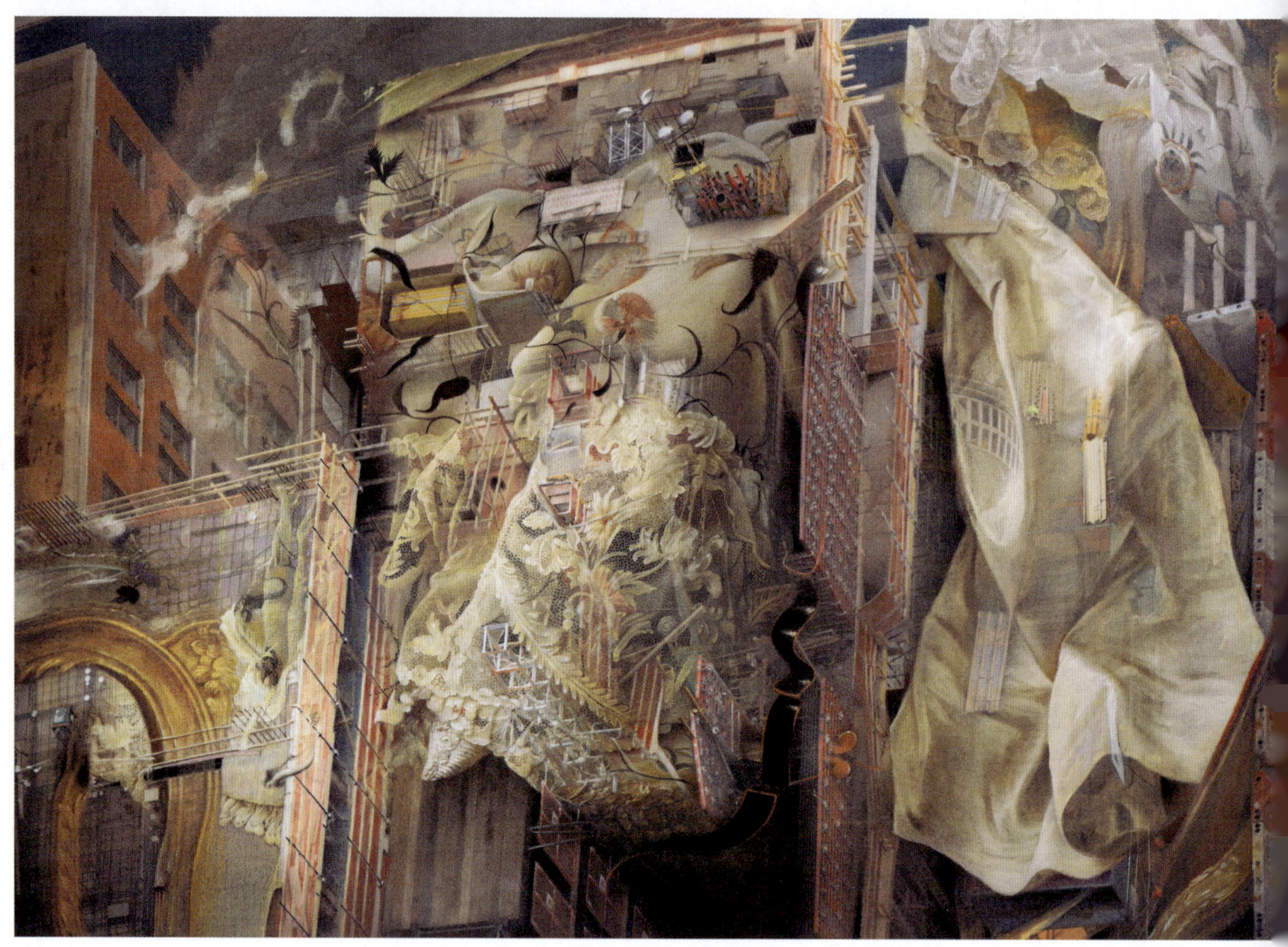

This drawing presents a seemingly chaotic yet carefully orchestrated scene, blending texture, figure, shape, and color into what appears to be a rooftop vista. From an undefined aerial perspective, a complex mix of scaled and unscaled figures fills a plane that seems both contained and infinite. Semi-structural objects are overlaid with delicate, lace-like elements, recalling old tablecloths that ripple across the urban parapet. The interplay of textures shifts the scale and viewpoint, suggesting both a first- and third-person perspective of a fleeting, indefinable past moment. Technique comes into question, as the scene feels like a print of a hand-burnished artifact, its softnes contrasting with the structured elements. A warm, golden glow suffuses the image, evoking a specific, yet surreal, moment of sunligh in the city. The drawing resists easy interpretation, blurring the lines between urban and domestic, structural and ephemeral.

Mark West

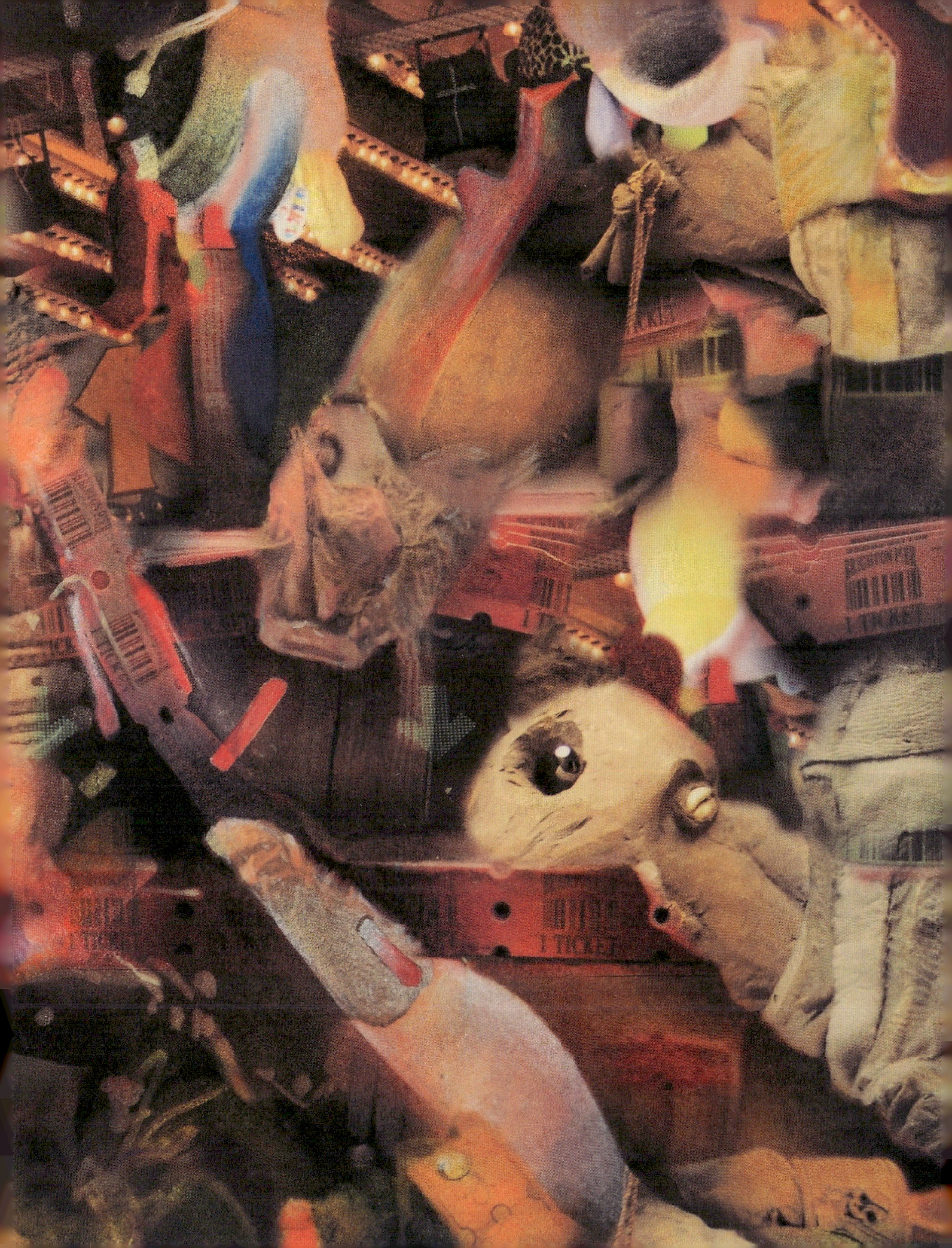

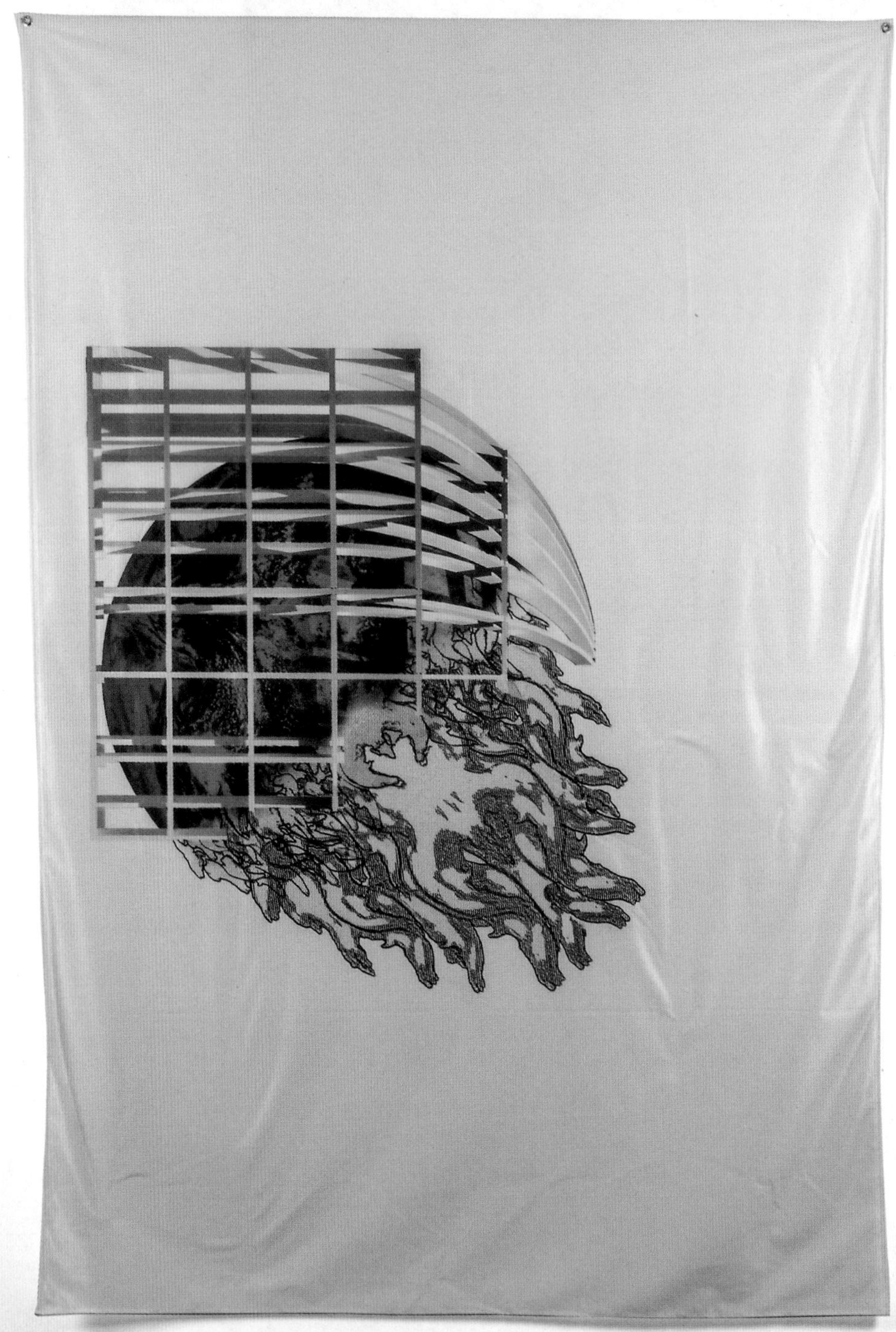

This striking image shows a black-and-white Earth engulfed in flames, encased within a dome structure that recalls "The Blue Marble," the iconic full-color photograph of our planet and a symbol of the environmental movement. Here, the absence of color abstracts the Earth, shifting it into a symbolic realm. The dome surrounding the fiery globe evokes the Pantheon's architecture, hinting at themes of shelter and containment while questioning humanity's stewardship of the planet. This powerful juxtaposition of scales—between the planetary and the architectural—challenges us to discern whether we're witnessing a literal or symbolic scene. Presented as a flag, the image intensifies its polemical message, acting as both a declaration and a[n] urgent call to action in response to the climate crisis.

Design Earth

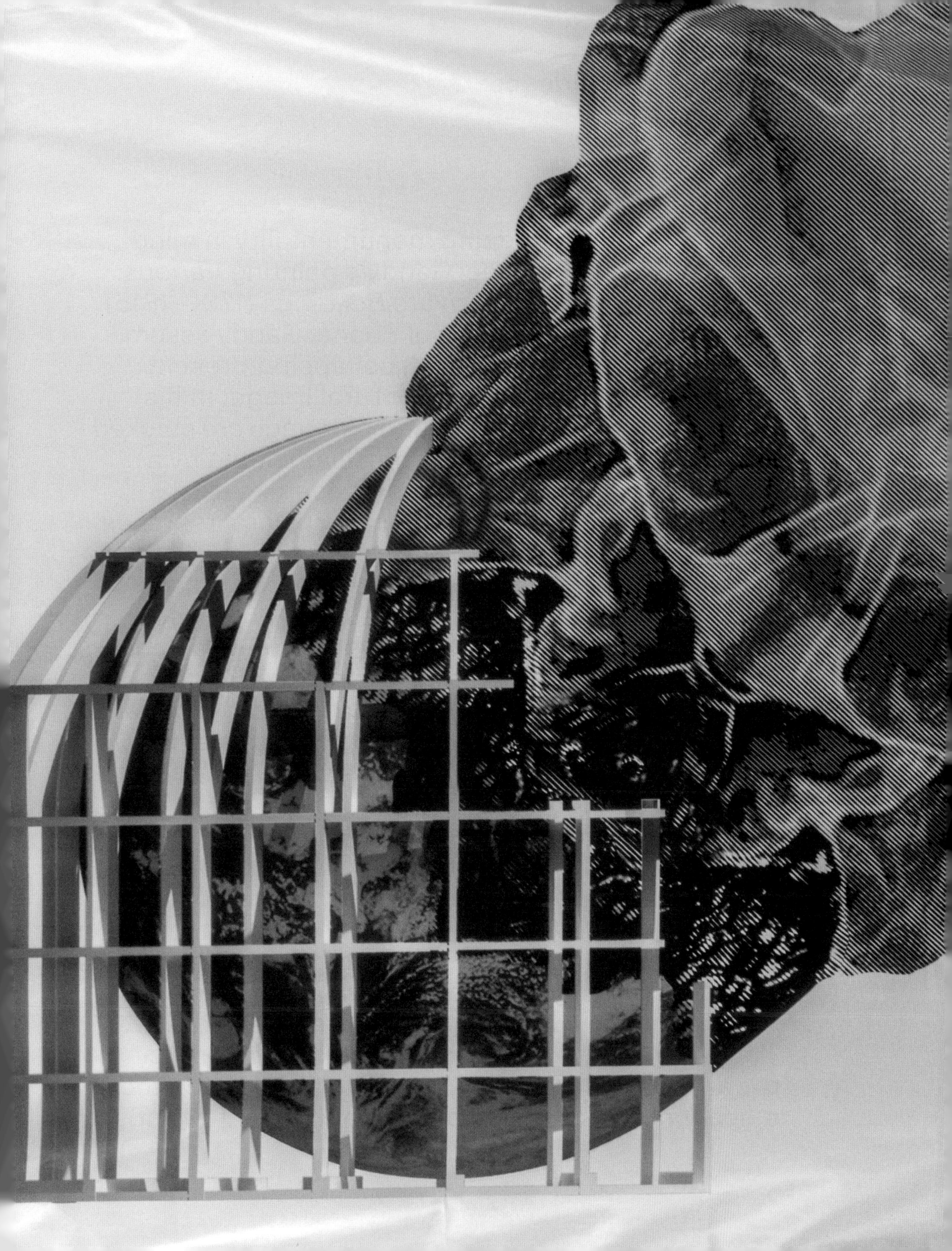

A camouflage of coincidence

With Cockerell's sweeping monumentality in mind, consider Joseph Michael Gandy's painting *Various Designs for Public and Private Buildings* (1780-1815). A collaborator and mentee of Soane, Gandy assembled his own representation, collapsing present and past into a single architectural image. In his work, architectural models and paintings are stacked atop one another in a dark room. Illuminated by a brilliant circular lamp, the models seem to exist simultaneously at their given scale and as a representation of some alternate urban reality. This collection of built and unbuilt work, cast in this light, raises a critical question regarding the nature of these projects' existence. Gandy views the models and drawings within his painting as primary. He conceptualizes this arrangement as a non-scalar, analogous configuration in which all the works exist in a shared physical plane.

Similarly, consider Adam DeTour's photographs for *Still Life*, Jennifer Bonner's 2016 catalog of Harvard GSD student work. In documenting the students' work, DeTour and Bonner drew on a wide range of sources, including sixteenth-century oil paintings, food photography, high fashion advertisements, as well as works by Caravaggio and Giorgio Morandi. They also experimented with color gels, referencing the artist Barbara Kasten.[1] By recontextualizing the student models in these photographs, Bonner and

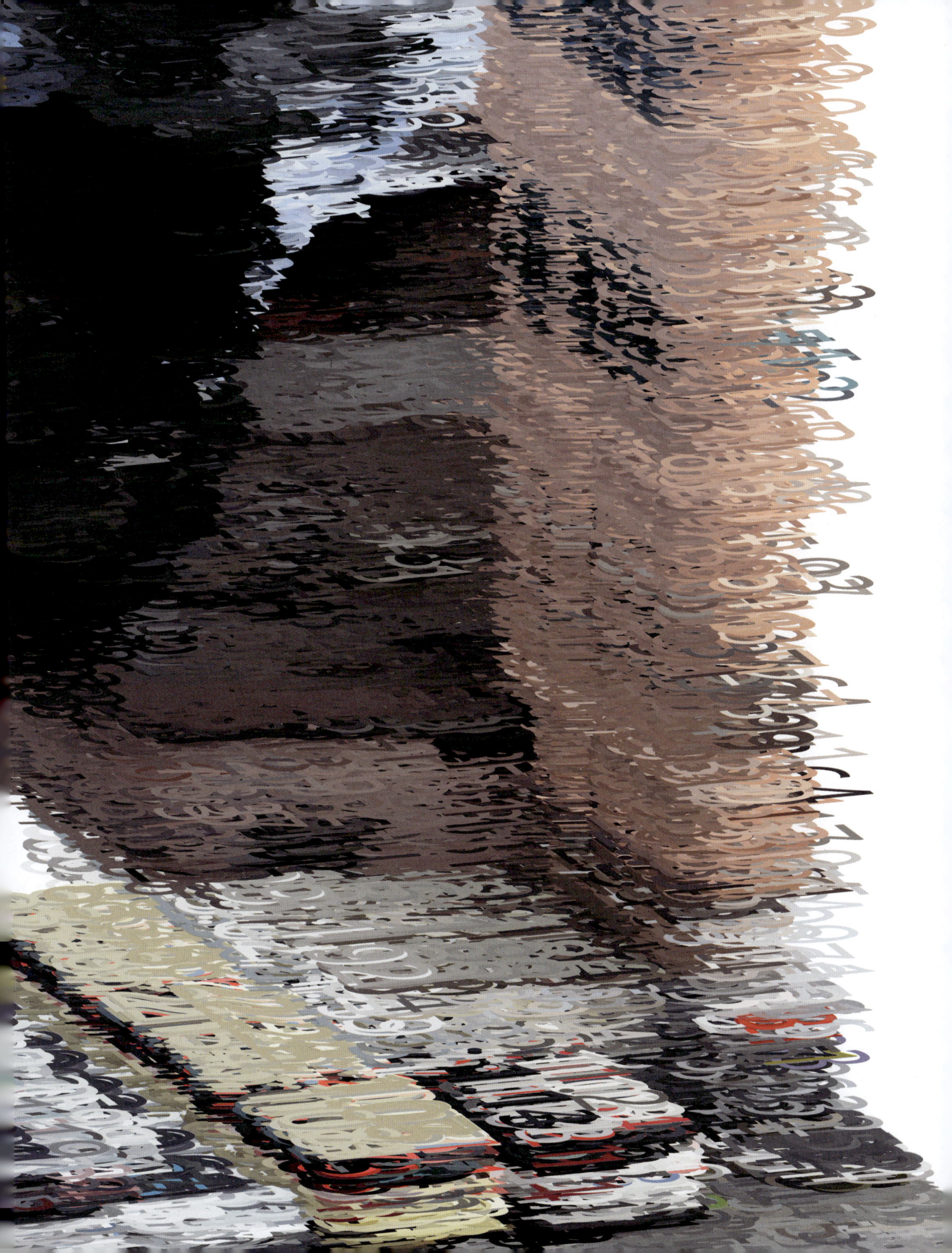

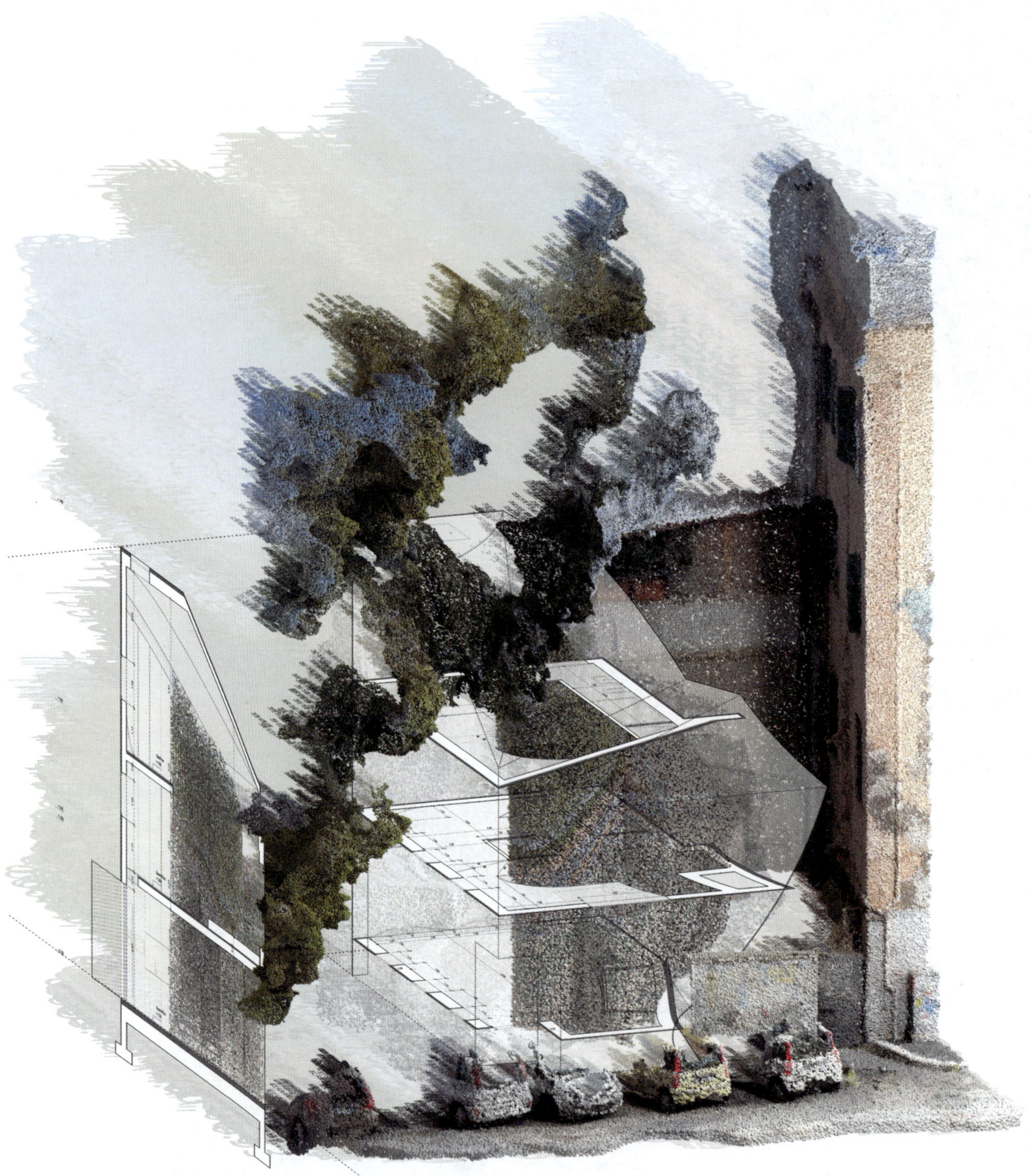

In this second image, the scene and resolution have shifted, with data now rendered as spherical grains, revealing a swirling mass of fine figures. Orthographic sections and plans—conventional construction drawings—have been integrated, creating a tension between the precise, idealized architectural proposition and the hazy, indeterminate point cloud. This contrast mirrors the difference between the clean, orderly vision of architecture before construction and the chaotic reality of a building site. A further tension emerges between surface and volume, between the real and the surreal. The crisp line of the architectural drawings clash with the blurred, vibrating forms the filled void, heightening the sense of ambiguity. The absence of a clear representation of the building's surfaces deepens the antagonism between the ideal and the real, surface and volume, architectu and its messy, unpredictable realization.

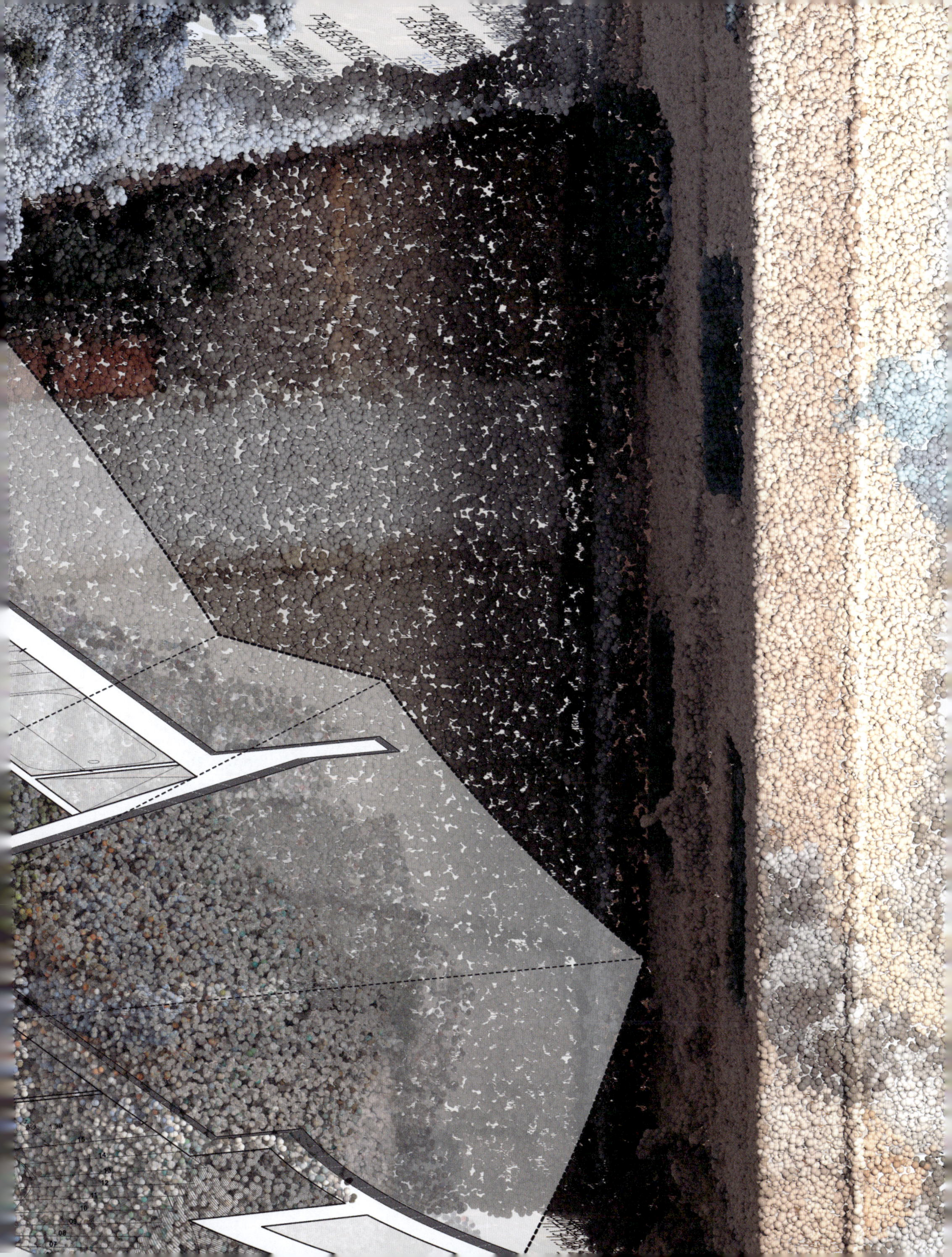

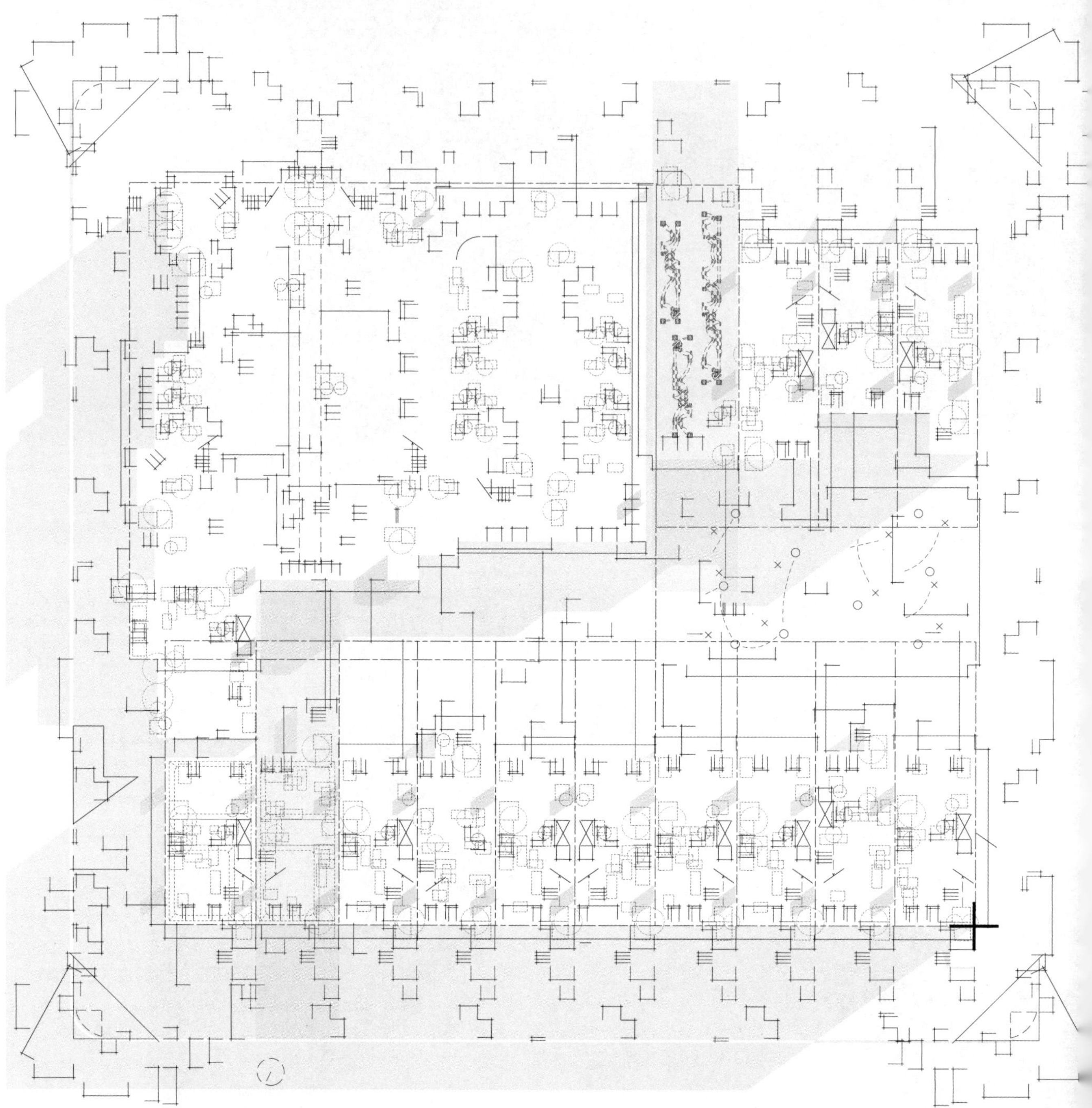

This architectural delineation operates within the conventions of technical drawing but introduces omissions so extensive that the work remains indeterminate, allowing the imagination to engage with boundless possibility. The drawing includes five types of annotation: first, a base point at the 0,0,0 coordinate in the lower right corner marking an apparent site boundary; second, property line notations defining repeating contiguous areas; third, dimensions that suggest proportional relationships without marked distances; fourth, hidden lines indicating clearances for open spaces; and fifth, shadows that in elevation and cardinal orientation. These shadows, subtle and light g introduce a familiar visual language found in architectural plan graph though their exact meaning remains elusive. By using only technical notations for construction alongside abstracted shadows from illustr tive drawing conventions, the piece blurs the line between function a abstraction, hinting at something precise yet entirely open-ended. T result is a work both hyper-determined and ambiguously expressive.

Studio Ames

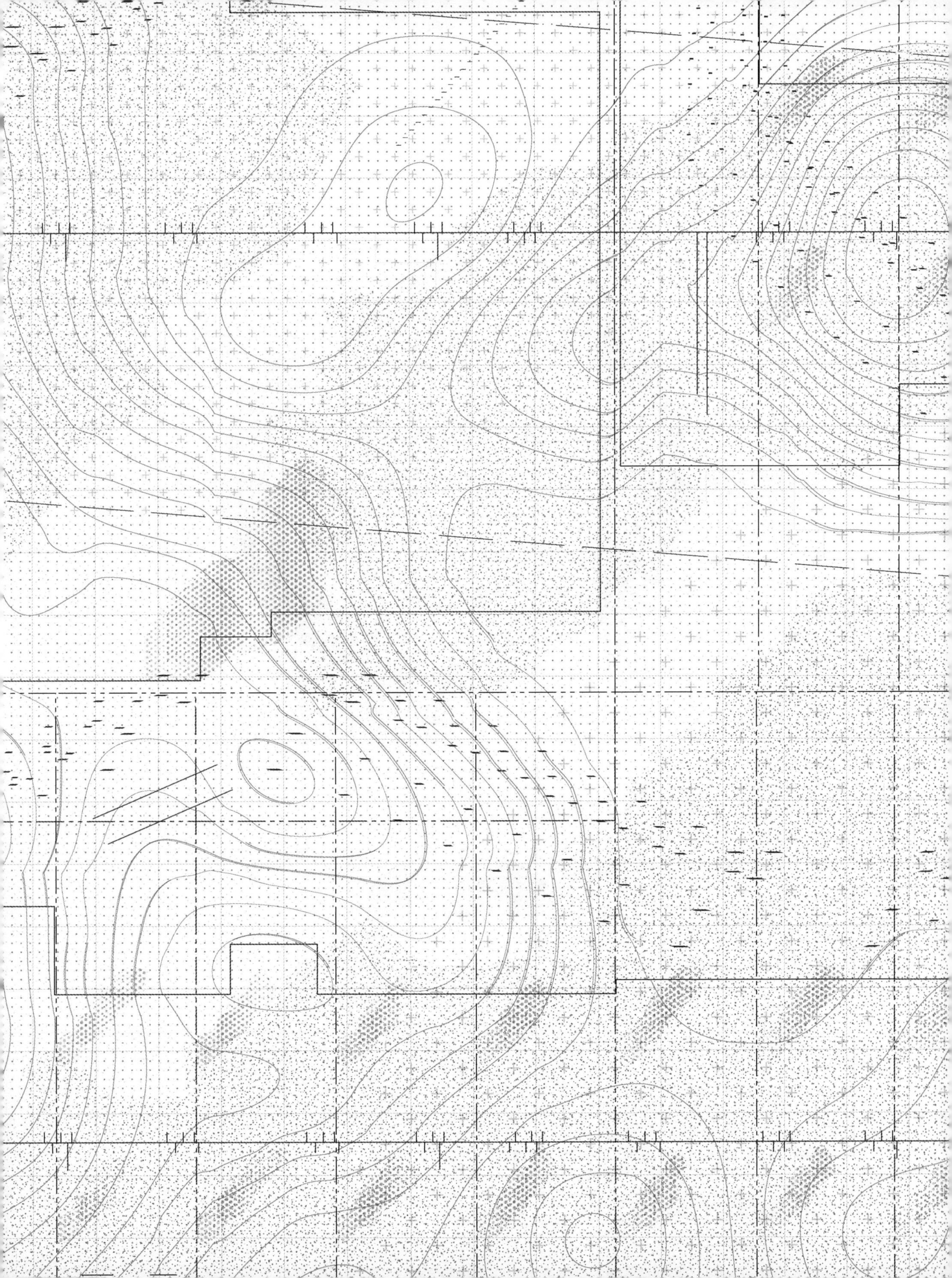

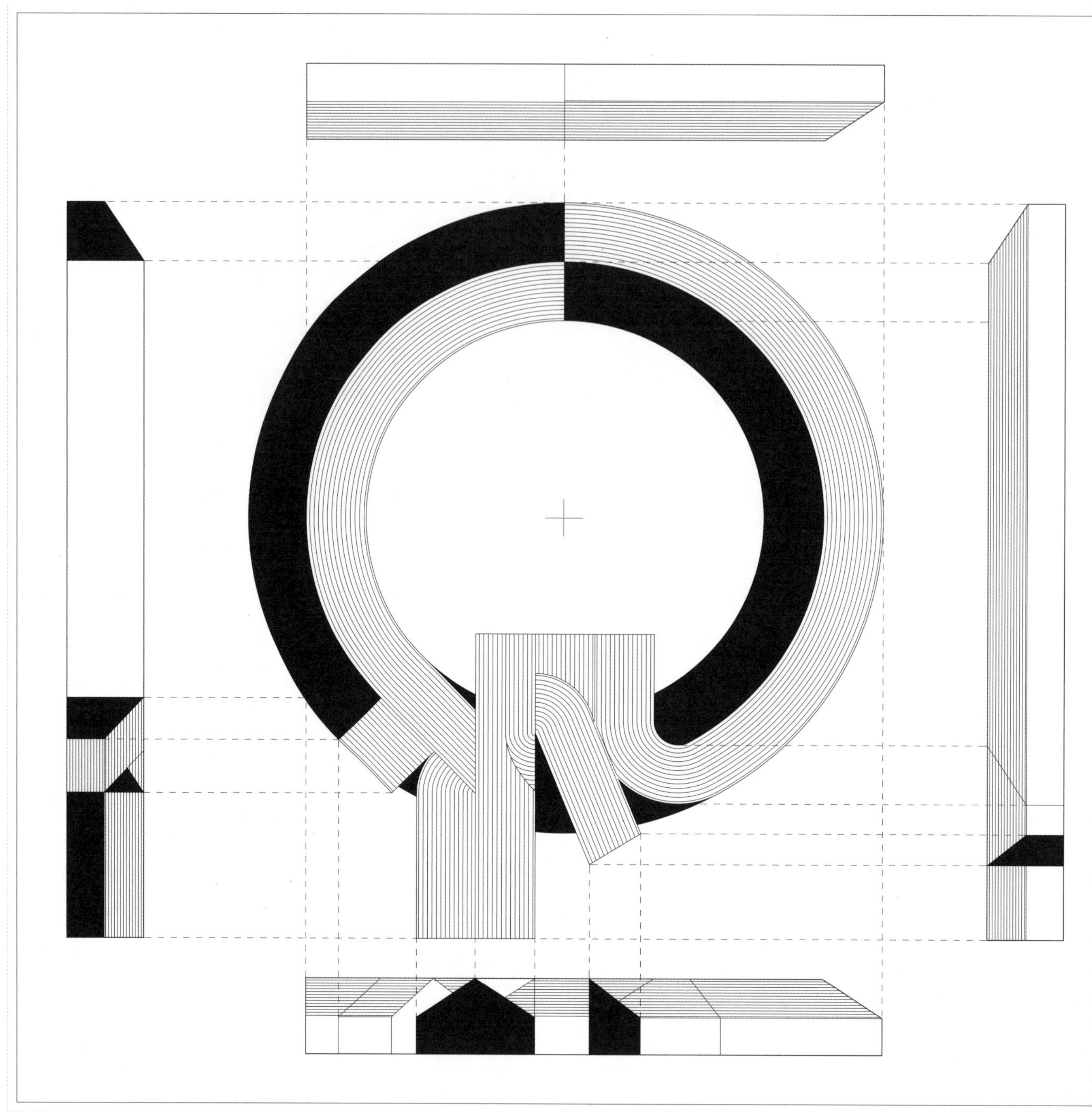

This drawing begins with a common yet rarely illustrated margin offset from its edges, a space defined by a center point connected to the margin through leader lines. The central focus is a contorted gabled form, bending beyond the limits of a conventional projection. The structure twists into two distinct knots resulting in a cyclonic, kaleidoscopic body split into two parts. This duality invites two potential readings: as a single form bent by space at the projective turn, or as a doubled gable, twisting into itself. Both interpretations challenge conventional spatial relationships. The recurring leader l marking the center emphasizes the significance of this origin point. The form, reminiscent of an ouroboros—a snake consuming its tail—creates a loop of infinity, where the twisted faces of the gable complicate the usual reading of front and back. The rotation itself becomes a meditative abstraction, rewarding deeper contemplatio

Studio Sean Canty

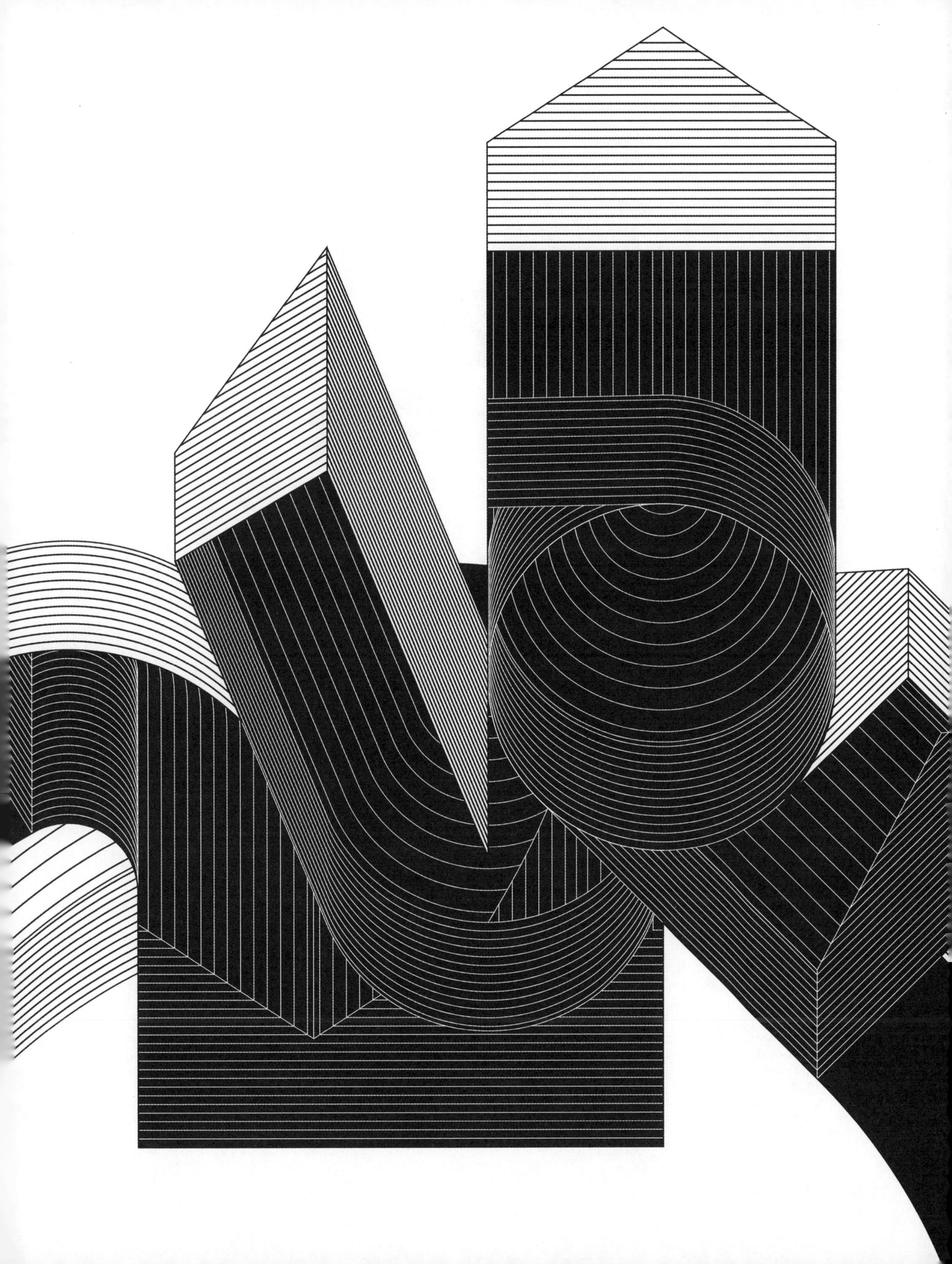

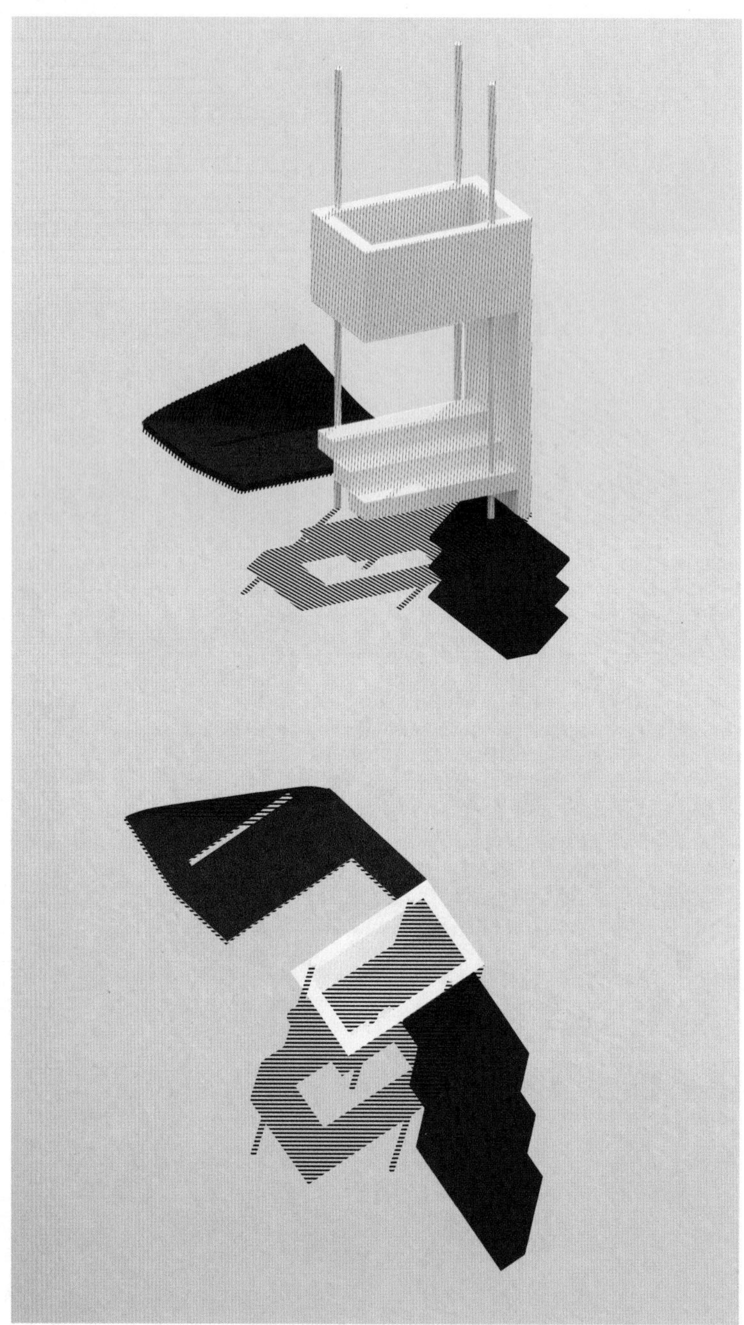

This image playfully blurs the boundary between the principal modes of visual representation, combining drawing and image into a single composite. The upright object carries ambiguous architectural qualities, featuring columns, a wall, a roof, and possibly a stair or a seat, evoking a sense of familiarity yet resisting clear identification. Beneath it, a soft, curling object appears to rise along a vertical surface, adding to the ambiguity. The rich, red texture of this surface, which seems thicker than a typical carpet, defies expectations as it drifts upward, suggesting the presence of hidden components—pe haps an unseen wall or element of a larger structure. The image pla with spatial perception and materiality, inviting us to question the boundaries of what we see. This "perfect imperfection" is a carefull crafted deception that challenges the conventions of architectural representation, merging the expectations of both isometric and pla projections into a single, disorienting visual experience.

Now Here

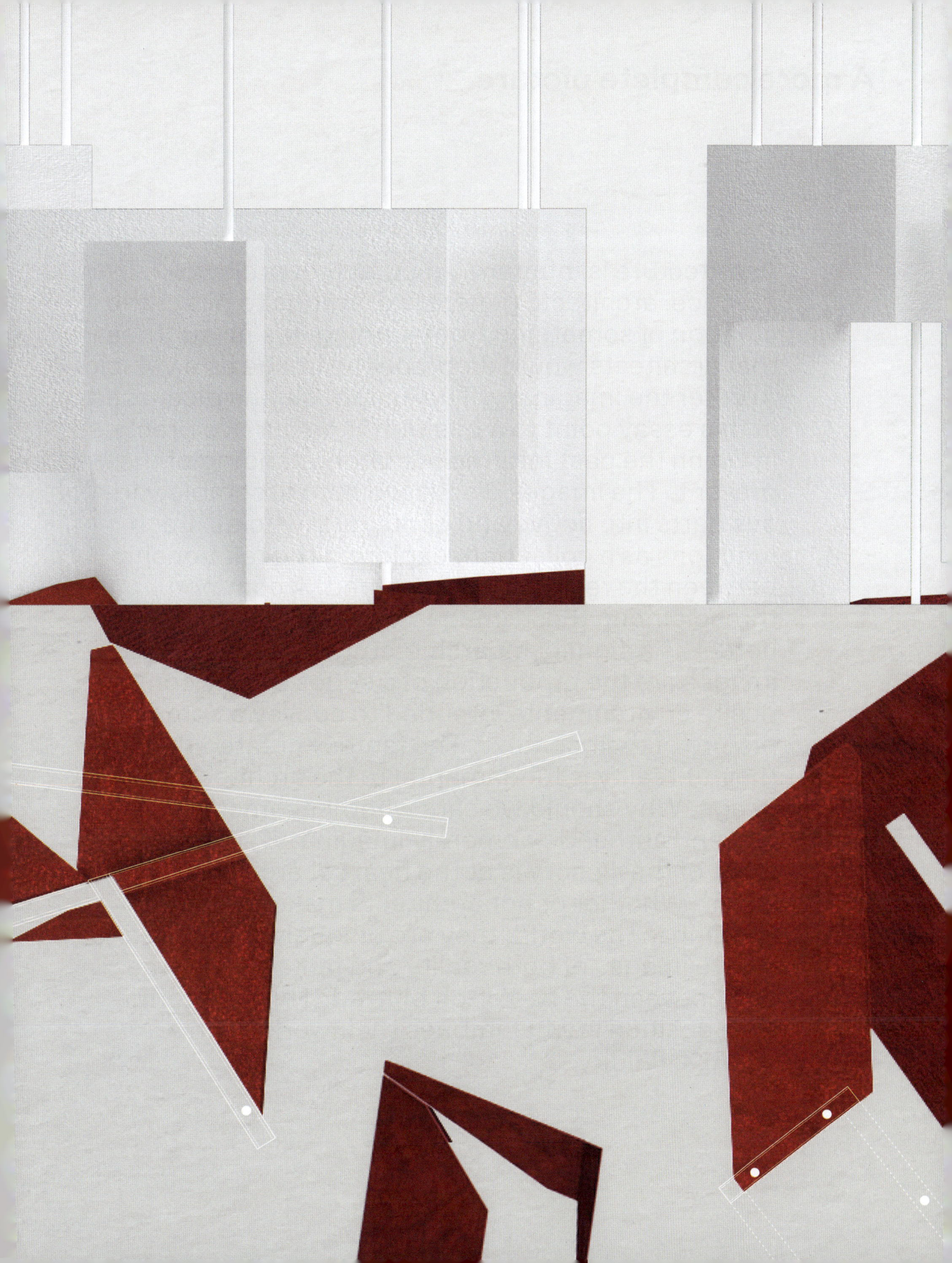

A more complete picture

Architecture is inherently a pursuit of projection. In practice, architects generate drawings to direct the creation of something from nothing. It's no surprise that architects would embrace the image as a vehicle to enter the imaginary. The juxtapositions discussed in this essay point to a position in discursive practice in which the past informs our understanding of the present. The images discussed here assemble various parts into fictive and contextual wholes. Each functions as a collection, exploring the relationship between the real and the imagined. A common thread among these images is the expression of the unreal as a significant architectural gesture. These images are the production of a series of fully composite environments intended to convey a complete picture of their context. The fantasy created through their unreality is fundamental to the architectural image. Why should we care whether something is real and authentic or merely imaginary? The embodiment of the illusory is at the heart of architectural intent. Whether or not architects make a mark by building in the world, they are uniquely positioned to create images of both reality and fantasy, with the line between the two often blurred. This indeterminate position is what imbues their works with a creative fluidity.

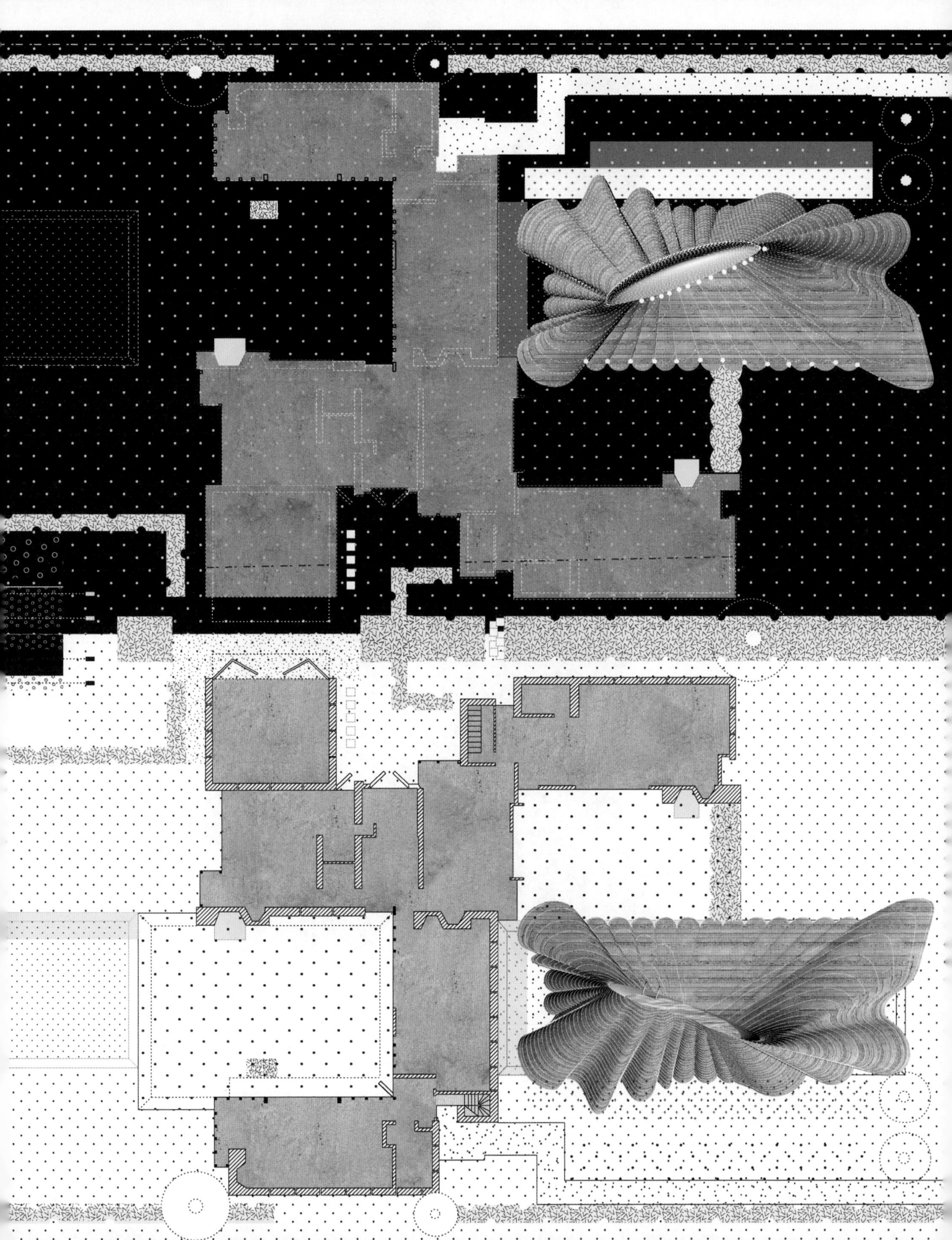

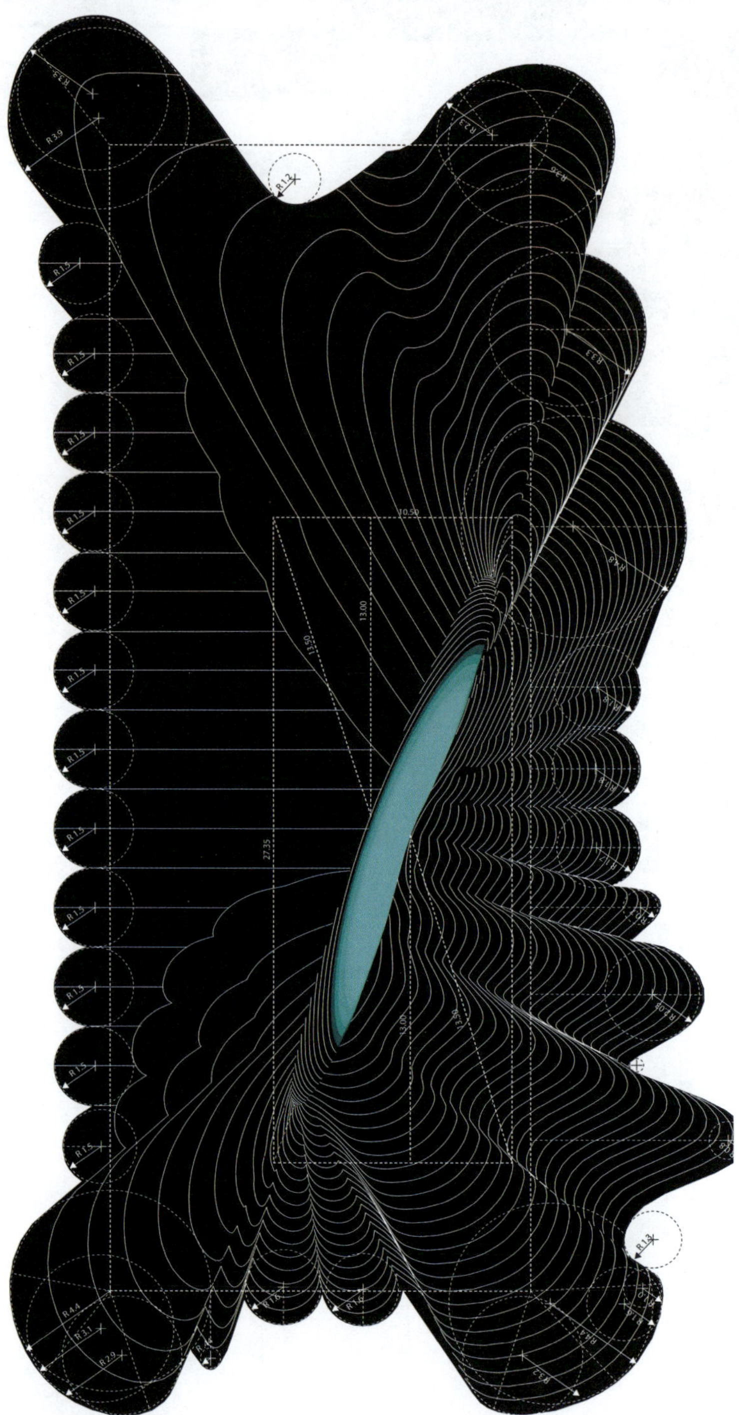

This drawing plays a mischievous counterpart to its mirrored partner, deepening the ambiguity of projection and spatial logic. At first glance, it seems like a conventional plan, with line segments and arcs conforming to regular dimensions. However, a second layer of linework—cast down onto the black figure—complicates the initial reading. The lines, reminiscent of contours, intersect irregularly, defying standard resolution. A blue fill resembling a body of water overlays the entire composition, adding to the sense of play. The drawing hints at a duality: is it a plan or a reflected ceiling plan? Th door to this misreading is opened by the use of both projections in previous drawing. Through this playful manipulation, the drawing resists a singular interpretation, inviting us to compare its orderly geometric notations with the mysterious spatial logic at work in its partner piece, where control and chaos coexist.

BairBalliet

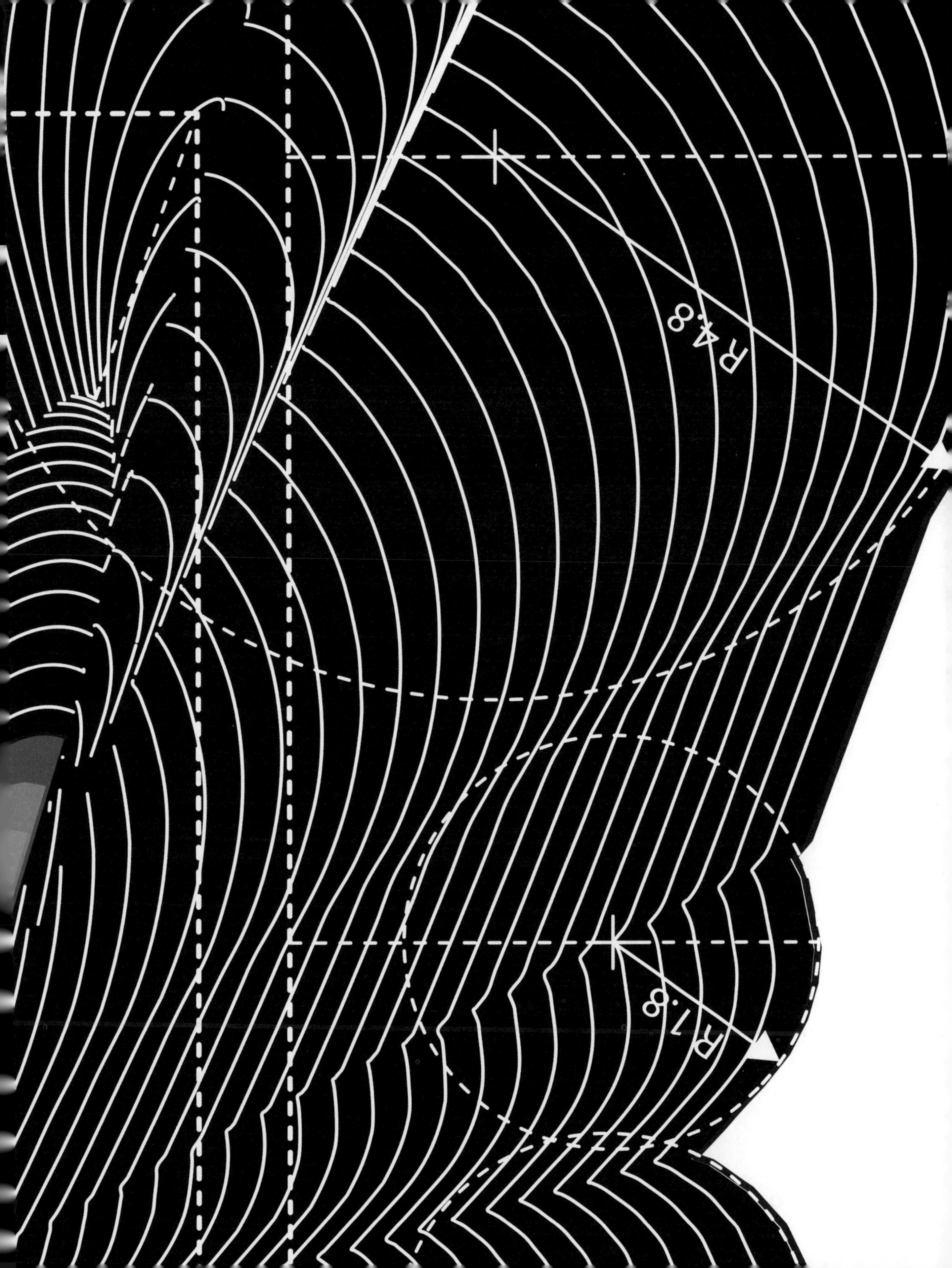
R4.8
R7.8

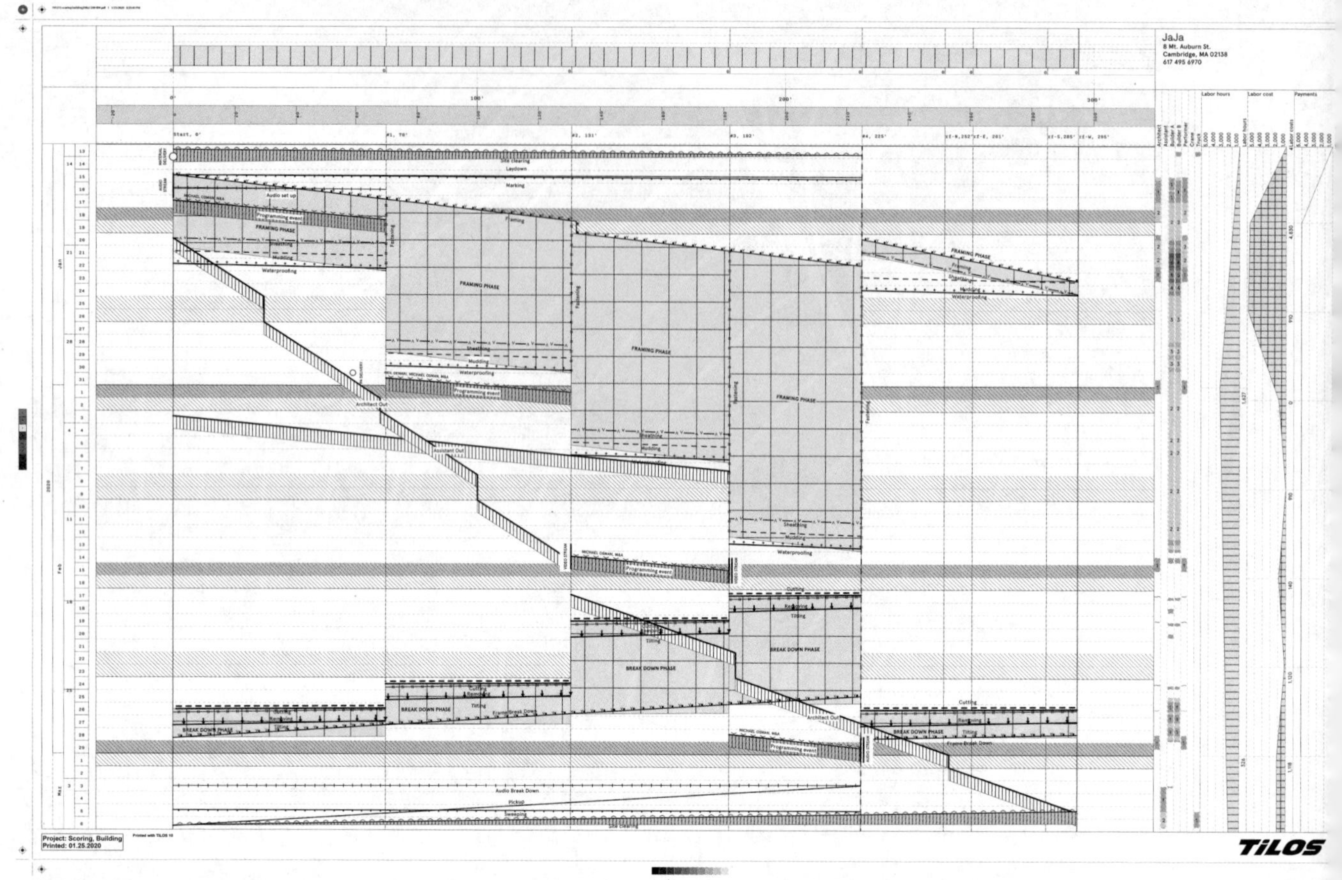

The drawing presents a project timeline, a tool used in construction management to coordinate between architect and builder. Typically, such timelines delineate expectations for the duration of various construction phases—framing, molding, spackling—tracking how far a building is from completion. Here, however, the schedule takes on an unconventional form. Rather than the standard activity-based approach, which sequences tasks, this timeline employs location-based scheduling, organizing work as a function of continuous speeds across space and time. This method allows for a rhythm of formal a material effects to emerge, sequencing material deliveries, payme room making, and color changes. The vertical axis reflects the passage of time, while the horizontal one represents the progress each phase. At a certain point, the timeline flips, transitioning fron construction to the breakdown phase, embodying a spatial logic th intertwines with the building's unfolding.

JaJa Co

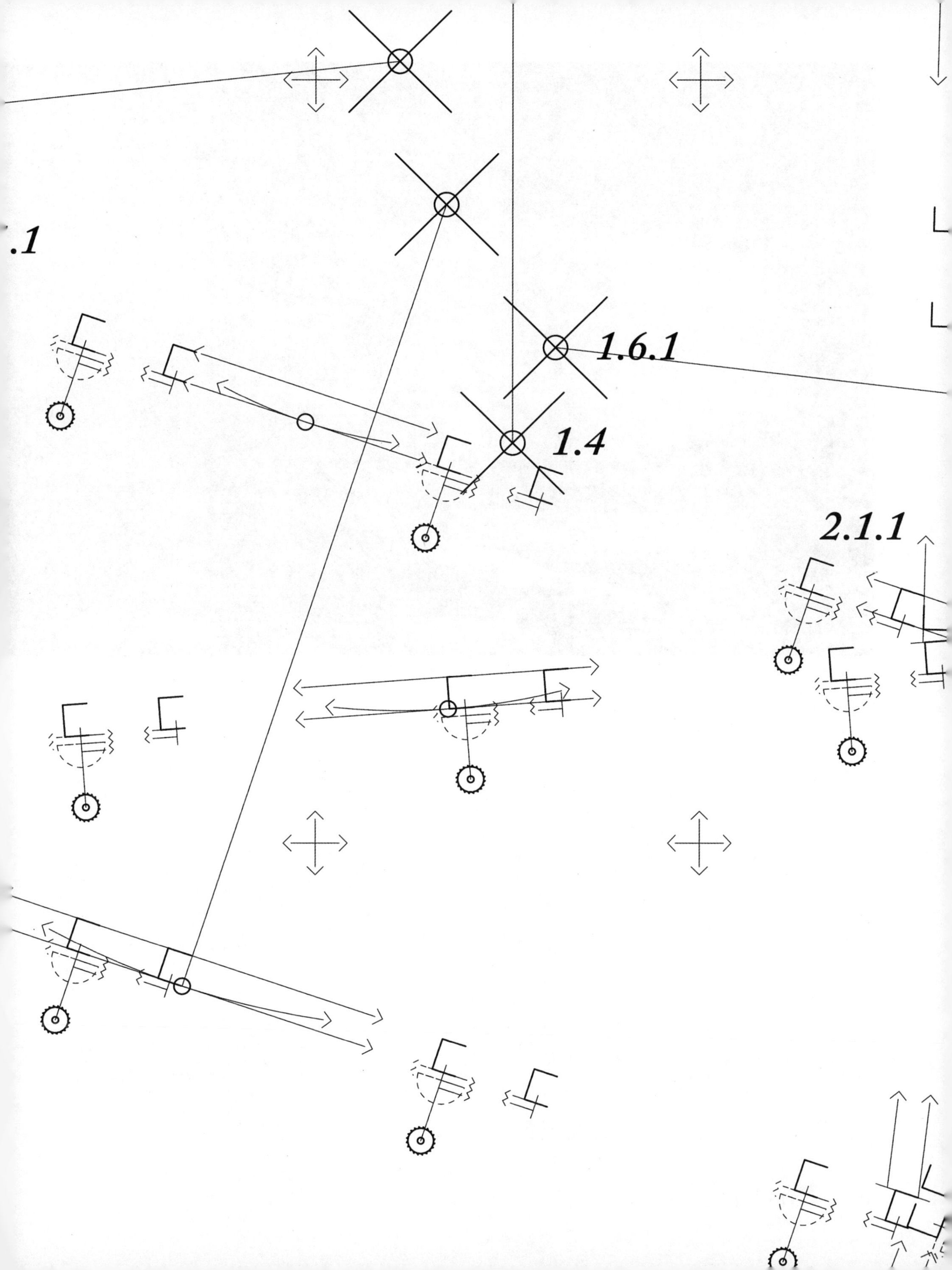

.1
1.6.1
1.4
2.1.1

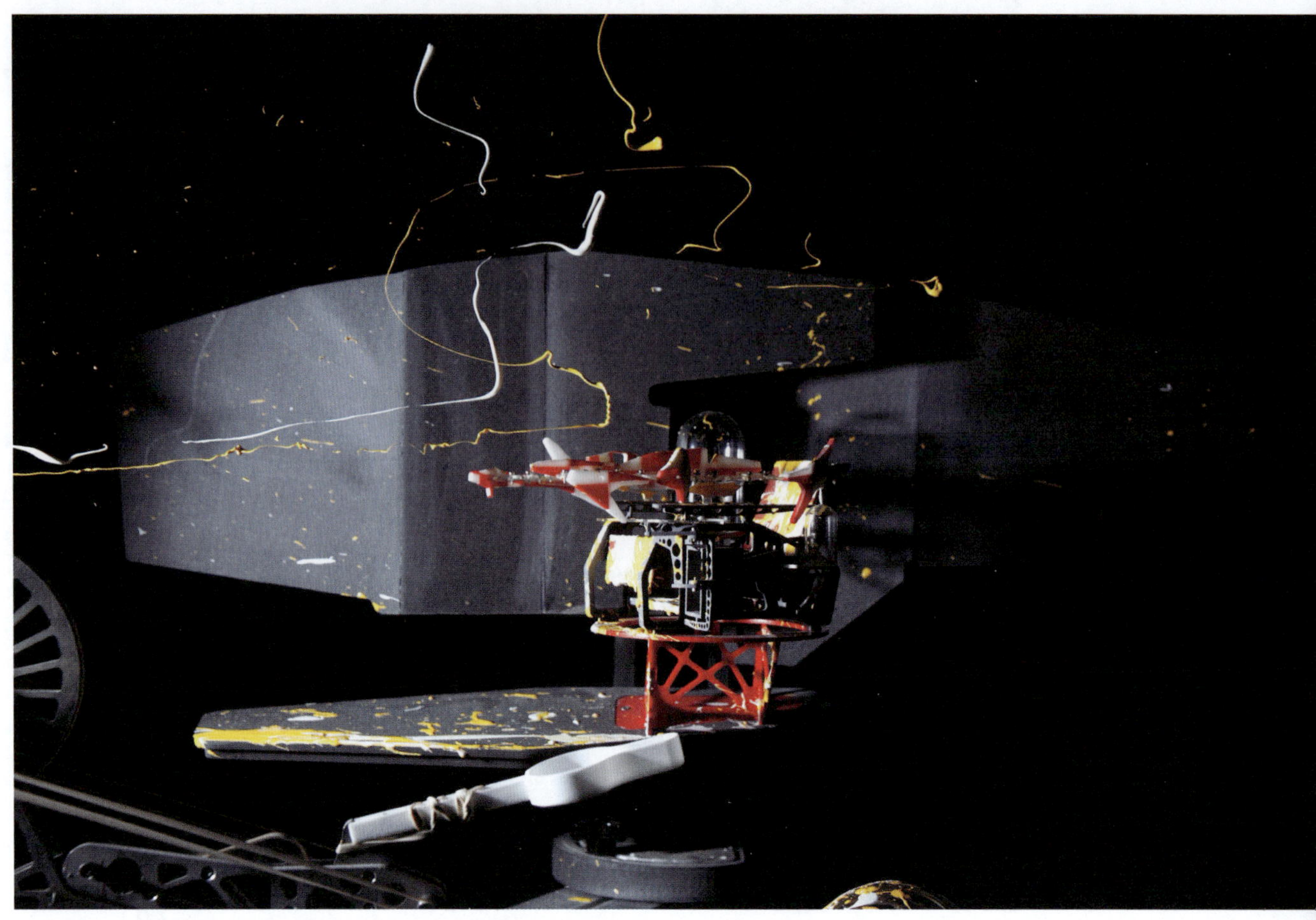

At first glance, the photograph appears to capture a moment in the life of a kinetic sculpture—an intricate assembly of parts, possibly rotating, just before being doused with streams of white and yellow paint. The setup resembles a scientific model, perhaps a mechanical planetarium, yet any markers of scale or context are absent, leaving the viewer to wonder about its true nature. The apparatus, toy-like in its composition, exudes a playful character as the splatters of paint disrupt the precision of the scene. This image seems to be an experiment in the interaction between controlled materials and th spontaneity of motion. The meticulous design of the components contrasts sharply with the randomness of the paint globs, highlig a dialogue between structure and chaos. Through this juxtapositi the piece may comment on the balance between precision and unpredictability in creative processes, reminding us of the spont inherent in even the most carefully planned designs.

Nat Chard

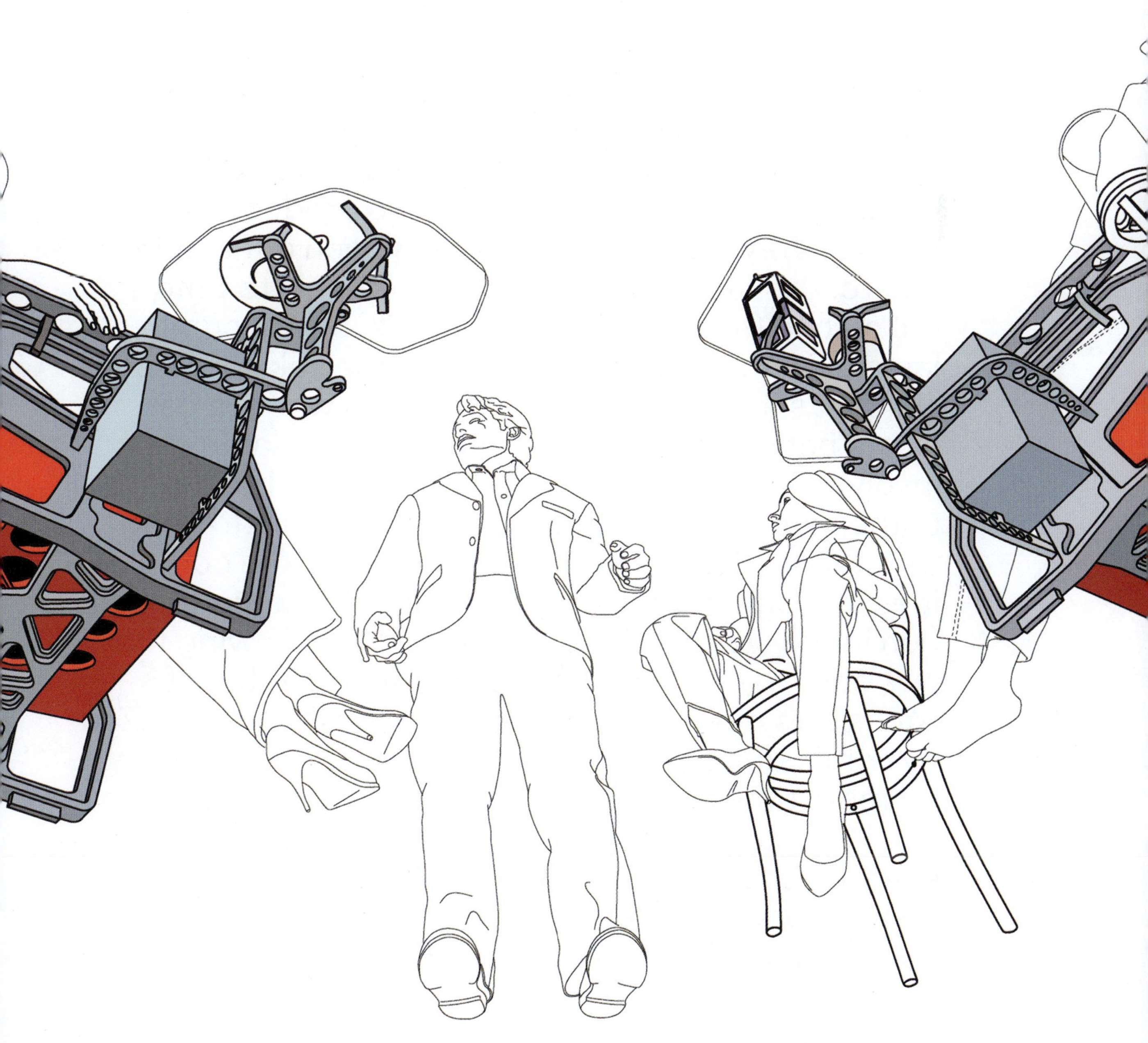

Appears easy, is difficult

I want to suggest four ways a drawing may be understood regarding the relationship between the actual labor required to create it and the audience's perception of effort. In two instances, the actual effort and the viewer's perception align—a drawing may have been either easy or difficult to make, and the viewer has the same impression. In the other two, the actual and perceived effort are opposed: a difficult drawing is perceived as having been easy to produce, or an easy drawing is seen as having been difficult to create. By "labor," I am referring not only to time but also to the resources, expertise, and accumulated skill imbued in the work. For the sake of discussion, let's focus on the two situations where a gap exists between the actual and perceived labor involved in creation. This dichotomy has been central to the mystique surrounding architectural drawing throughout its history. It also highlights the complexities of architectural production and its commodification in the world around us. Consider a drawing that was easy to produce but is perceived as difficult. Architects often work within a paradox characterized by conflicting demands on their resources. They bill for more time while expending less effort, and value efficiency while projecting an image of unwavering expertise. As a result, there is a growing tendency to create work that seems challenging but is not actually complicated. The tools of our profession have been marketed under this premise over the last several

1/2” LINE; 1/4” LINE; 1/8” LINE

the piece, the more elusive its creation seems, yet there it is—unmistakable and compelling.

In my view, this second approach has gained increasing value. The methods of production have become simpler, more readily available, and, in some respects, commercially commodifiable. By carefully authoring and controlling the methods of creation, it's possible to embed value in the work without sacrificing individuality. In this case, the difficulty arises from the intelligent deployment of labor rather than brute control. The complexity inherent in the drawing accumulates over time, resulting in a piece that is both ordinary and yet entirely unique.

–KH

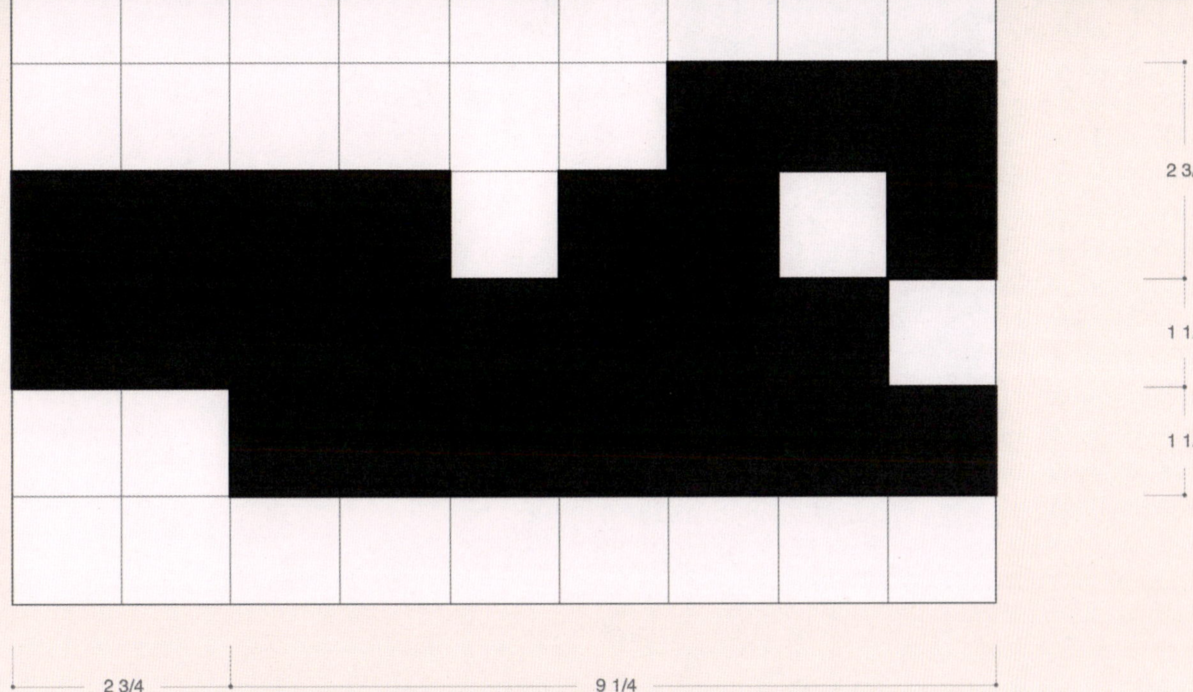

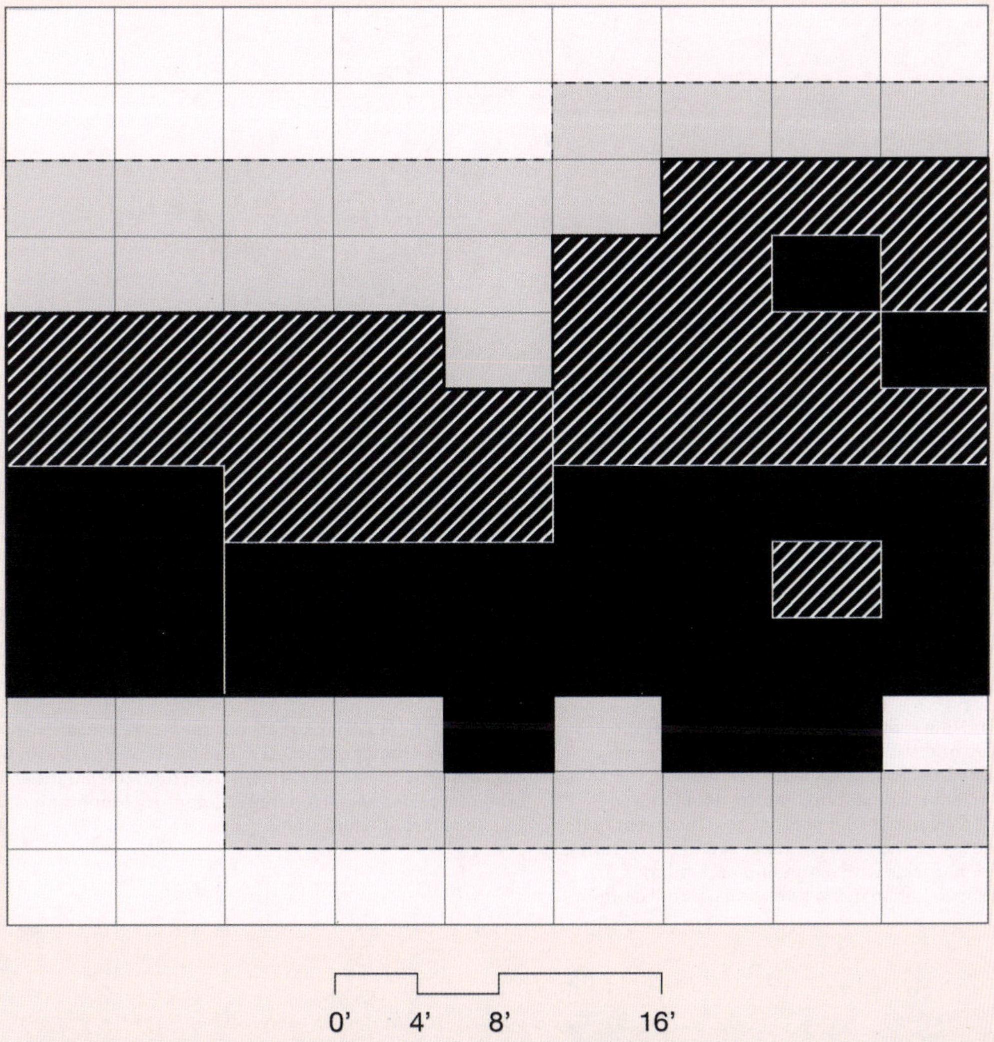

0' 4' 8' 16'

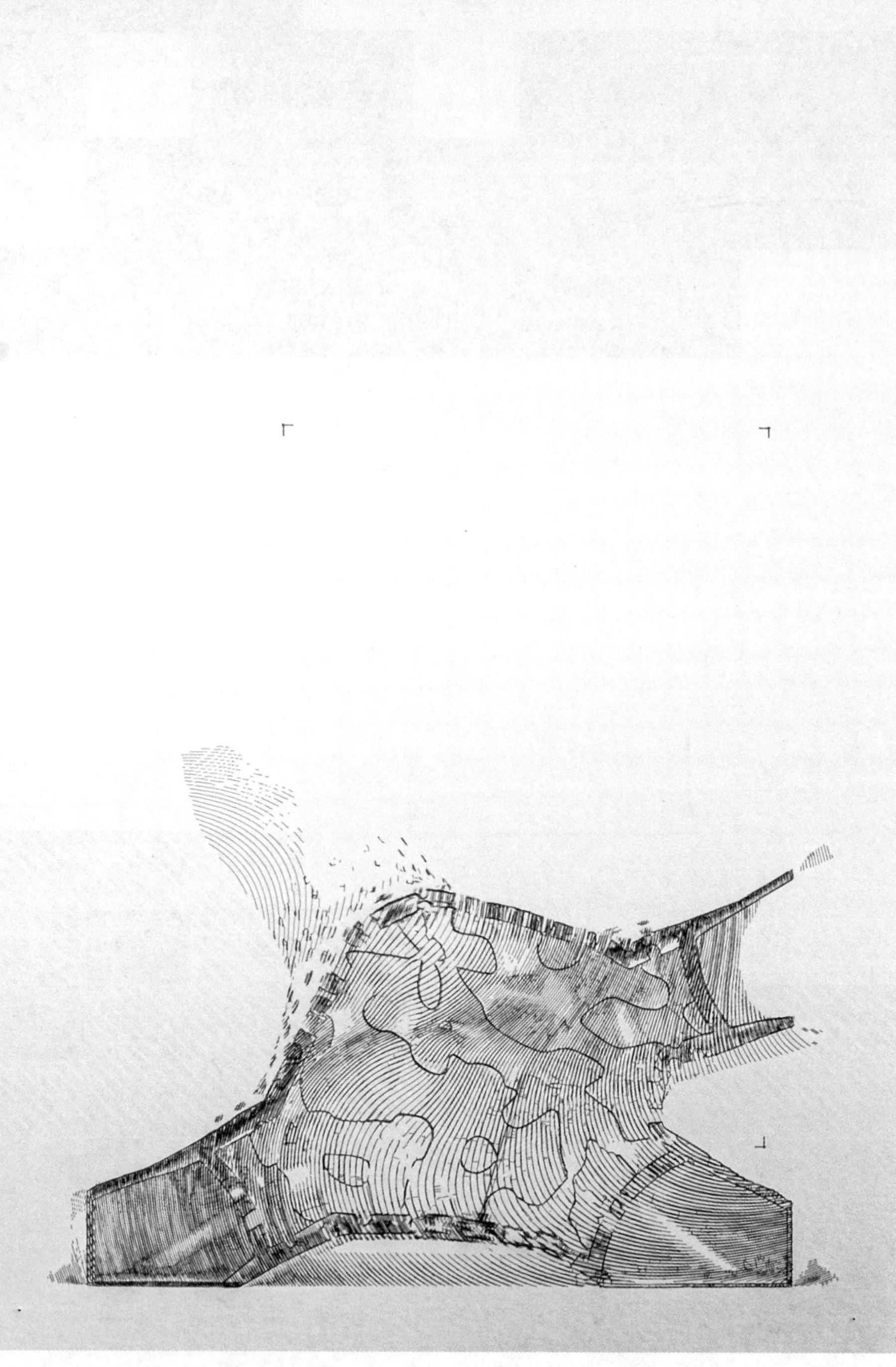

This drawing, a contoured line sketch, represents an early stage of a compostable product designed to collect water and support tree growth in the wild. Despite the casualness of its delineation, the lines exhibit a mechanical precision, suggesting that the drawing was produced in hybridity with a computational process. The object rests on an unseen ground and is cut into an elevational section. The form, reminiscent of a geode or barnacle with extending appendages, is defined through surface articulation using swerving parallel contours. These contours reflect material density or pattern rather than following a logical geometry. The lines, clearly drawn with a pen, introduce a physicality absent from digital techniques. The paral radiating lines recall nineteenth-century lithography, articulating surface through line alone.

HouMinn

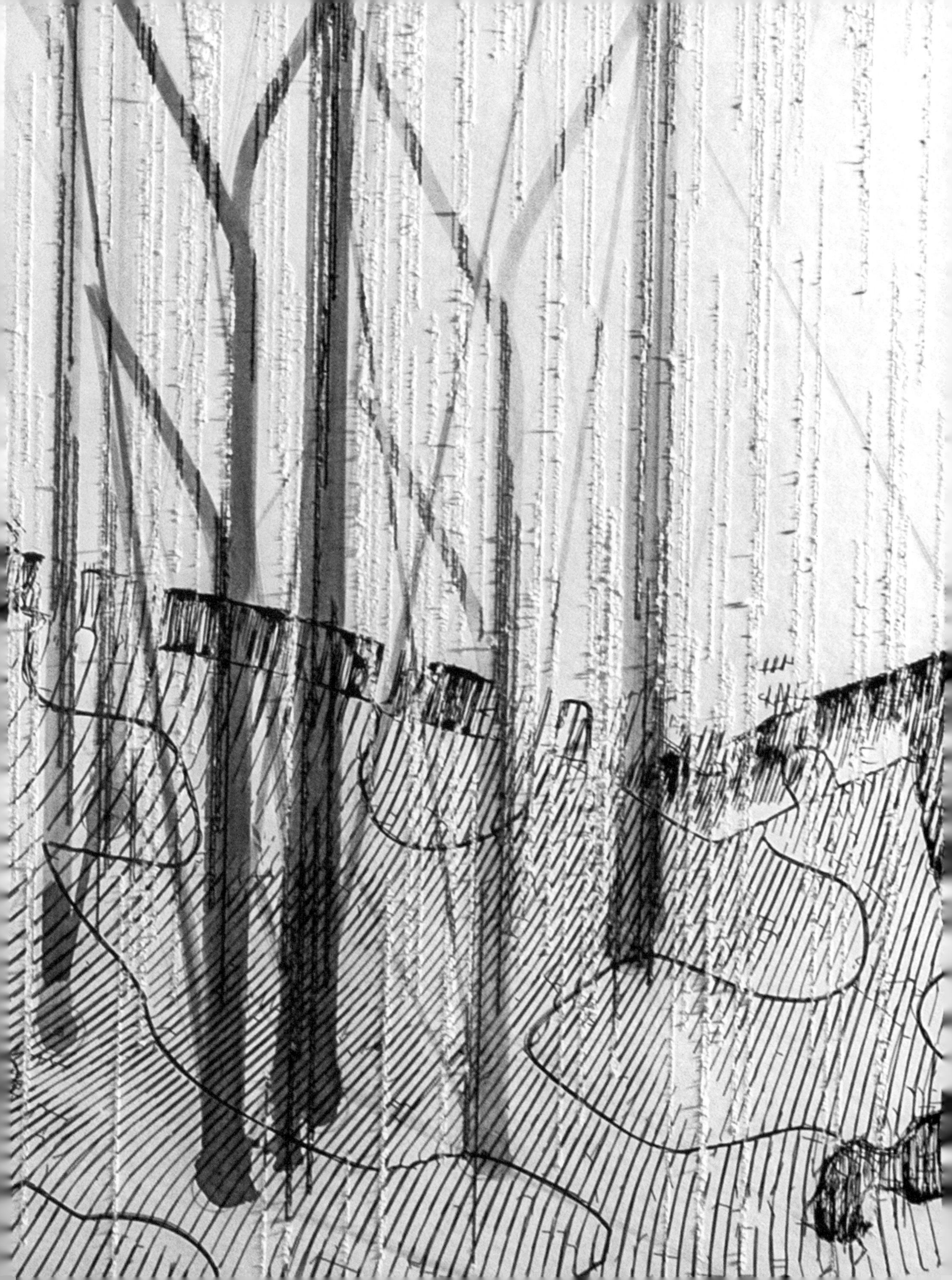

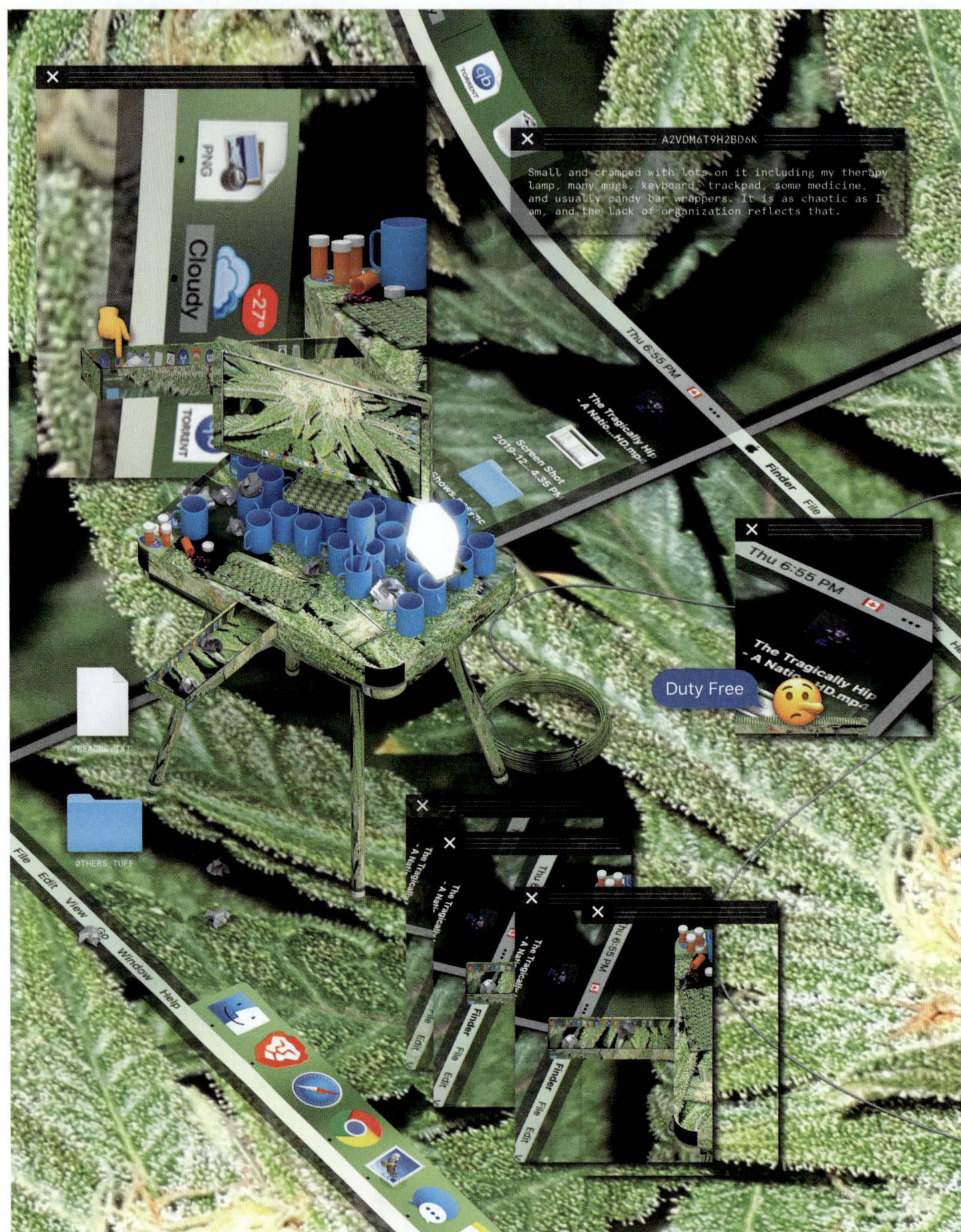

This composite image presents a desktop rendered onto itself, blending the physical and digital realms in a surreal overlap. Objects typical of a busy, perhaps chaotic, workspace—coffee cups, prescription bottles, folders, a budding marijuana flower, and crumpled paper—are scattered across the surface. Despite the evident artificiality of the scene, there's an undeniable sense of a lived-in reality, capturing the frantic energy of long hours of labor. The layering of digital windows, images of windows, and desktop icons evokes a visual loop, transforming the familiar desktop interface into a patterned wallpaper that dominates the composition. A Pinocc nose emoji declares "duty-free," adding a whimsical yet puzzlir element. The collapsing of the literal desktop into the image of the desktop creates a camouflage effect, where objects blend i their own digital representations. Familiar tools and iconograp such as blue folders and mugs, blur together, commenting on t mundane yet vital rhythms of modern work life and domesticity

EXTENTS

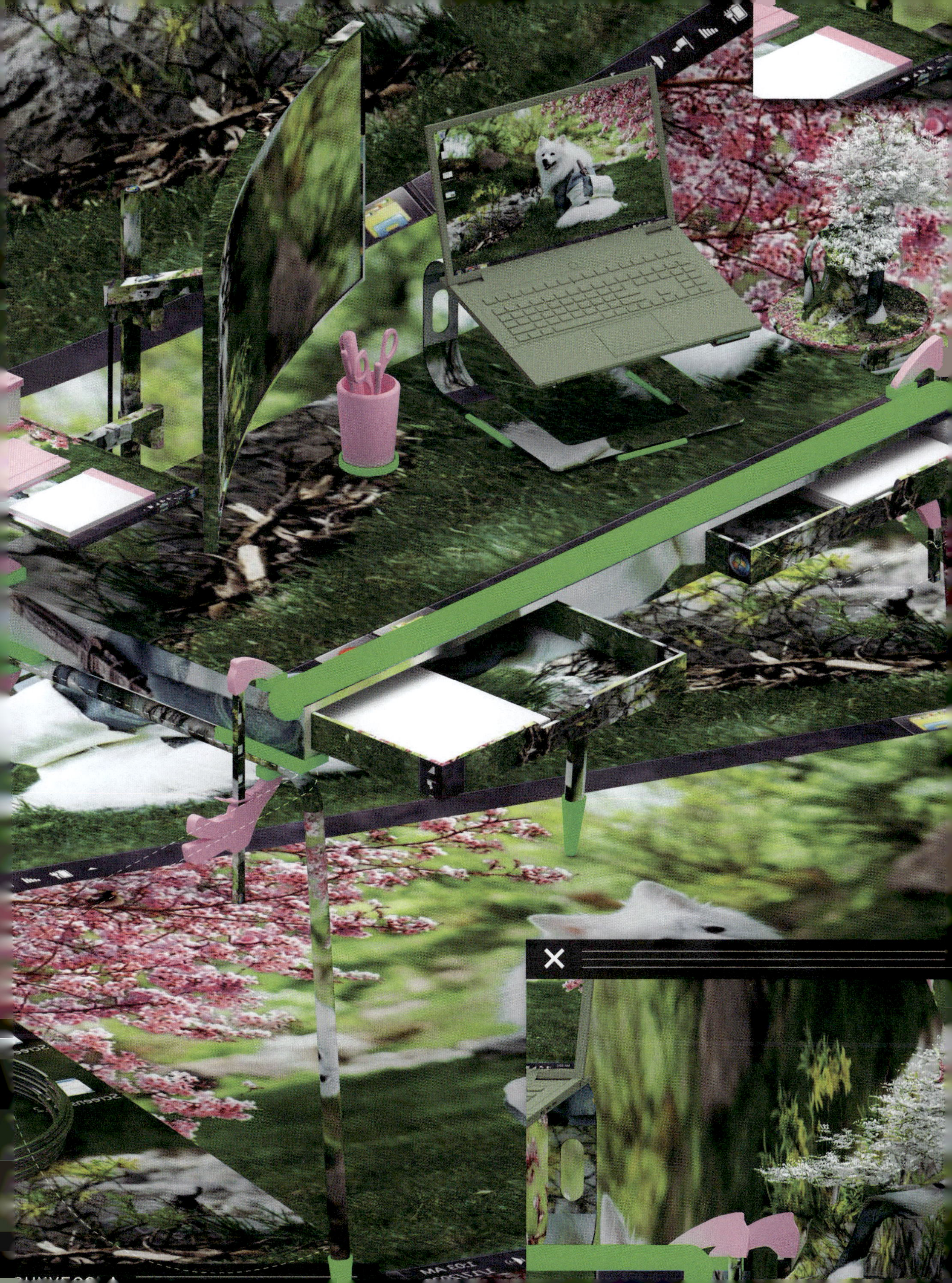

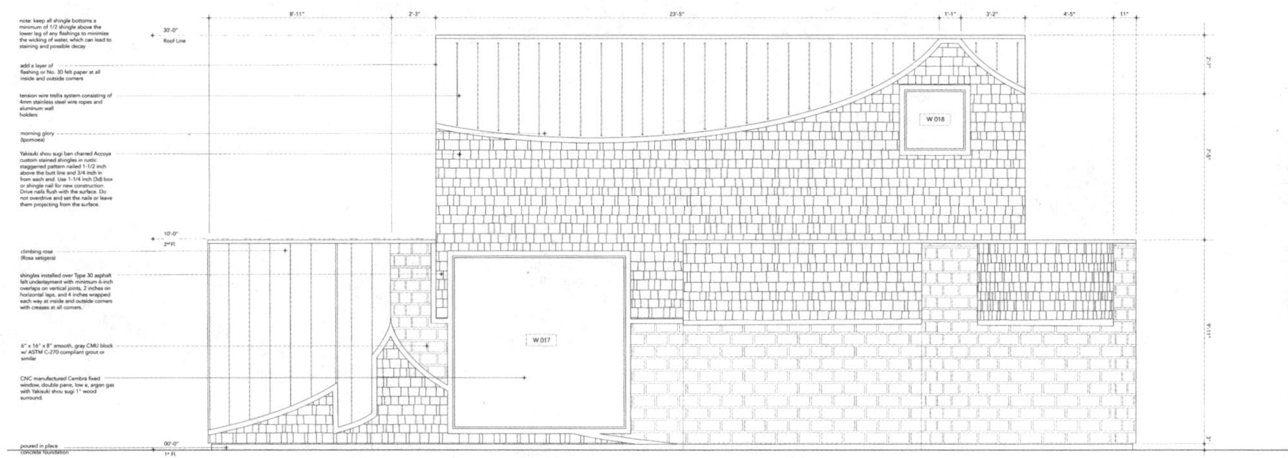

This carefully crafted construction drawing adheres to the precise standards expected of an architectural elevation, depicting a small, domestic-scale structure. The building's base is made of concrete block, with shingles continuing up the façade, and its apparent roof is clad in a wire scrim designed to support climbing plants. The introduction of organic plant matter into the assembly adds an unexpected layer to the structure, as does the subtle curvature of the roof, which interrupts the seemingly straightforward elevation. Two windows puncture the façade, positioned at odds with the underlying geo Despite its precision and clarity, the drawing introduces an elem of ambiguity with the apparent roofline's curious curve, which in presents as a conventional pitched roof but, upon closer inspect reveals itself to be a flat wall with three distinct materials flowing its surface. This blend of the conventional and unexpected make elevation both functional and intriguing.

Hume Architecture

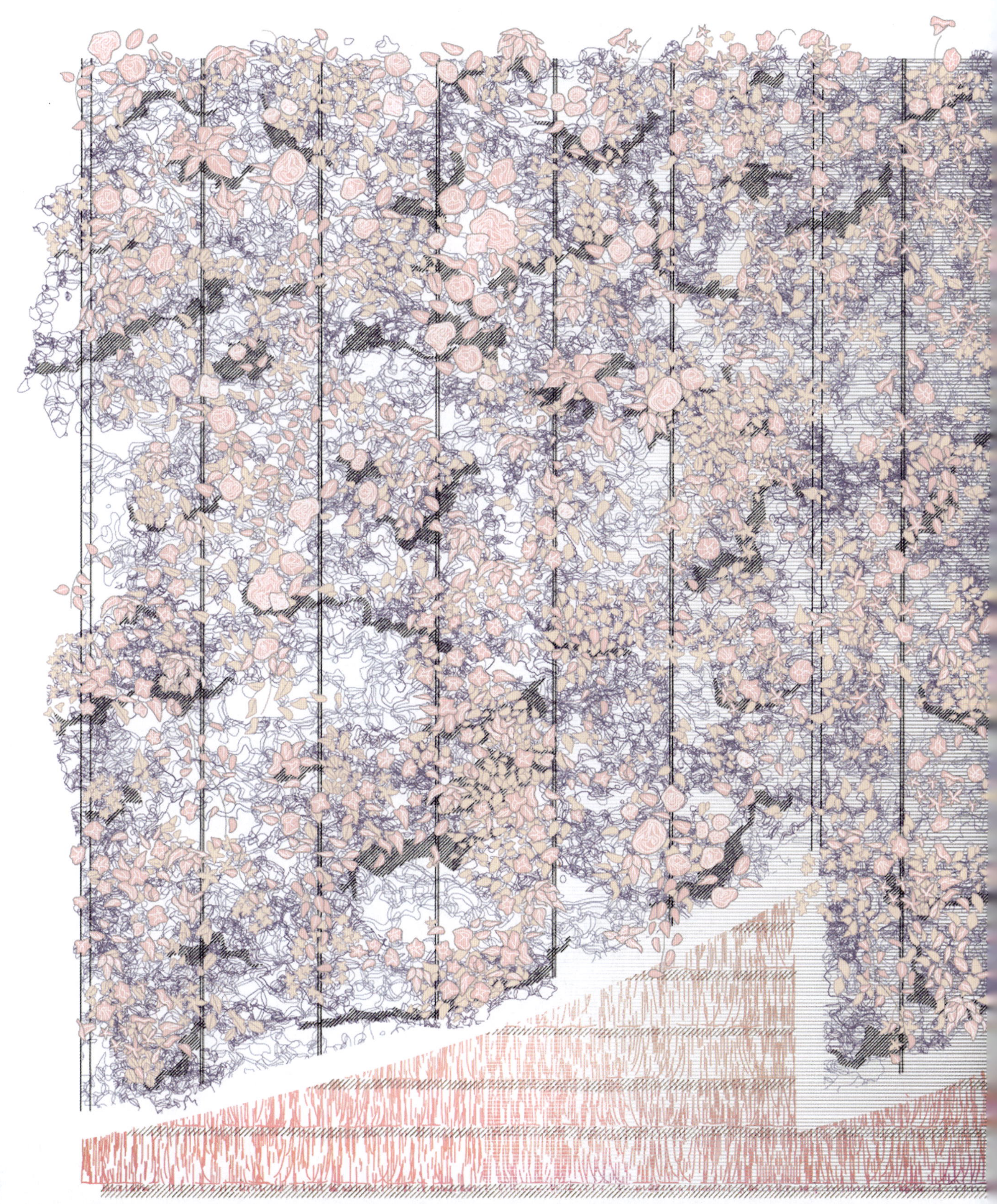

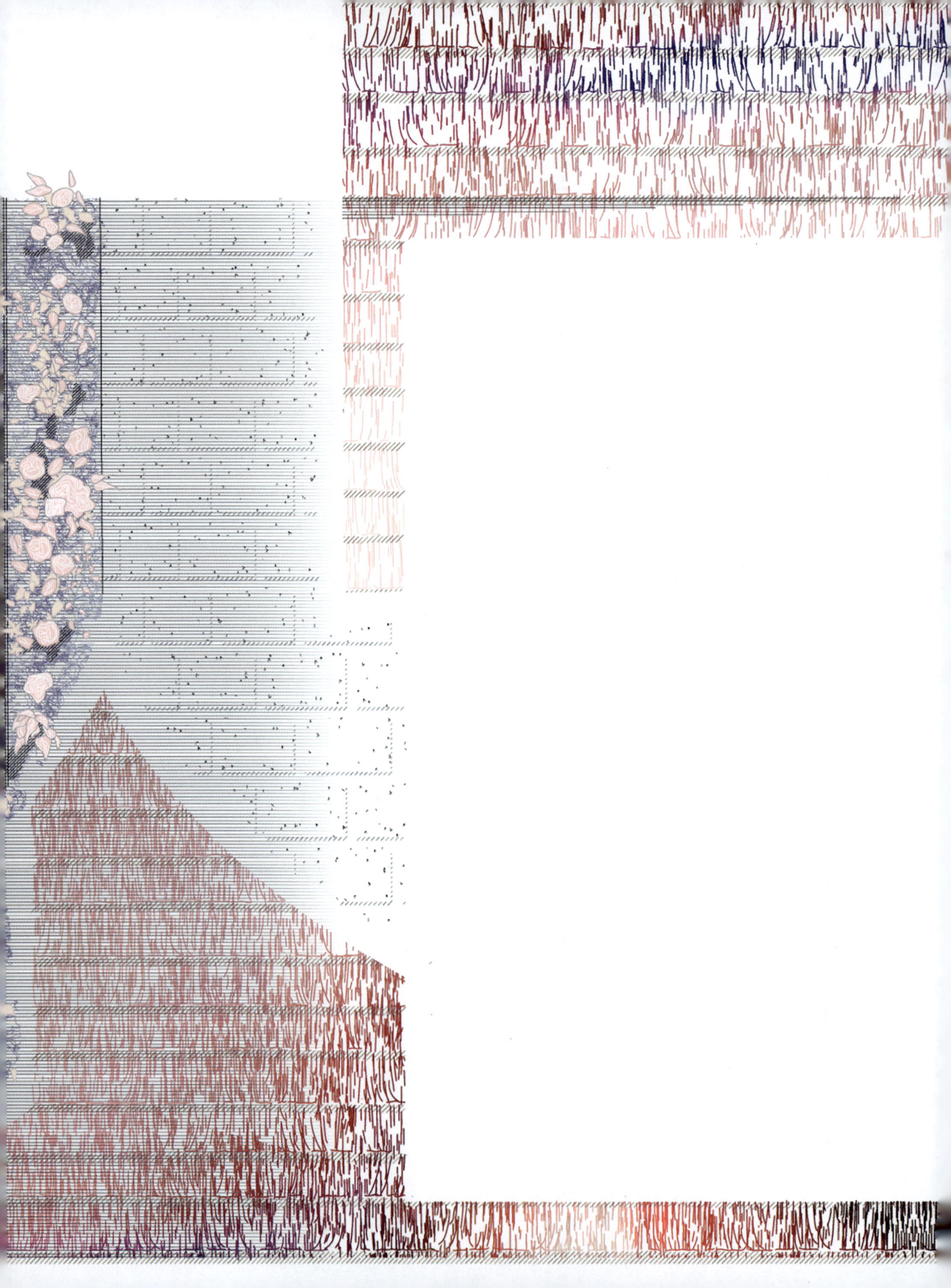

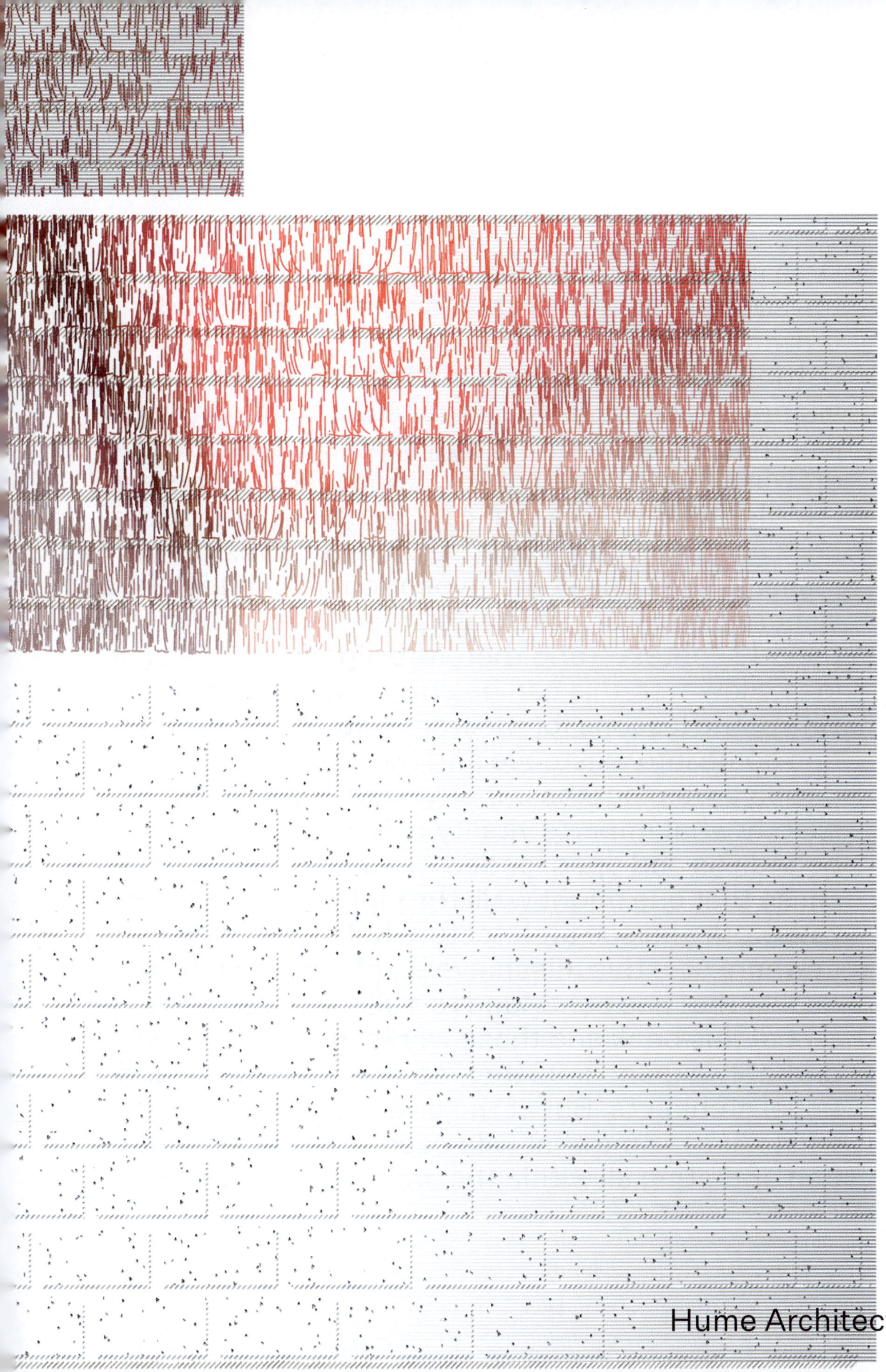

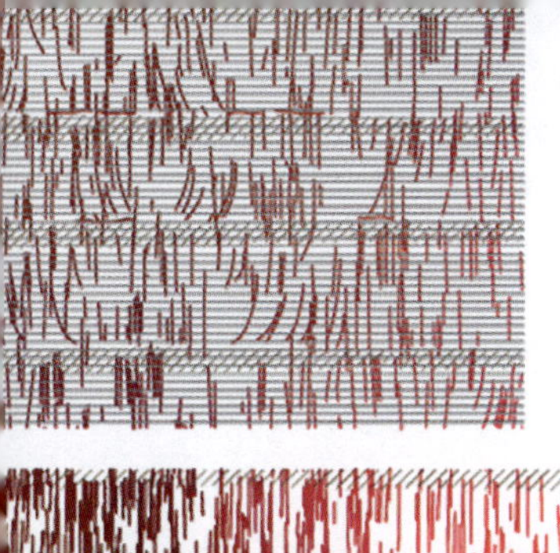

Hume Architecture

Improper / Proper

Drawing is an act of enhancing individuation. With the constraints of natural pragmatism removed, drawing can be a powerful act of self-declaration. Setting aside attempts to categorize, to pull into alignment, or to make a larger statement on the trajectories of the culture around us, let us assume that drawing can truly be entirely open-ended. There are few disciplinary acts that can carry that weightlessness and then, on a dime, become fully vested with realism. The consistent invocation of architecture as a linear history of interrelated ideas can be useful to provide context—and therefore significance—to an idea. However, this can be equally just as paralyzing. One of the lessons for me from watching the exhibition come into existence and then just as quickly dissolve was that the impermanence of drawing is exactly what imparts vitality to it. Likewise, the boundless and open-ended nature of drawing gives a sense that one might walk through a room crowded with work and see architecture both everywhere and nowhere. It is this mischievous, ghostly, vaporous quality that has continued to pull me back to the content of this book and these works. If I could, I would probably expand it further, adding works from additional architects. But at the end of the day, this is what it is: a somewhat wild cacophony of individuation operating all within the architectural imagining.

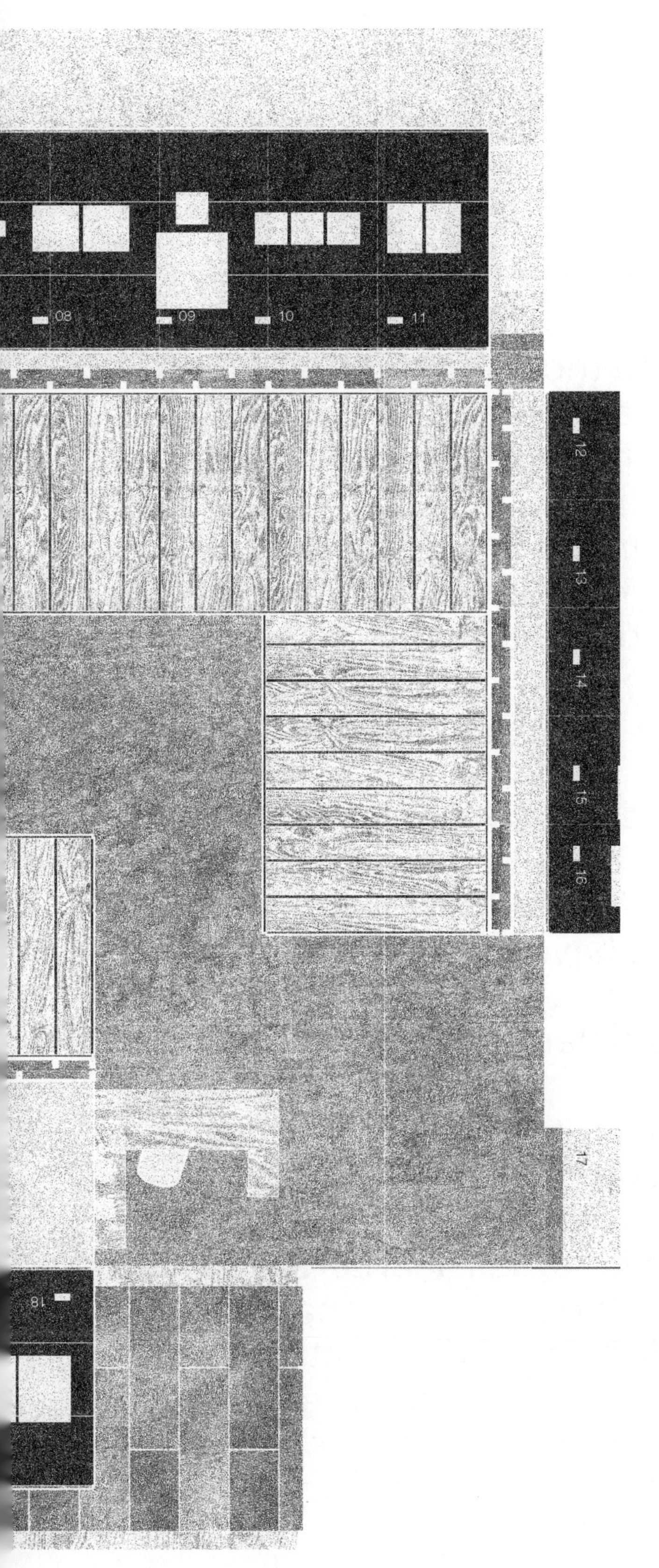
08
09
10
11
12
13
14
15
16
17
18

The Promise of Drawing

In this time of image ubiquity and oversaturation, when everything is visualized in countless ways across a jarring spectrum of infinitely tweaked approaches, media, and techniques, true invention is nearly impossible. We can hand-draw, digitally draw, model, collage, animate, and even create through feeding words into artificial intelligence, all with increasing speed and precision, and with a decreasing need for technical knowledge or training. Almost anyone can produce something eye-catching in the blink of an eye.

If anyone can draw, why teach it in architecture school? Is it to help students secure jobs upon graduation? To enable them to communicate their ideas and intentions accurately? Or do we do it simply because that is what we have always done?

Or can drawing serve a different, deeper purpose?

Noam Chomsky famously states that the purpose of education is "...to help people determine how to learn on their own." In other words, education should foster independent thinkers, self-learners, and lifelong questioners, nurturing a mindset that does not take the "way we do things" for granted. In contrast, he notes that in prevailing models of education, "...there have been many measures taken to try to turn the educational system towards more control,

Marc Swackhamer

are mischievous. They don't provide clear answers. In themselves, these drawings are acts of dissent, modelling not a specific aesthetic, but rather an approach for students and more, broadly, for education.

The work in this amazing catalog has never been more important than it is now.

Contributors

Current Interests is a Los Angeles-based architectural design studio led by Matthew Au and Mira Henry. Matthew and Mira are on the design faculty at the Southern California Institute for Architecture.

Perry Kulper is an architect and a professor of architecture at the University of Michigan's Taubman College of Architecture and Urban Planning.

Frank Fantauzzi is the Department Chair of the Architectural Design department at the Maryland Institute College of Art. Charlie O'Geen is a lecturer at the Taubman College of Architecture and Urban Planning at the University of Michigan.

CJ Lim is a Professor of Architecture and Urbanism at The Bartlett Faculty of the Built Environment at University College London.

LANZA Atelier is a Mexico City-based architectural design studio led by Isabel Abascal and Alessandro.

NEMESTUDIO is a San Francisco Bay Area-based architectural design practice led by Neyran Turan and Mete Sönmez. Neyran Turan is an associate professor at the University of California, Berkeley.

Norman Kelley is a Chicago and Cambridge-based architectural design practice led by Carrie Norman and Thomas Kelley. Thomas Kelley is an associate professor at the University of Illinois Chicago. Carrie Norman is an assistant professor at the Massachusetts Institute of Technology.

office ca is a design research collaborative led by Galo Canizares and Stephanie Sang Delgado. Galo is an assistant professor at the University of Kentucky College of Design. Stephanie is an assistant professor at the School of Public Architecture at Kean University's Michael Graves College of Design.

WOJR is an organization of designers based in Cambridge led by William O'Brien Jr. William is an associate professor at the Massachusetts Institute of Technology.

The Open Workshop is a multidisciplinary design workshop in San Francisco and Toronto led by Neeraj Bhatia. Neeraj is an associate professor at the California College of the Arts.

Outpost Office is a design practice in Columbus led by Ashley Bigham and Erik Herrmann. Ashley and Erik are assistant professors at The Ohio State University.

T8Projects is a Texas-based design practice led by James Micha Tate. James is an assistant professor at Texas A&M University.

Nada Subotincic is the cofounder of the Montreal-based design practice Ceci n'est pas un musée.

Sort Studio is the Denver-based architectural design and art practice led by Brian Dale and Meredith Dale. Brian is a lecturer a the University of Colorado Denver.

Anca Matyiku is the co-founder of the Cincinnati- and Calgary-ba design practice MOTE Projects. Anca is an Assistant Professor a the University of Cincinnati.

Variable Projects is the New Orleans-based design practice led b Adam Marcus. Adam is an associate professor at Tulane Univers

Mark West has taught architecture at a variety of universities in the USA, Canada, United Kingdom, Europe, and Turkey since 19 Mark is founder of the Montreal-based design practice Surviving Logic.

DESIGN EARTH is the Cambridge- and Ann Arbor-based resear practice led by Rania Ghosn and El Hadi Jazairy. Rania is an ass professor of Architecture and Urbanism at the Massachusetts In of Technology. El Hadi is an associate professor of Architecture the University of Michigan.

A/P Practice is a Florence- and Wuppertal-based architectural design practice led by Daniele Profeta and Maya Alam. Maya is Chair of Theory and Discourse in Design at the School of Archite and Engineering Bergische University Wuppertal. Daniele is the Architecture Program Director at Syracuse University in Floren

Studio Ames is the New York City-based architectural design an research practice led by Daisy Ames. Daisy is a member of the f at Yale University and the Cooper Union.

Studio Sean Canty is the Cambridge-based architectural desigr practice led by Sean Canty. Sean is an assistant professor at Ha University.

Now Here is the Los Angeles-based architectural design practic led by Katy Barkan. Katy is a member of the faculty at the Unive of California-Los Angeles.

This book is made possible through the support of the University of Colorado Denver College of Architecture and Planning.

Published by Axiomatic Editions

Axiomatic Editions
an imprint of ORO Editions
Publishers of Architecture, Art, and Design
Ashley Simone: Editorial Director
www.axioeditions.com
info@axioeditions.com

Author: Kevin Hirth
Managing and Text Editor: Toby Gardner
Proofreading: Sarah Fingerhood
Design: Office of Luke Bulman
Production Manager: Jake Anderson

First Edition
ISBN 978-1-961856-59-2

Prepress and print work by Axiomatic Editions, an imprint of ORO Editions Inc. Printed in China.

The publisher makes a continuous effort to minimize the overall carbon footprint of its publications. As part of this goal, ORO, in association with Global ReLeaf, arranges to plant trees to replace those used in the manufacturing of the paper produced for its books. Global ReLeaf is an international campaign run by American Forests, one of the world's oldest nonprofit conservation organizations. Global ReLeaf is American Forests' education and action program that helps individuals, organizations, agencies, and corporations improve the local and global environment by planting and caring for trees.

instead a product of process, a form of internal meditation and practice? Or is it a facet of public posture, a way of positioning a proposition or translation for public consumption and enjoyment in its own right? These objectives are increasingly conflated as our methods of working become more diverse and less reliant on a singular standard. To me, this is not only productive but also projective. No drawing is improper if it is ultimately useful or productive in its own right.

The works presented here are a compilation of fifty-six original pieces by twenty-eight architects who were asked to respond to the following prompt: *make something dutiful; make something mischievous*. This deceptively simple and seemingly frivolous premise was crafted to intentionally sidestep questions of pragmatism and propriety while simultaneously engaging them. To my continuing delight, in response to the prompt, we received photographs, renderings, images, sketches, collages, and graphs. For the purposes of this book, the term drawing intentionally encapsulates all forms of media contained herein. The body of work presented on these pages, diverse in both scope and limitations, represents a thesis about architectural drawing in our present, one that is increasingly inclusive, aware of its compartmentalization, and curious about the utilities of certain conventions. The featured architects and thinkers were not assembled to establish a canon or provide a comprehensive view of what can and should be done in our confused present. Rather, this is an optimistic cross section, a diverse set of

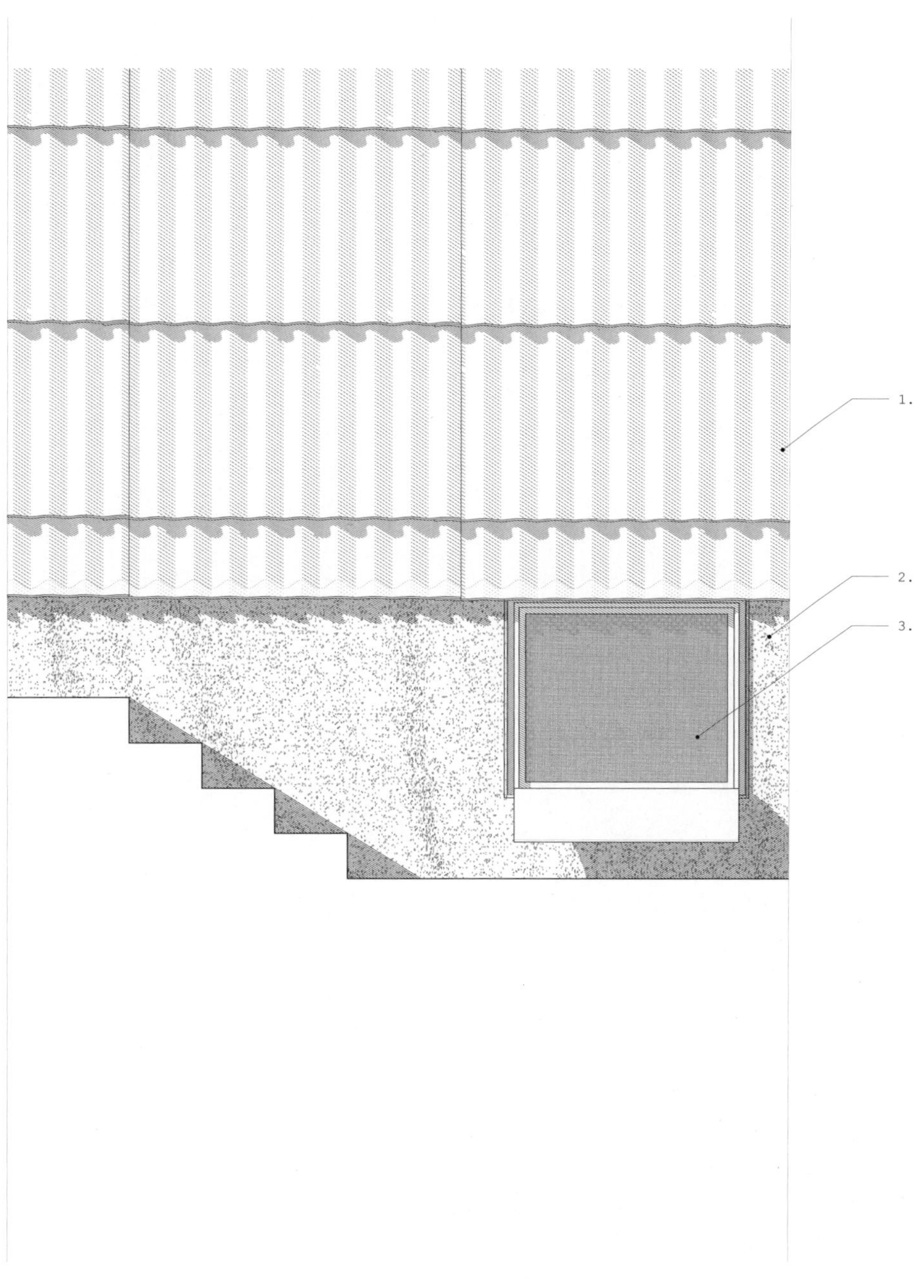

We see a stair, a window, and a pattern denoting projected shadows and material textures rendered as a hatched overlapping composition. The drawing is pragmatic and rational, adhering to the expectations of a construction document. The geometric elements' precision reflects a rigorous approach to assembly. Seams are aligned, stair treads and risers meet at crisp angles, and the window displays a clear logic of construction. The hatch aligns with the projected angle of the sun's cast shadows, corresponding to the rise-to-run ratio of the stair. The dashed finish of the stucco lower surface is applied with minimal visible tiling, enhancing the realism and reinforcing the precise intentionality of the overall design.

Current Interests

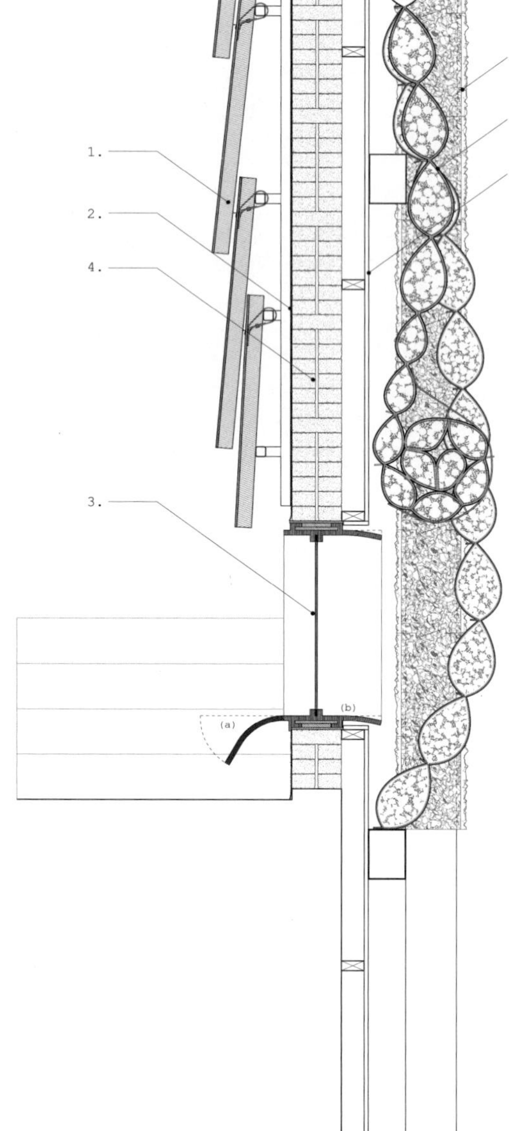

1. Rainscreen: Corrugated 0.25″ Fibre-Cement Shingle w/ Urethane Dipped Tip (color: Dark-Tone, Red; Dark-Tone, Green); 0.15″ Leather Strap; 1.5″ Steel Tube Purlin Frame(color: PC Black).

2. Stucco, Dash finish (color: Dark-Tone, Green).

3. Window(Gasket): Urethan Rubber, Shore A, Density: 30lbs(a), 50lbs (b) (color: UV Black); 0.25″ Pilkington Mirropane Glass.

4. Unreinforced Masonry Wall, existing.

5. Interior Wall: 2x4 Framing @ 16″ OC; 0.625″ Gypsum; HG Enamel Top Coat (color: Ultramarine)

6. Interior Structure: 6x8 Timber Column/Beam; 0.125 Aluminum Composite Cladding (color: Ultramarine), 1.5″ Flexible Urethane Foam Sleave, (color: Ultramarine Pigment).

7. Insulation Blanket: Tyvek Fabric (color: Silver); Wool Insulation, R20.

Upon initial examination, this section is identified as corresponding to the previous drawing. What appears rational and straightforward in the partial elevation reveals itself to be far more complex. The building is shown to be a recladding of an existing unreinforced masonry wall. Both the interior and exterior finishes prove to be more intricate than they first seem. The precision of the exterior cladding is achieved through a hanging system that enables large-scale shingling of materials.
The window, initially perceived as a simple feature in the elevation, is actually a custom rubberized unit, intentionally designed to produce material sagging. Inside, the cladding functions not only as insulation but is also apparently performative, gesturing toward informality.

Current Interests

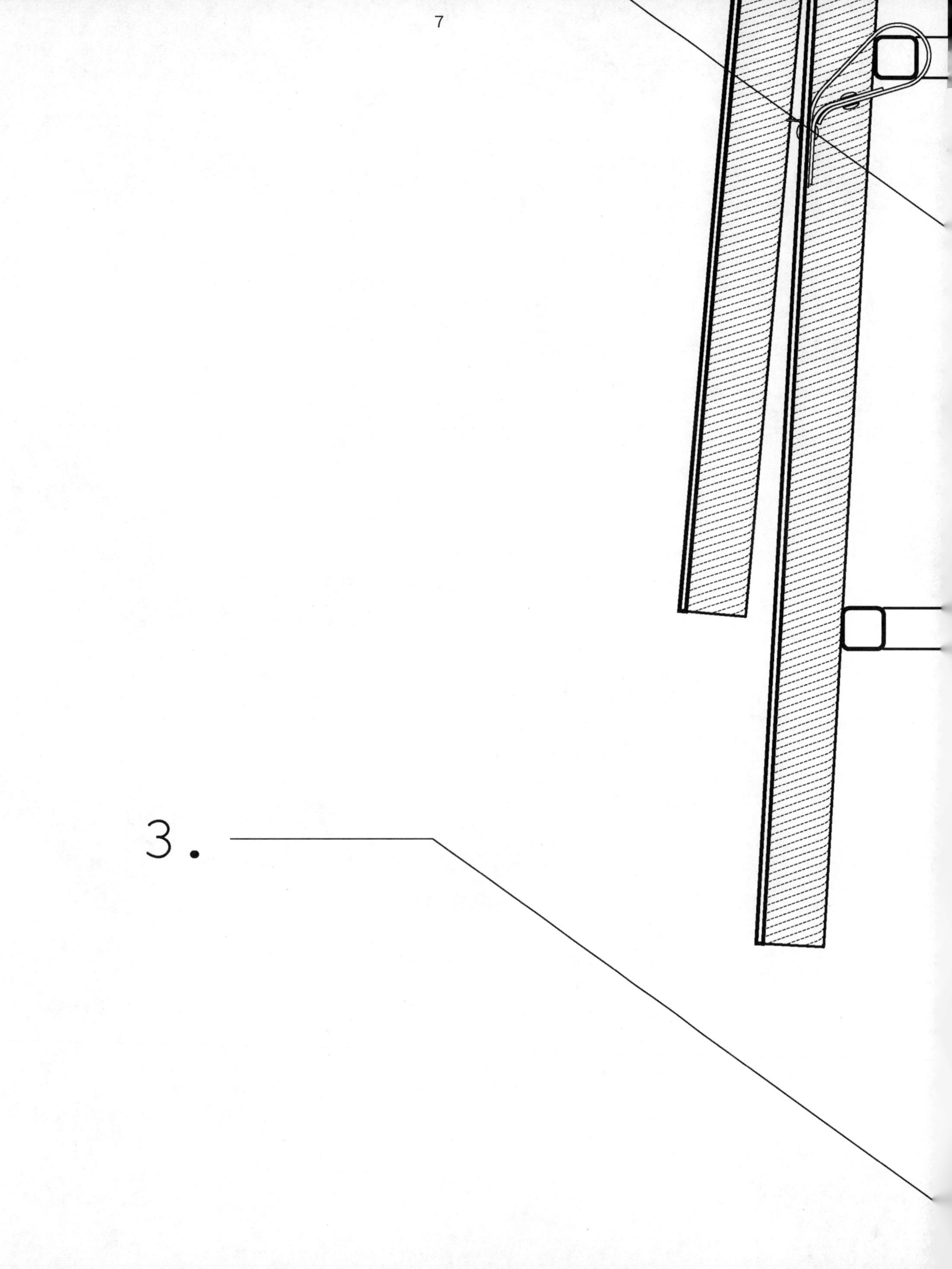
3.

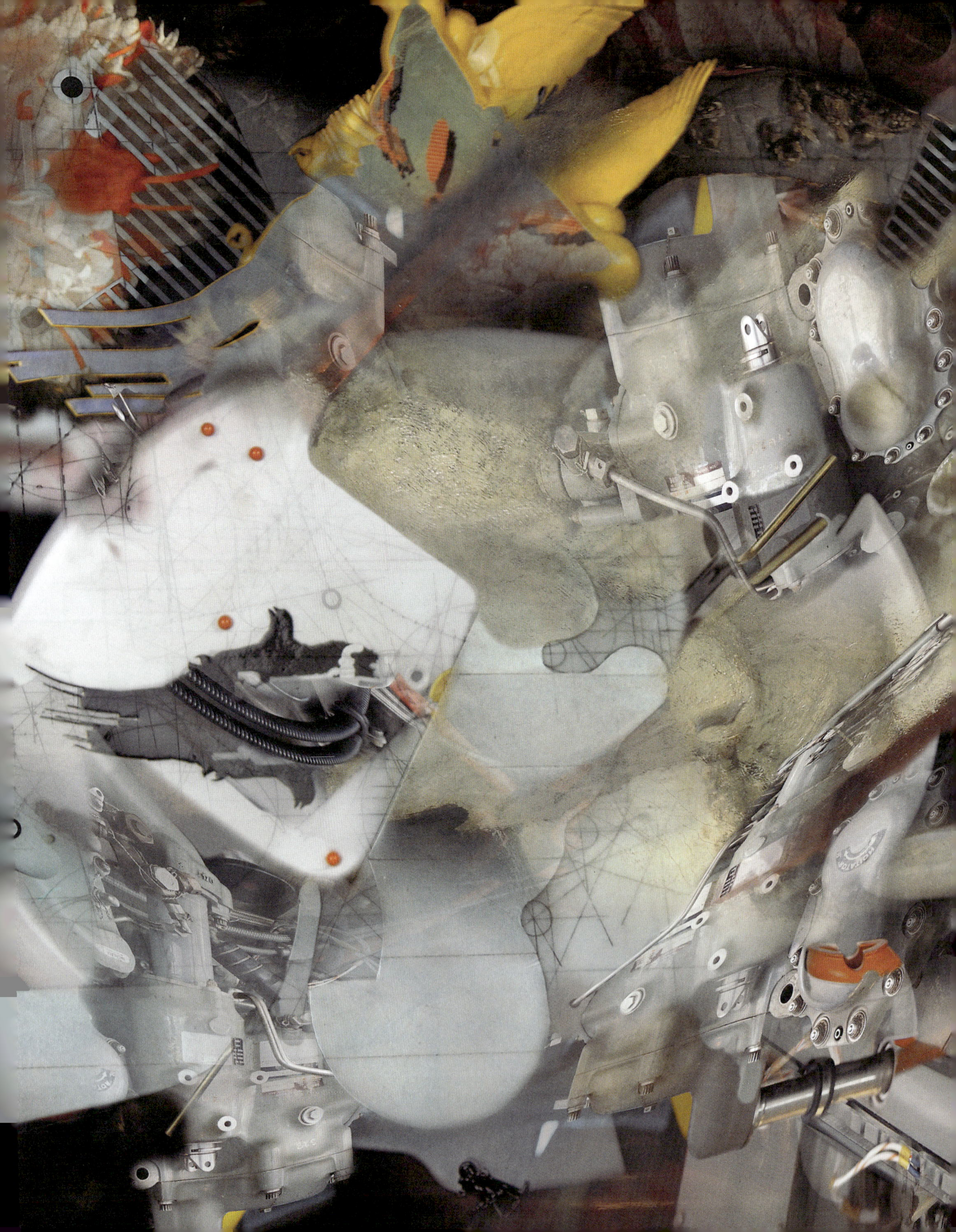

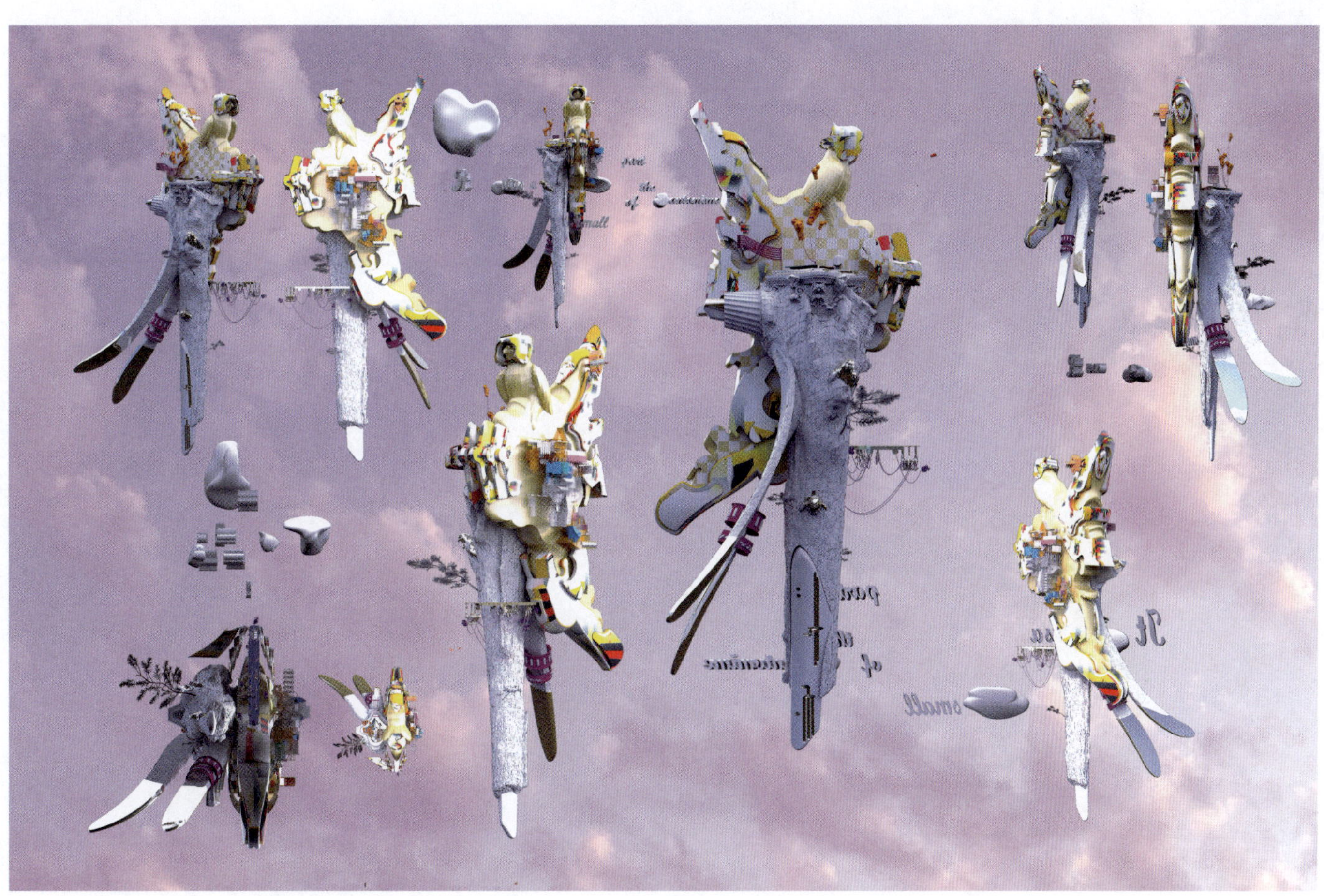

Objects float on a cloud-like background, surrounded by a collection of illuminated and floating figures. The placement and orientation of these mechanical and biological objects initially suggest an elevational or perspectival space, where gravity seems irrelevant. The complexity of these figures is undeniable. A referential collage takes shape in their form, where fragments of column capitals, plastic birdhouses, text objects, and mannered figural forms exist in concert. The image appears to be a pure rendering, collaged into a rosy photograph of the clouds that these figures inhabit. The use of clear figuration, such as a bird or alpine foliage, blurs the boundary between the artificial and the organic. Upon closer inspection, the image presents a projective ambiguity: are we viewing ten distinct variants, or simply duplicates rotated and isolated on an ultimately flattened plane?

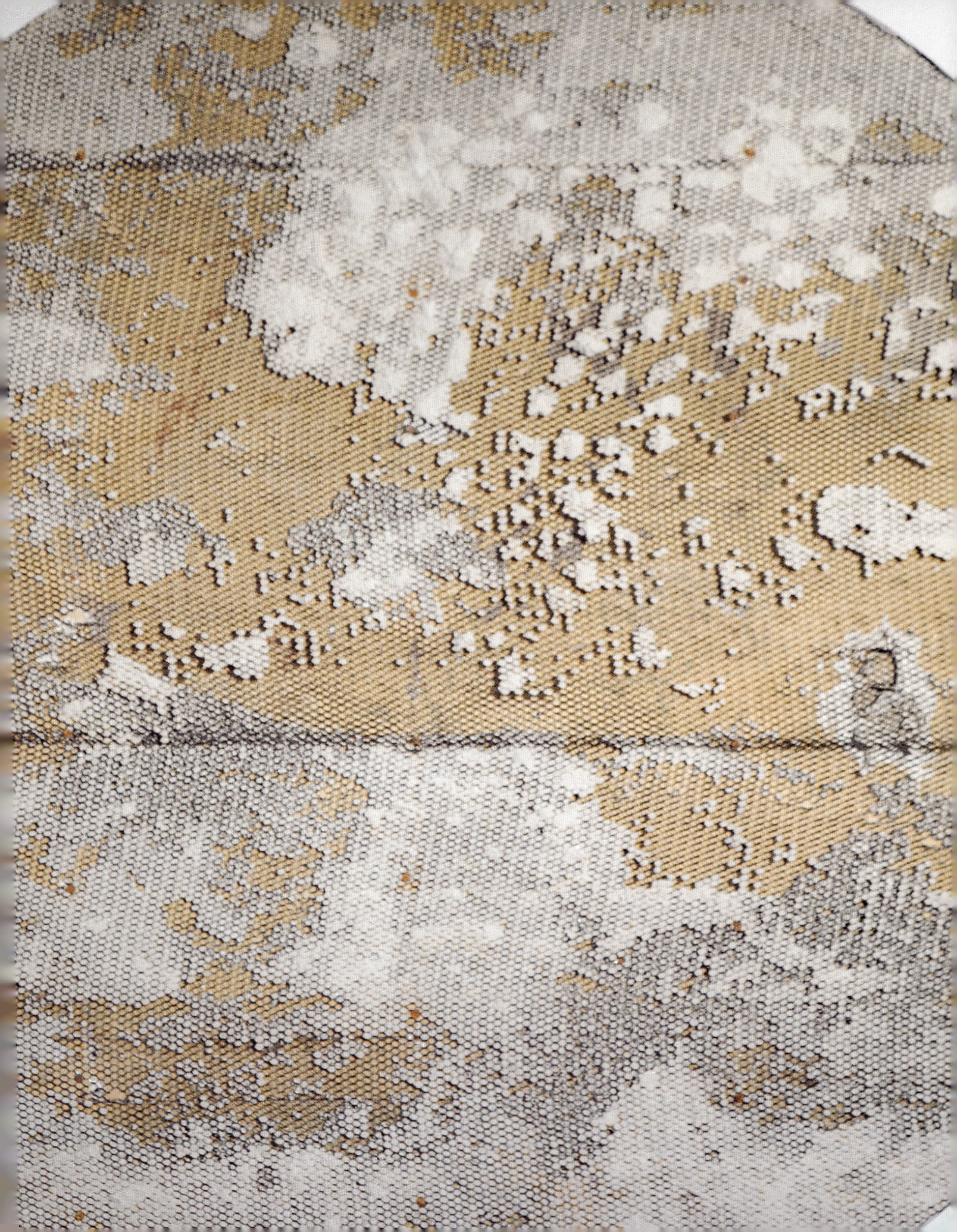

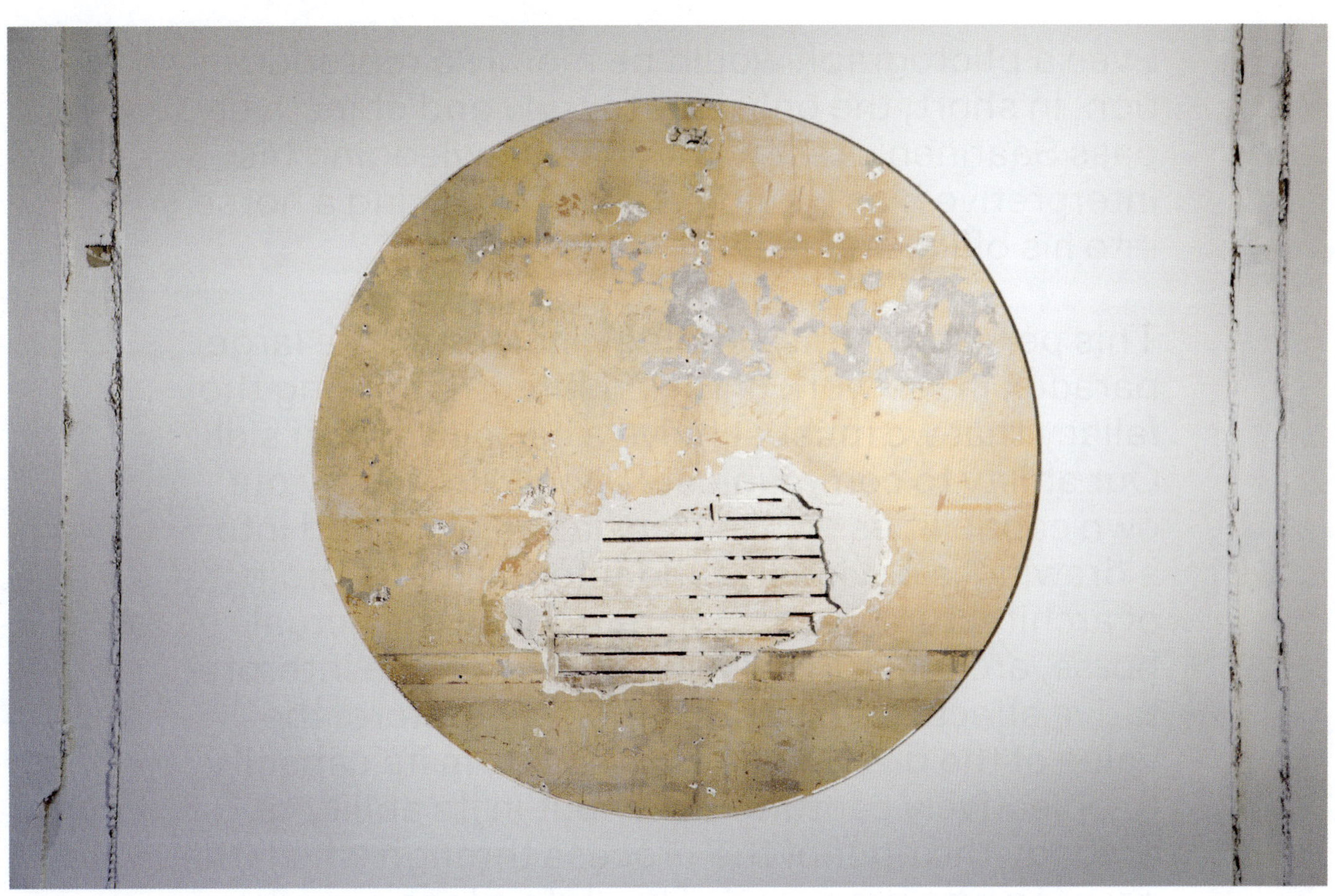

This image initially seems more straightforward than its twin—two vertical bands frame a circle of exposed plaster, chipped away in one area to reveal the supporting lathing. Yet the composition maintains an uncanny quality, a careful destruction. The broken wall within a perfectly inscribed circle appears to result from a very deliberate, almost obsessive technique. The fidelity of these images as photographs is striking; close examination reveals little evidence of Photoshop tampering, suggesting they exist as stand-ins for the true drawings—the inscribed circles themselves. This ambiguity between the artifact documenting the drawing and the drawing itself raises a playful question about authenticity and reproduction in architectural production. The normal brutality of demolition here takes on a precise, clinical quality, pointing toward sustainability and preservation, reimagining what might ordinarily be discarded as a delicate object of art.

Even a photograph would be merely a reproduction. In short, the only way to truly and objectively pass Saarinen's test without acknowledging his interpretive bias would have been to bring a horse into his office and leave it in his lobby.

This perhaps clumsy analogy illustrates the larger paradox in the work of the architect, exposing the fallacy that we must achieve a certain level of skill. Our ability to communicate is only limited by our own capabilities. While translating our world into a drawing is obviously fundamental to the project of architecture, unless we reproduce the actual horse, architecture will always rely on the interpretative effects of this translation. Therefore, the value of the drawing doesn't reside in its capacity to objectively capture reality but in its ability to embody the rigor of the process through which the drawing was produced. This extends to any form of architectural drawing and ultimately depends on the author's ability to embed their identifiable voice into what they have created. In doing this, the drawing can exist in its own right and accept various interpretations without degrading in value. If done cleverly, the drawing becomes an exercise in pragmatics, accepting both objective and subjective readings without losing the fidelity of the final intent.

All of this is to say that architectural drawing can, and should, exist outside the boundaries of evaluating success purely in terms of the resolution and articulation of an objective end. There is value in the small, the incomplete, or the frivolous.

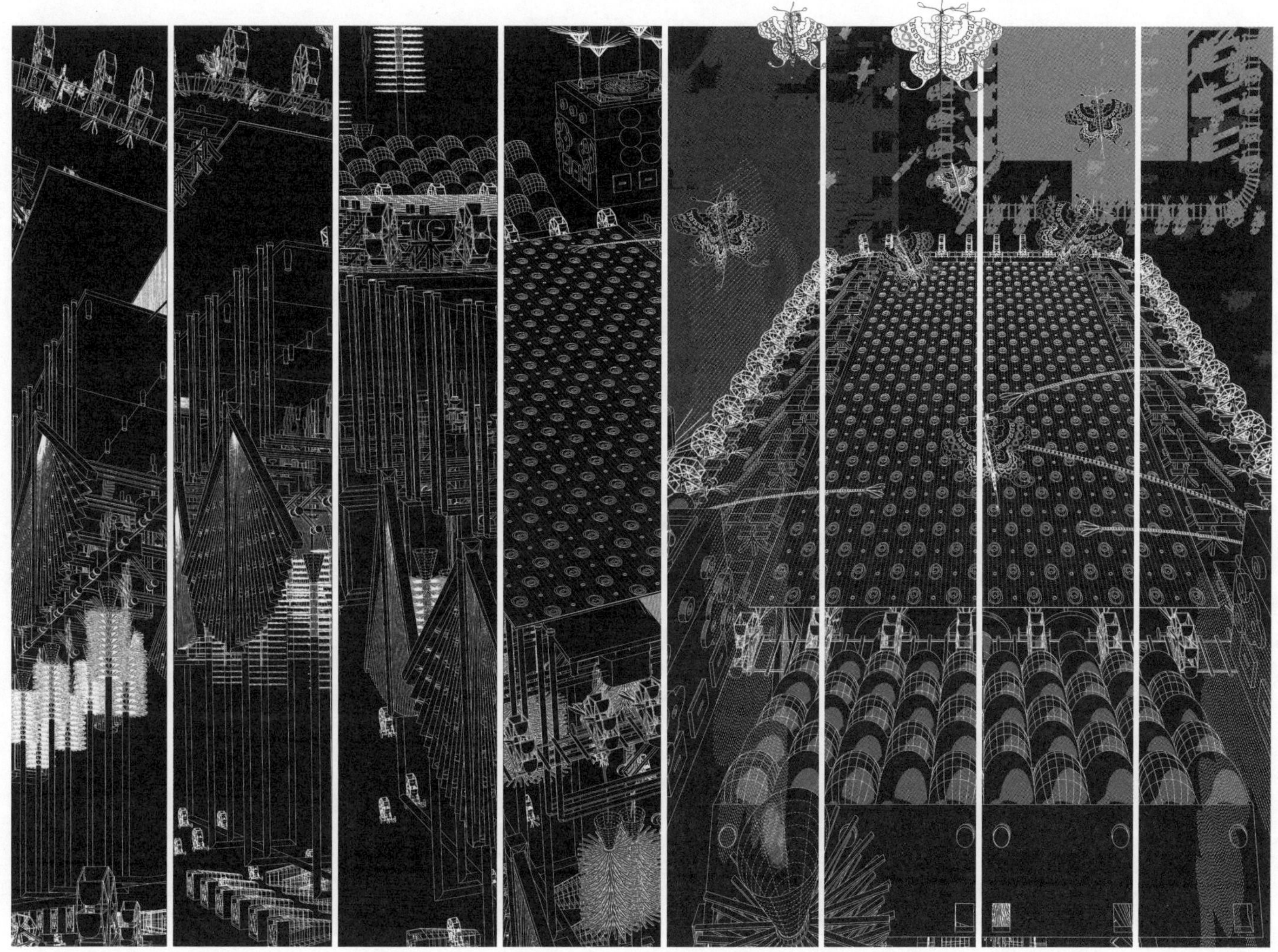

The illustration narrates its story across eight panels, vertically divided into two sets. The first four panels indicate a shifting viewpoint through repetition and varying perspectives, introducing a dynamic sense of movement and time. In the second set of four panels, a single perspectival drawing is divided into four parts, creating a compositional framing of view. This arrangement emphasizes both spatial and temporal shifts. Utilizing simple single-weight solid white lines and hatching on a black background, the scene evokes themes of domesticity and industry, presenting a juxtaposition of references. The white lines on a black background enhance the image's registration, allowing the divided scene to remain abstract while expanding beyond the frame. The framing, therefore, operates not only to structure the image but to introduce multiple viewpoints within the same narrative flow.

CJ Lim

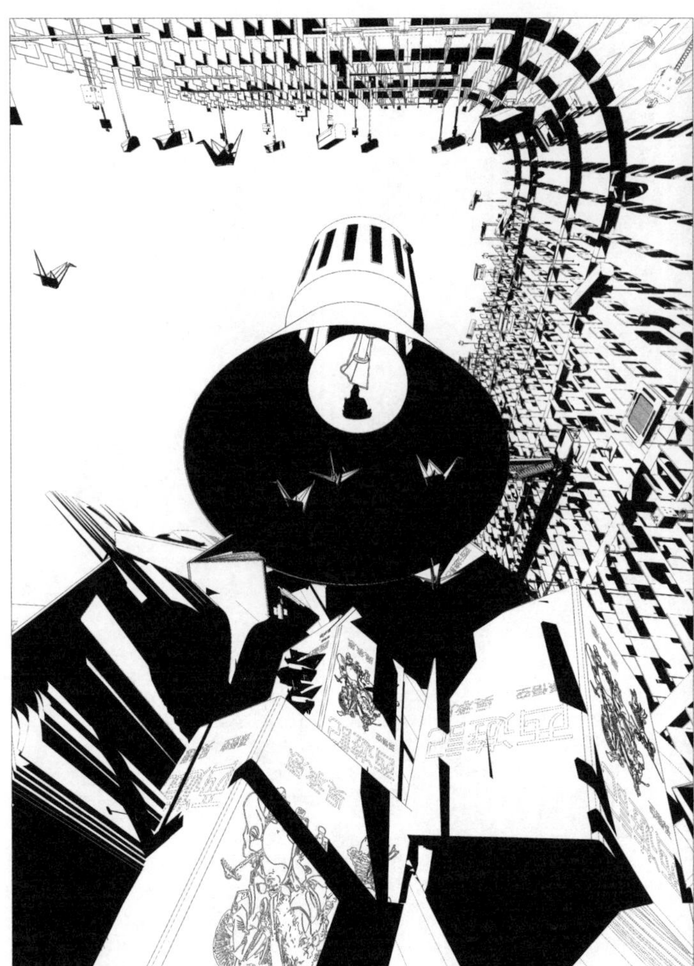

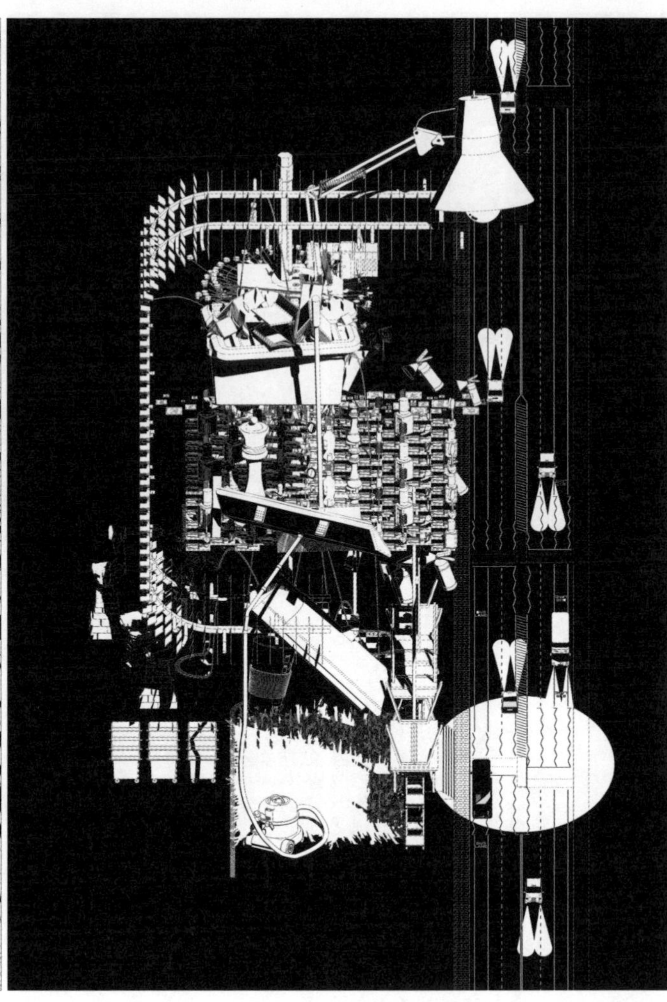

This illustration creates tension between its two vantage points. The left-hand panel presents a perspective that evokes a sense of surveillance: a drafting lamp looms above, incongruously dominating a seemingly urban environment. The floating origami cranes and an assortment of security cameras add to the quality of unease. The right-hand panel changes the viewpoint to an oblique projection of what appears to be the same scene. The lamp is now shown hanging ominously over a car-filled street. Joining the scene are less foreboding domestic objects—books, chess pieces, toys, a vacuum. In both panels, the scales of the urban and the domestic overlap, the public and the private collide, and the result is an overall sense of paranoia as even an object of intimate space is rendered as a potential instrument of surveillance. The convolution of scale in the drawing raises questions about the relation between subject and object as well as the viewpoint of this drawing relative to its counterpart image

CJ Lim

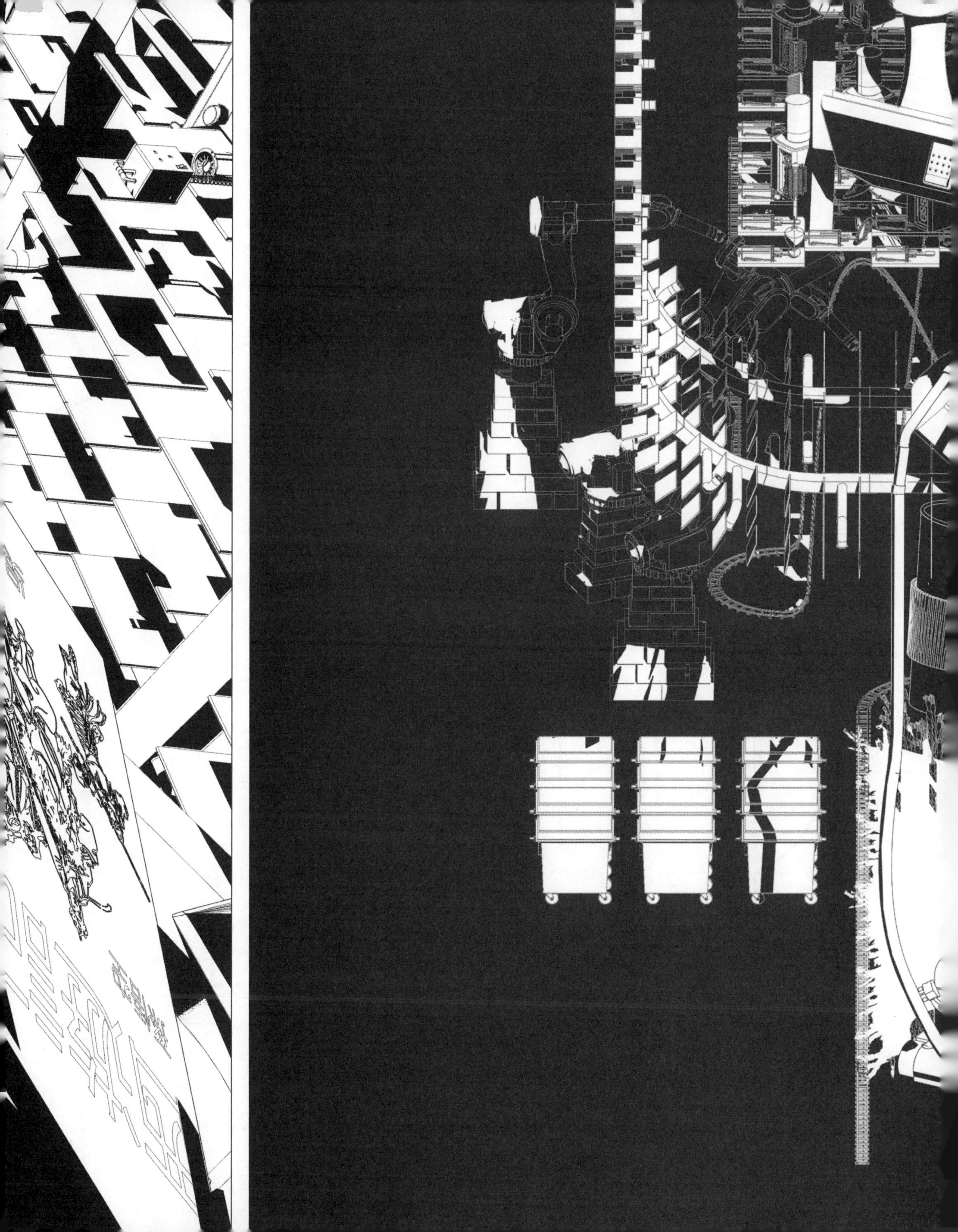

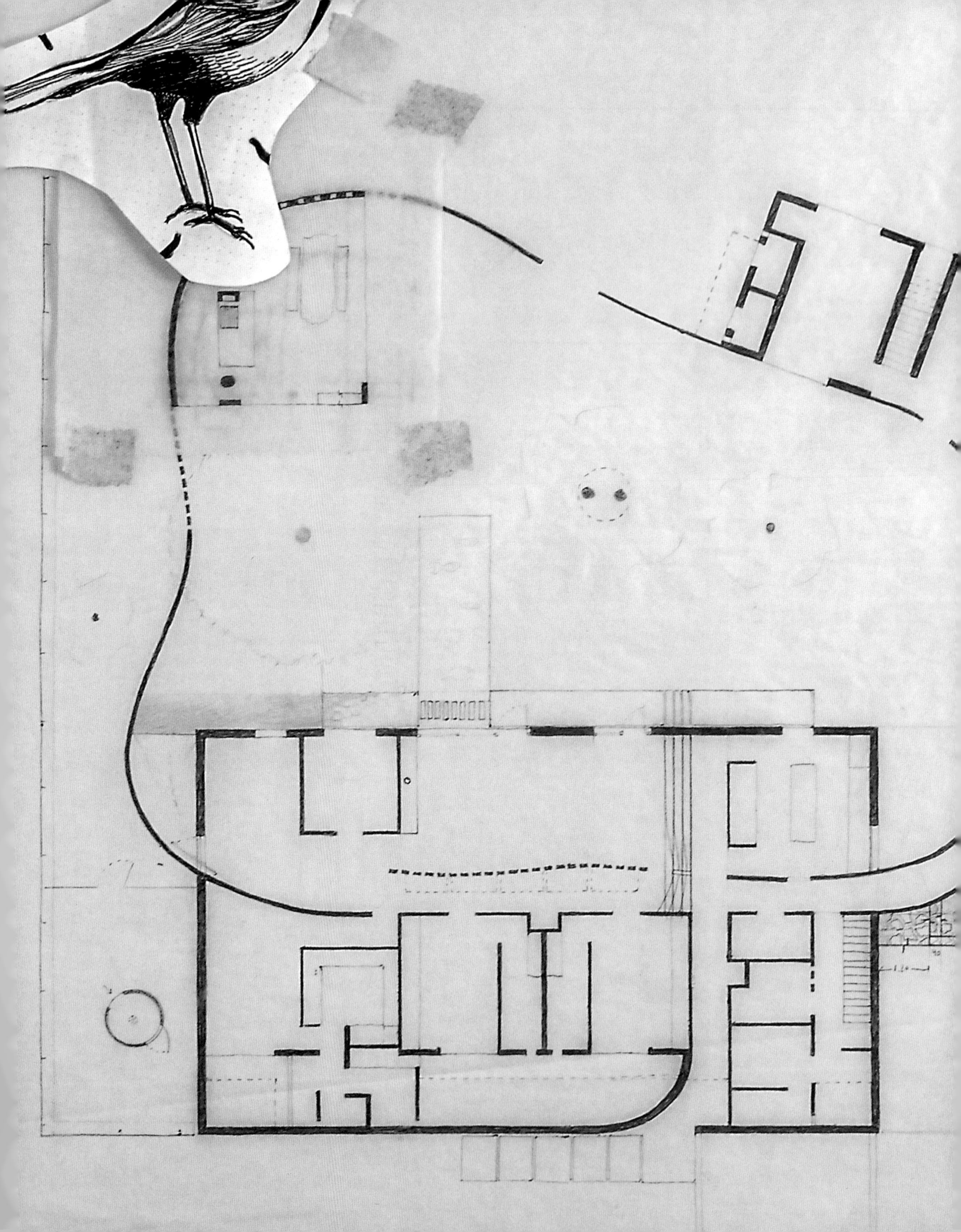

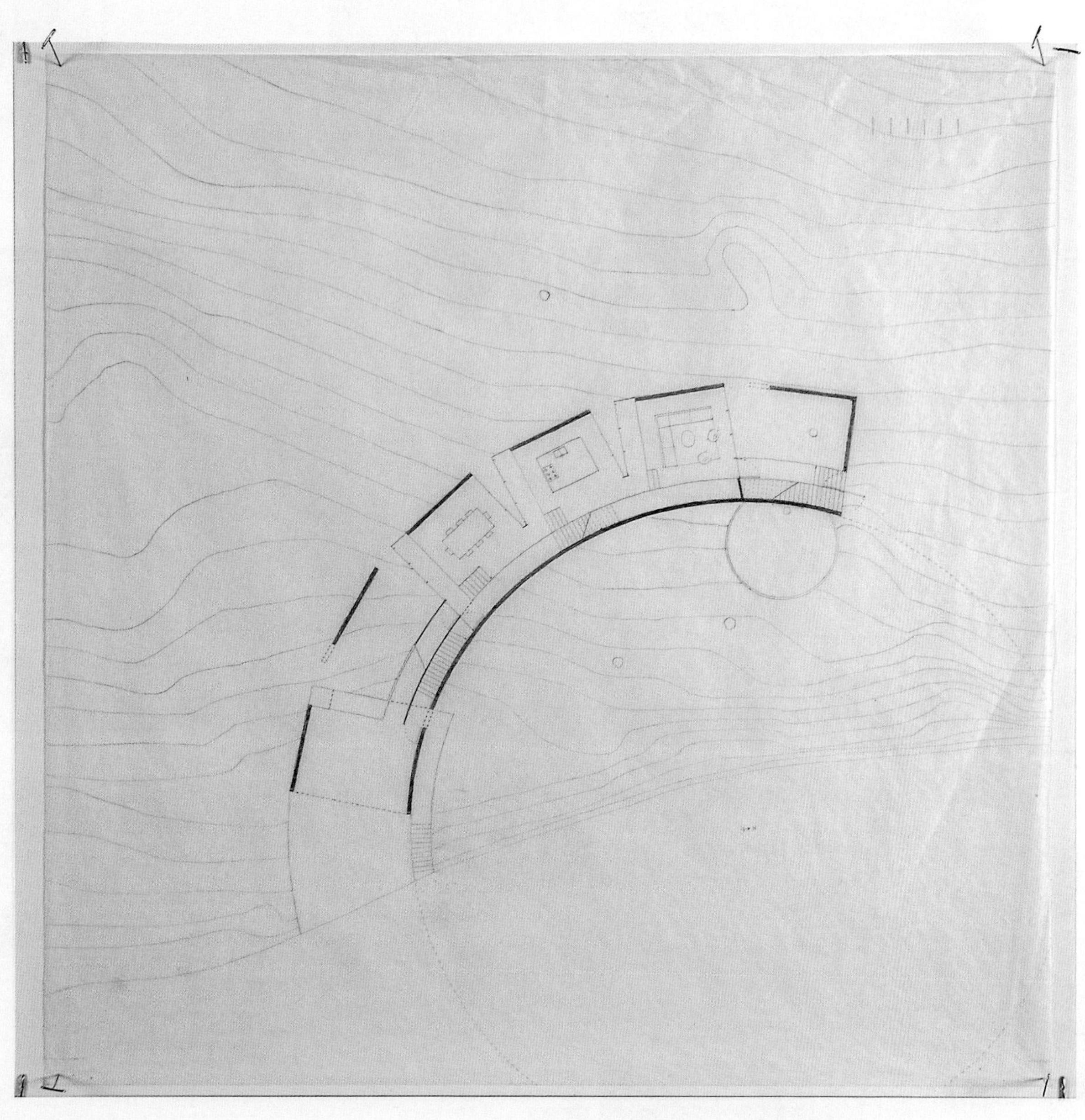

A gentle slope, outlined by faint pencil marks, is overlaid with a floor plan for a semicircular house that sweeps across the topography. The innermost curve defines an exterior wall and shapes the staircase that navigates the slope. Beyond that, another line marks the edge of the interior circulation, with rooms branching outward. Six exterior walls enclose these rooms, creating two interior courtyards. The drawing is clean, precise, and untouched. Unlike the previous drawing, which shows signs of being worked and reworked, this one is untouched and precise. Its purity and balanced organization suggest a complete and singular vision, in contrast to the more personal and contingent negotiations evident in the first drawing.

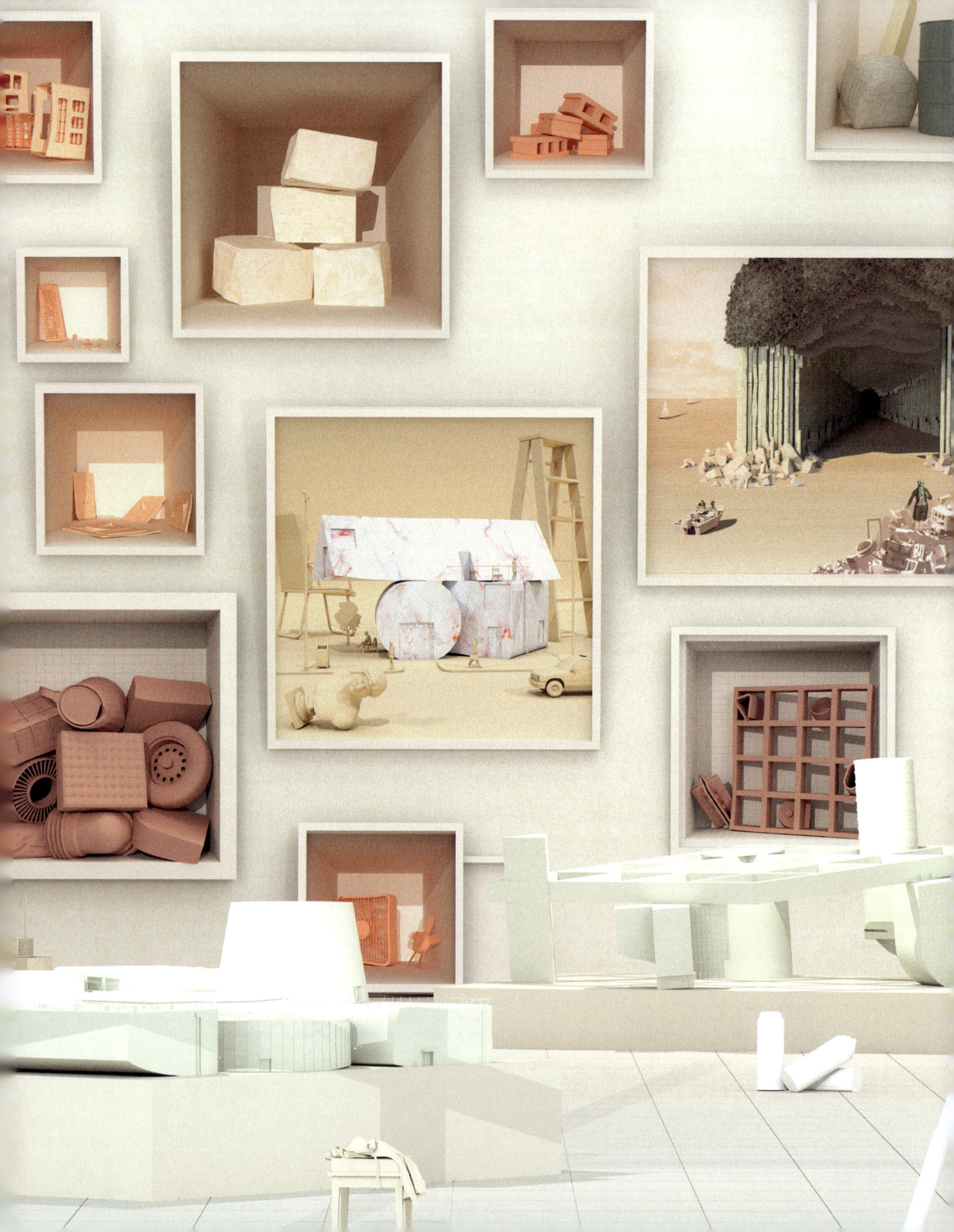

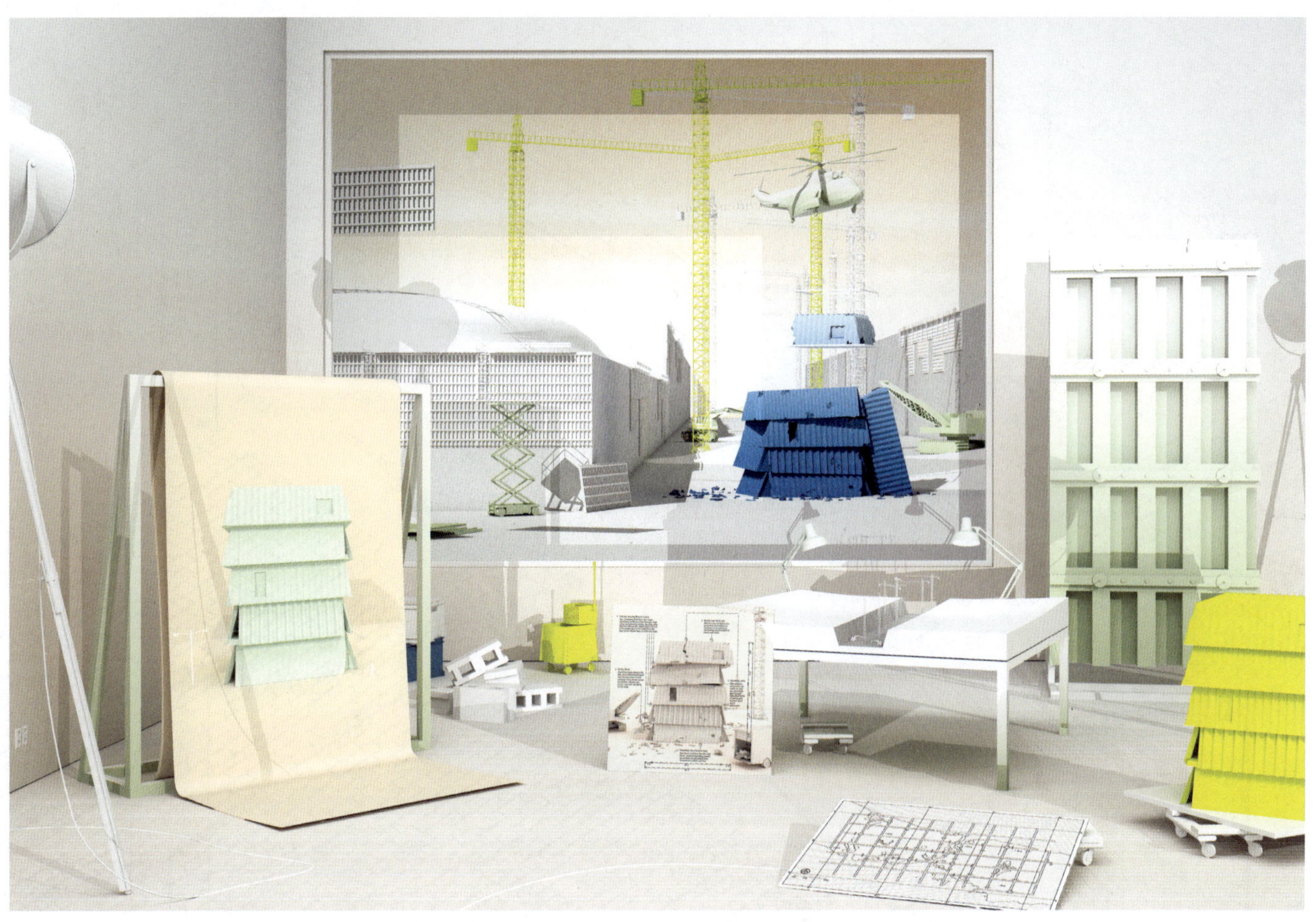

If the previous image was explicitly about space, this second image presents another kind of performance, seen primarily through the lens of time. Different moments in the lifecycle of a relic are on display. In the foreground, a conceptual rendering and a material mockup gesture at this structure's ideal state, either at its inception or in its future condition. Meanwhile, a drawing is labeled with instructions for the care of the fragile monument through a window, a helicopter is holding a piece in midair. The direction of time's arrow is ambiguous—are we witnessing assembly or deconstruction? The surrounding buildings indicate that this may be a film studio lot. Like its counterpart, this is an intentionally composed scene that simultaneously appears haphazard. The careful composition is meant to make the scene look lived in. The aesthetic provided by the choice of color and lighting draws the viewer in, inviting us to gaze more closely.

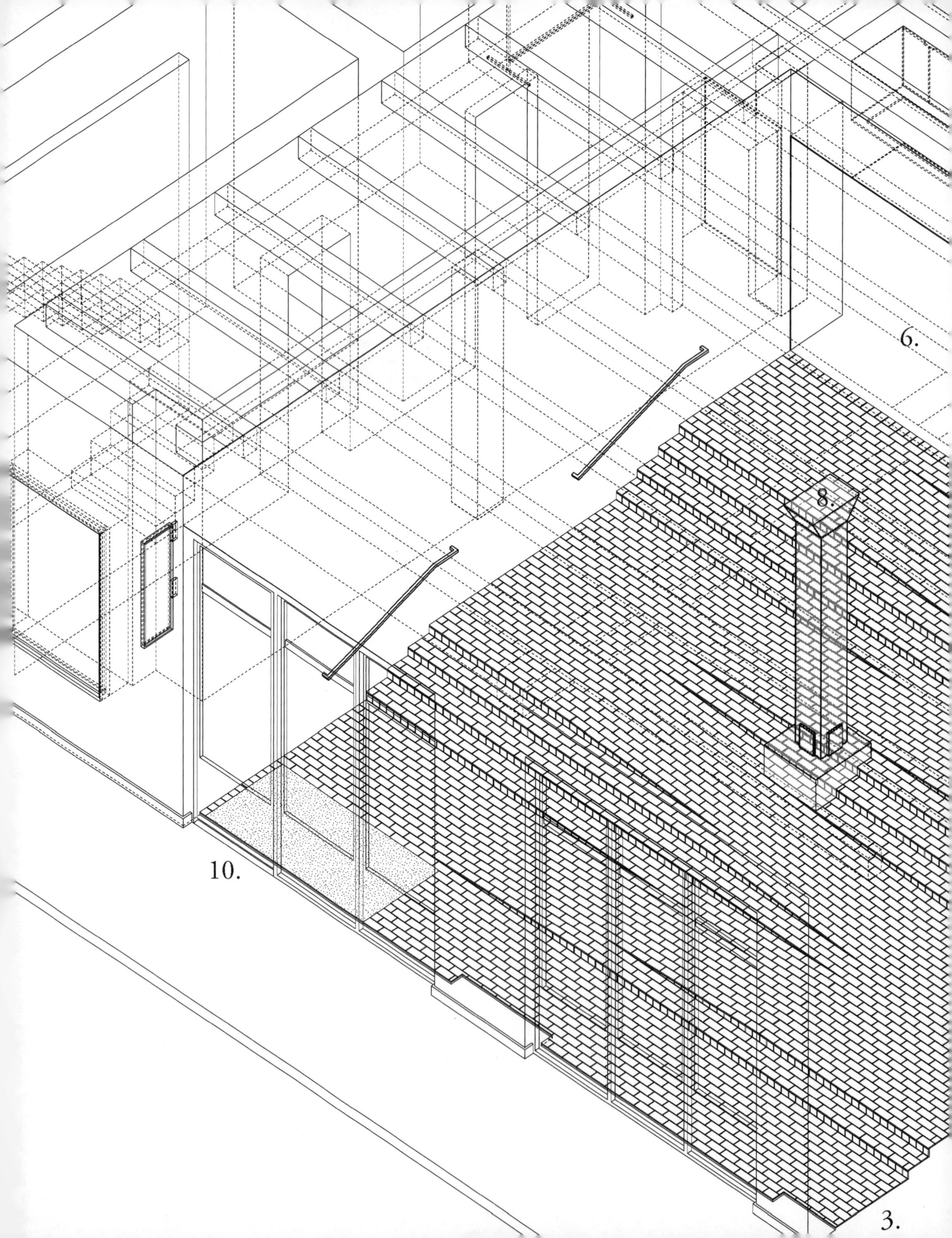
6.
8.
10.
3.

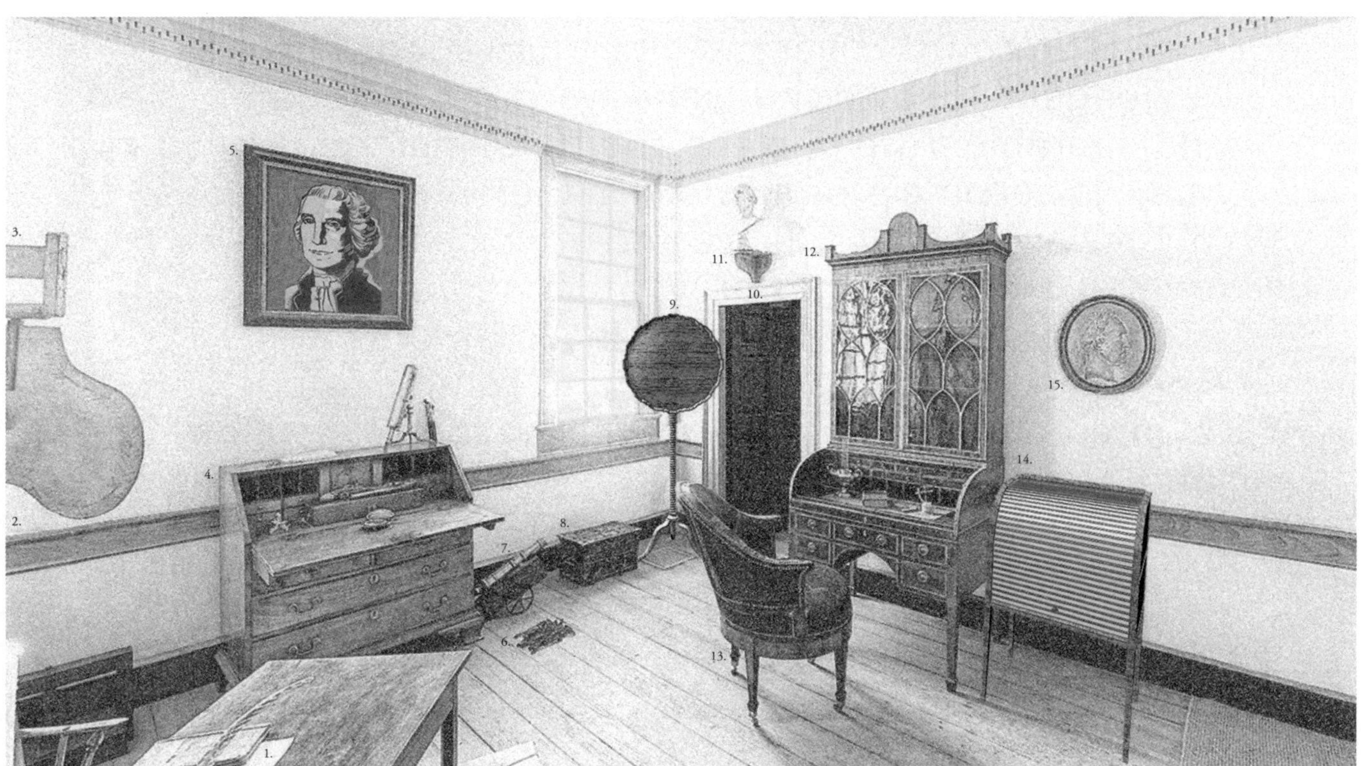

1. Desk
2. Oak chair rail
3. Fan Chair
4. Secretary Desk
5. Portrait of George Washington, by Roy Lichtenstein
6. Surveyor chain
7. Canon
8. Iron box
9. Fixed Tilt-Top Mirror Table, by Norman Kelley
10. Treasure closet
11. Bust of John Paul Jones
12. Secretary Desk
13. Presidential Chair
14. Rolltop Armchair, by Norman Kelley
15. Portrait of George Washington

This scene depicts an interior of furniture and objects dating to the eighteenth century. The provided key gives the impression that this may be a period room found in a museum, with most objects labeled simply "desk" or "iron box." However, a large portrait of Washington is attributed to Roy Lichtenstein, while two other pieces were made by Norman Kelley. In this one room, serene vernacular anonymity is disrupted by the announcements of contemporary artistic authorship. The tension between past and present, or the appropriation of the past in the present, permeates this scene. The way the designed objects are integrated into the scene is at once dutiful and mischievous. Without the key, the interventions blend in. With the key, we are invited to ponder and examine these new artifacts further.

with little control over their interpretation. They no longer "speak a thousand words" or offer an indisputable truth of place and time. Instead, they've become promiscuous in their representations of time and reality. Elusive and often concealing deeper truths, images prevent immediate understanding. Passed from individual creators into collective consciousness through complex webs of interaction, images frequently evade authorship and become detached from the moment they may represent. Often manipulated and artificial, the images of the twenty-first century are illusions.

Artists and architects have a long history of crafting architectural images into resonant fantasies. By embracing permissible falsehoods and candidly acknowledging the fabricated nature of architectural imagery, architects often demonstrate their technical skills while navigating familiar architectural tropes and exploring innovative concepts. This process of cycling through and reusing common techniques helps the audience to understand the subject while also requiring increasingly diverse narrative forms. The image of architecture is always a collection of parts bringing about a whole. Whether it's a straightforward photograph of a new building on an existing site or a collage of disparate objects unified into a single composition, architectural imagery combines both synthetic and occasionally authentic elements. It is a composite of parts forming a whole. This act of visual assembly, which constructs an artificial context, is central to the work of the architect.

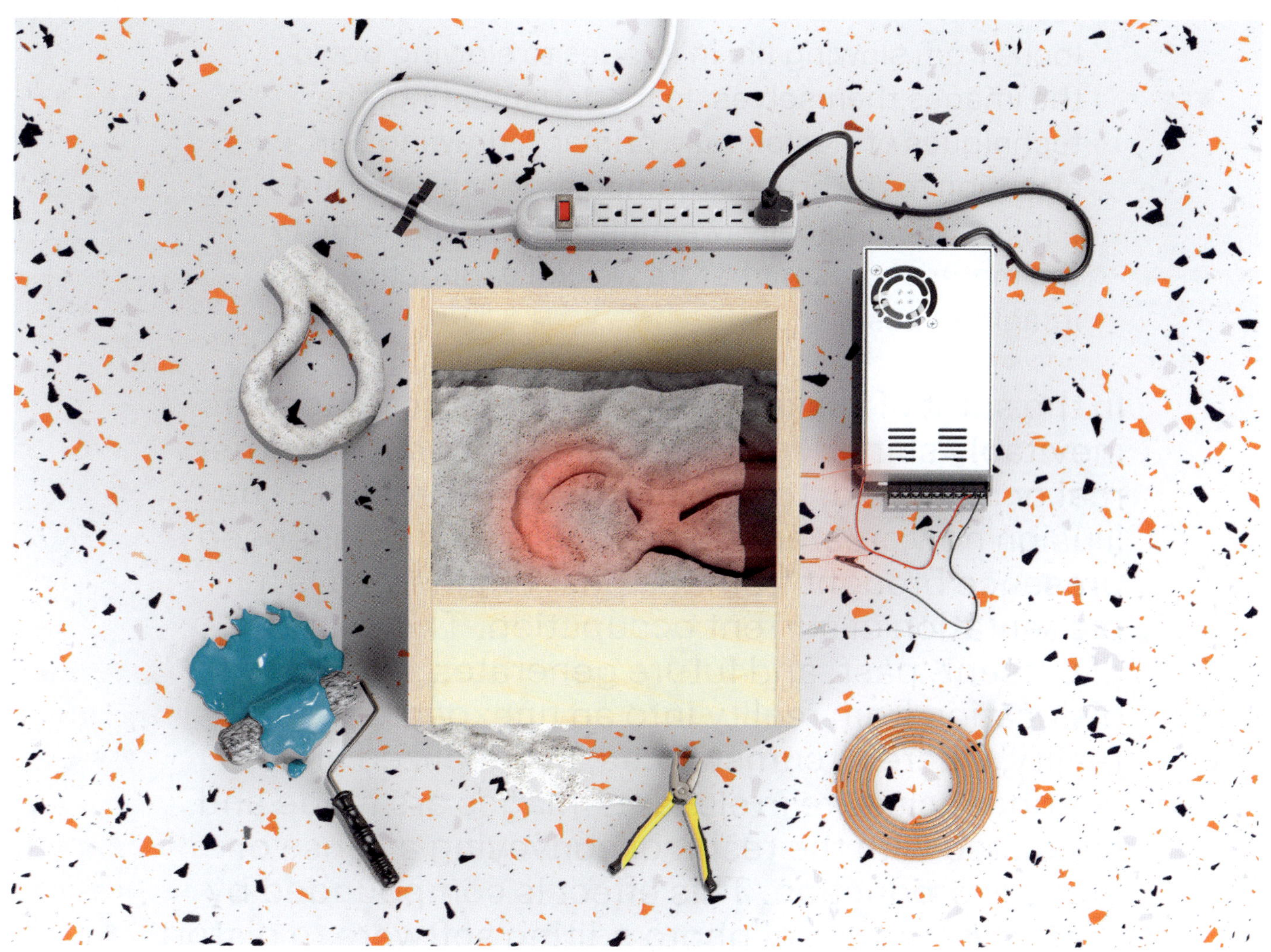

This meticulous rendering presents an overhead view of various objects arranged on a terrazzo surface, blending hyperrealism with an unsettling artificiality. A box connected to a power source holds an object nestled in a bed of gray powder, with its wires seemingly electrifying the contents. Surrounding the box are needle-nose pliers, a roller smeared with glossy blue paint, and a tubular object, each rendered with such exacting precision that they almost defy reality. The glossy texture of the paint and the soft, powdery substance in the box heighten this tension between realism and artificiality, creating an uncanny atmosphere. The careful organization and sharp detail of this composition contrast with the mystery at its center: what's inside the box? The image suggests an ongoing material experiment, but the ambiguity of its purpose and process invites endless speculation, making it both precise and enigmatic in equal measure.

office ca

> focus from slowing life in images to slowing down the images themselves. In modern painting, the techniques of illusion take primacy, drawing our attention to the artist's method as much as to the subject. Ideologically, we must first pay homage to the material present before we can experience the imagined past.[1]

In the spirit of Hickey's observation, the image has inevitably shifted from recording the past, whether real or imagined, to transmitting the present. The illusion now created is no longer one of transposed presence brought from the past but instead is a presentation of current occupation. This blurring of present, past, and future generates an effect of dislocation from reality into an unexpected meta-reality, where circumstances are idealized and contingencies are irrelevant. Images are made and circulated with the result of conveying a sense of endless production. This effect is compounded by the pervasive use of photo editing software to distort an image to provoke the strongest response from a captive audience. The production, editing, and circulation of images occur at an astounding rate, feeding a consumptive culture of architectural imagery. By accepting that the image is no longer a bearer of intentional truth, the author and audience of a given image acknowledge that they are viewing an alternate reality. Much like the spectators at a magic show, we suspend disbelief and embrace a false reality to enjoy the experience.

This is evident in a wide range of recent works, such as William O'Brien Jr.'s photorealistic renderings for

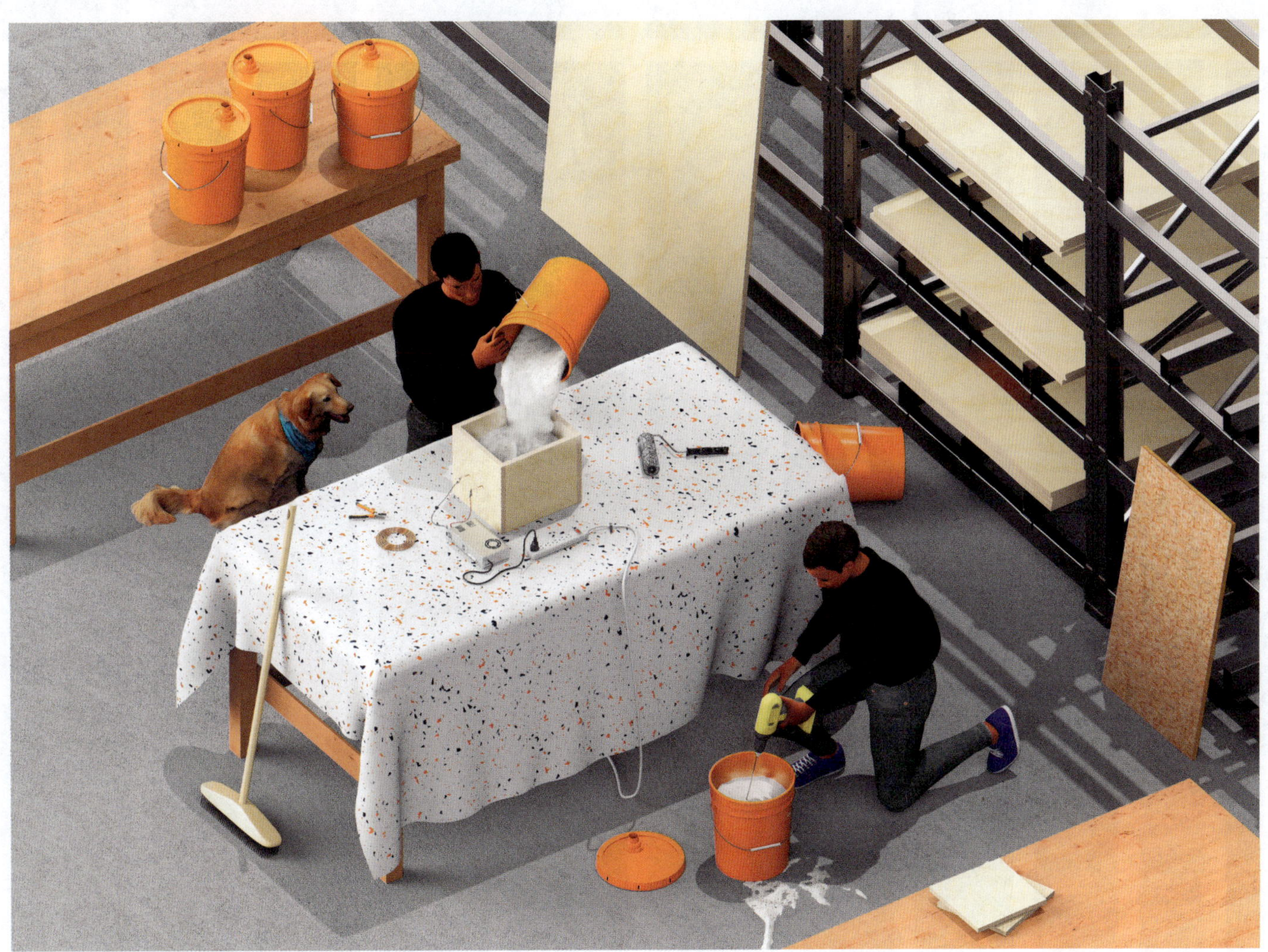

This expanded scene reveals more context to the process hinted at in the earlier image yet deepens the sense of mystery. A terrazzo sheet now drapes over a shop table where two nearly identical figures, dressed alike, perform tasks in an industrial setting. One figure stirs the gray powder, while the other pours it into a box like the one seen earlier. Adding an incongruous touch, a golden retriever with a blue bandana watches attentively. Despite the precise hyper-realistic rendering—down to the diagonal paint roller and casually rotated bucket—the scene remains enigmatic. The orange tubs, the unknown scale of the space, and the missing connections between the process and its purpose all provoke questions. The controlled composition, juxtaposing crisp detail with deliberate omissions, suggests a commentary on the artifice and ambiguity of creation, where the familiar meets the unsettling.

office ca

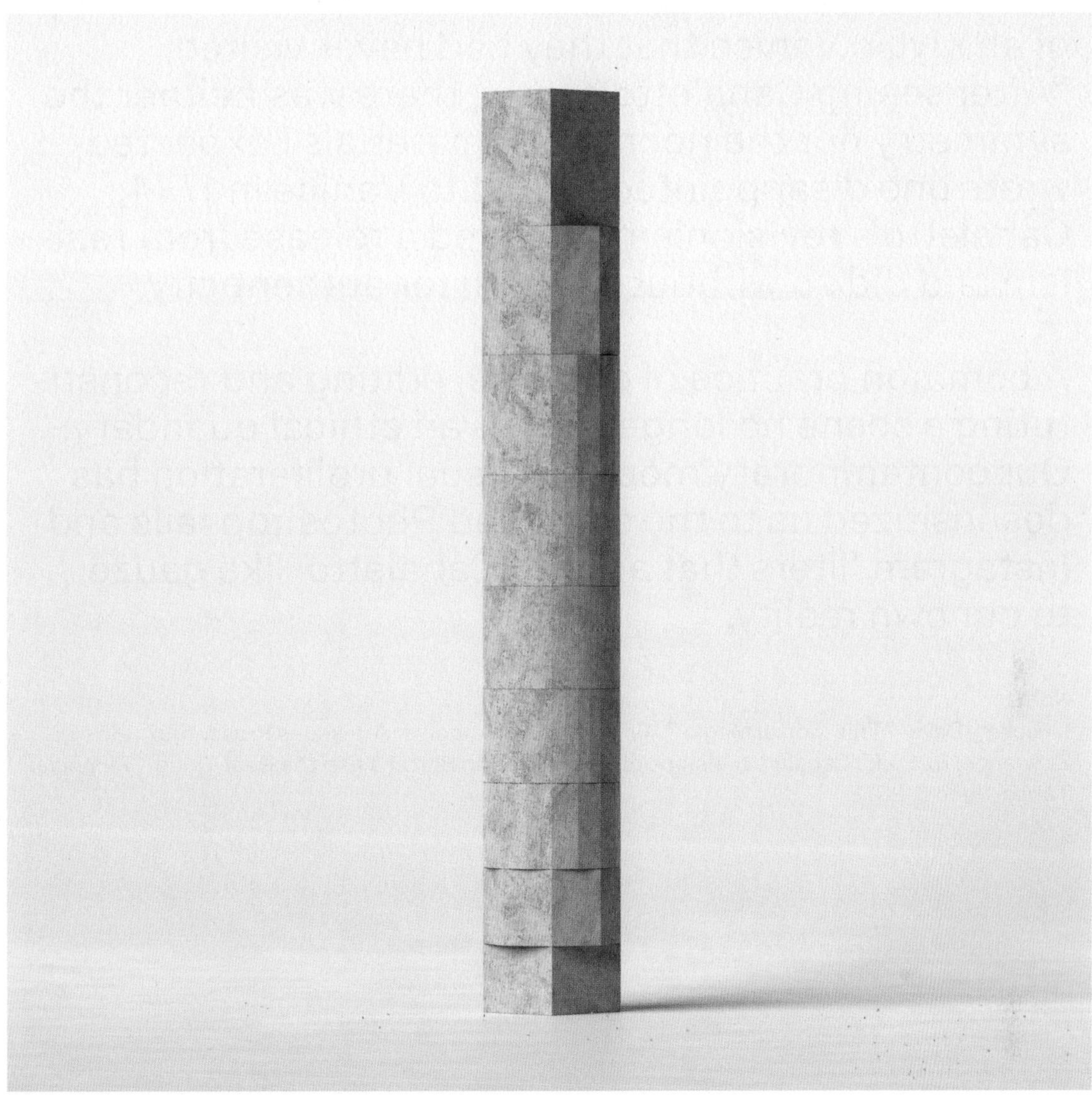

In the paired image, a meticulously detailed obelisk stands against a stark, horizonless white background. Its scale is ambiguous yet imposing. Rendered to appear as cast masonry, the column stands as a high-fidelity depiction of the vector drawing, a realistic rendering set within an artificial, infinite environment. Faint specks of debris add a touch of realism, grounding the object within the surreal space.
The composition of the obelisk reveals an intriguing progression: from bottom to top, it divides into segments of increasing, then decreasing, facets. This rhythm is a visual manifestation of resolution itself, as the column transitions from smooth surfaces to increasingly articulated forms, showcasing the interplay between detail and structure. The obelisk ultimately serves as an exploration of resolution, segmenting a circular form into facets at varying densities, and demonstrating how detail can transform as scale shifts.

of an idyllic Venice that they had never visited. "After seeing Canaletto's view, there was neither the symmetry nor the richness of materials I expected," wrote one disappointed tourist to Venice in 1774.[2] Canaletto's revisionism provided a release from realism and did so without concern for authenticity.

A common practice of our time, editing and reconstituting a scene no longer poses an ethical quandary. Our contemporary model of visual proliferation has desensitized us to the so-called Photoshop fails and Instagram filters that apply a Canaletto-like gauze to our own reality.

Notes
1. Hickey, Dave. "This Mortal Magic." *Air Guitar*. Los Angeles: Art issues Press, 1997, 185–86.
2. Spence, Rachel. "Canaletto: Visions of a Venice Even Better Than the Real Thing." *Financial Times*, June 6, 2017.

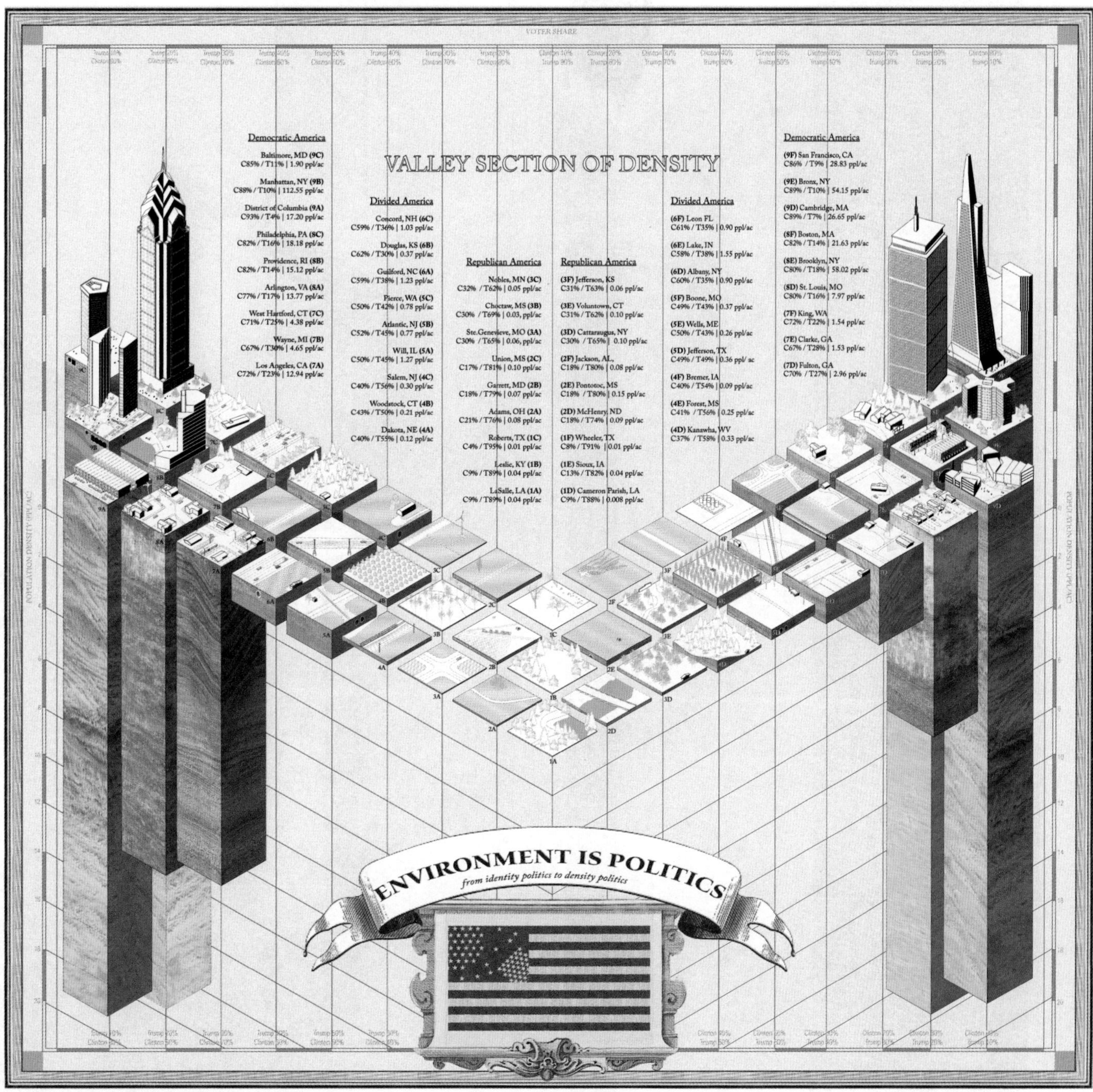

These three drawings can be considered as a triptych, or a single composition, offering a striking visualization of how spatial organization influences political leanings. Inspired by the 2016 election, which revealed correlations between population density and voting patterns, the images examine how proximity to neighbors can predict political affiliation. Isolating emblematic one-acre plots from counties with distinct density patterns, the drawings connect spatial layout to political tendencies, suggesting that the distance between homes shapes both social interactions and political landscapes. Each composition integrates a range of scales and modes of representation, including geologic and cartographic elements, as well as isometric views of urban and rural environments. Borrowing from the conventions of nineteenth century newspaper lithography, one could imagine these drawings as broadsides, framing architecture and urban planning as inherently political acts. Together, they reveal that built environments actively shape collective identities and civic behaviors, underscoring how design and geographic location influence beliefs and social alignment.

The Open Workshop

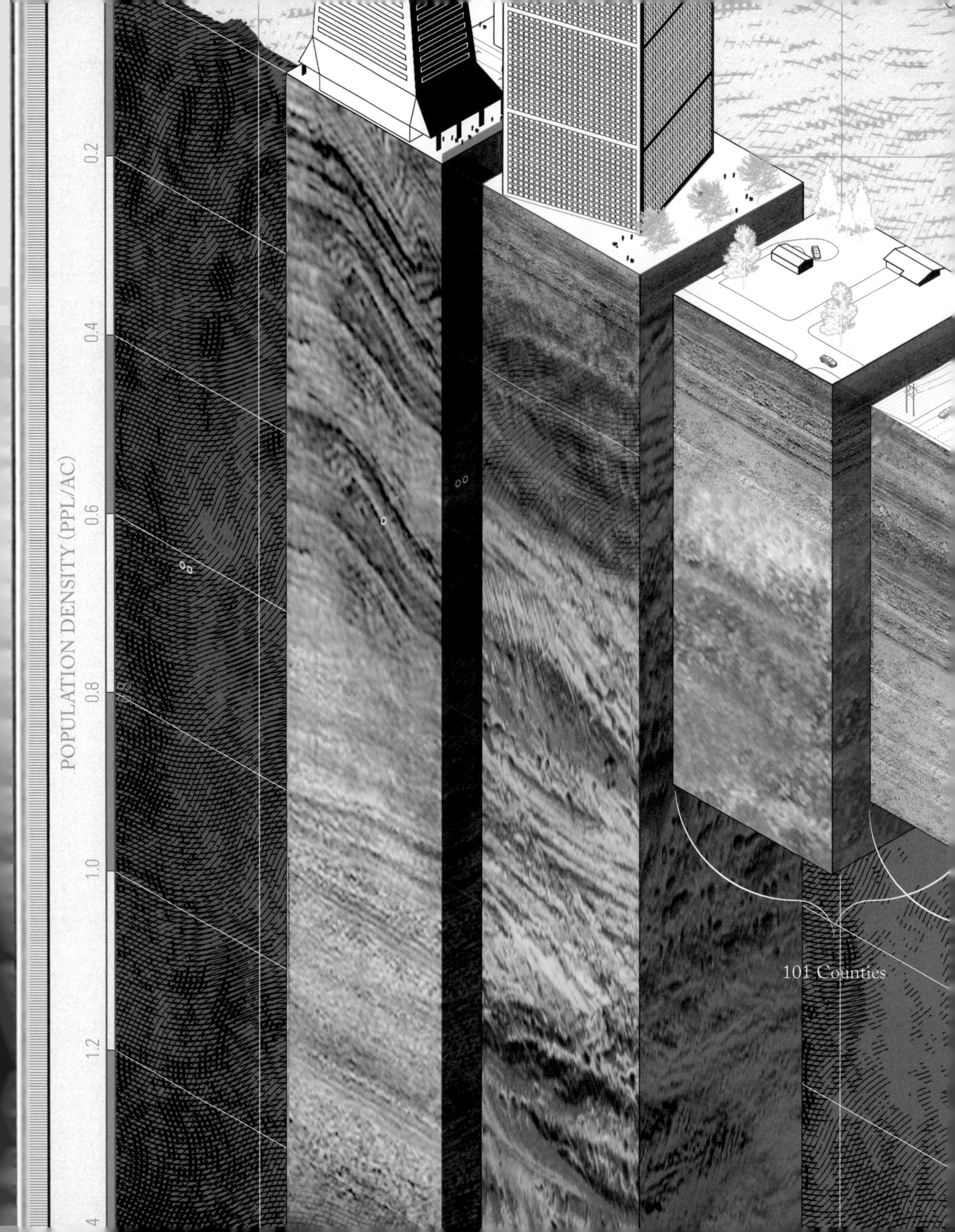
POPULATION DENSITY (PPL/AC)
0.2
0.4
0.6
0.8
1.0
1.2
101 Counties

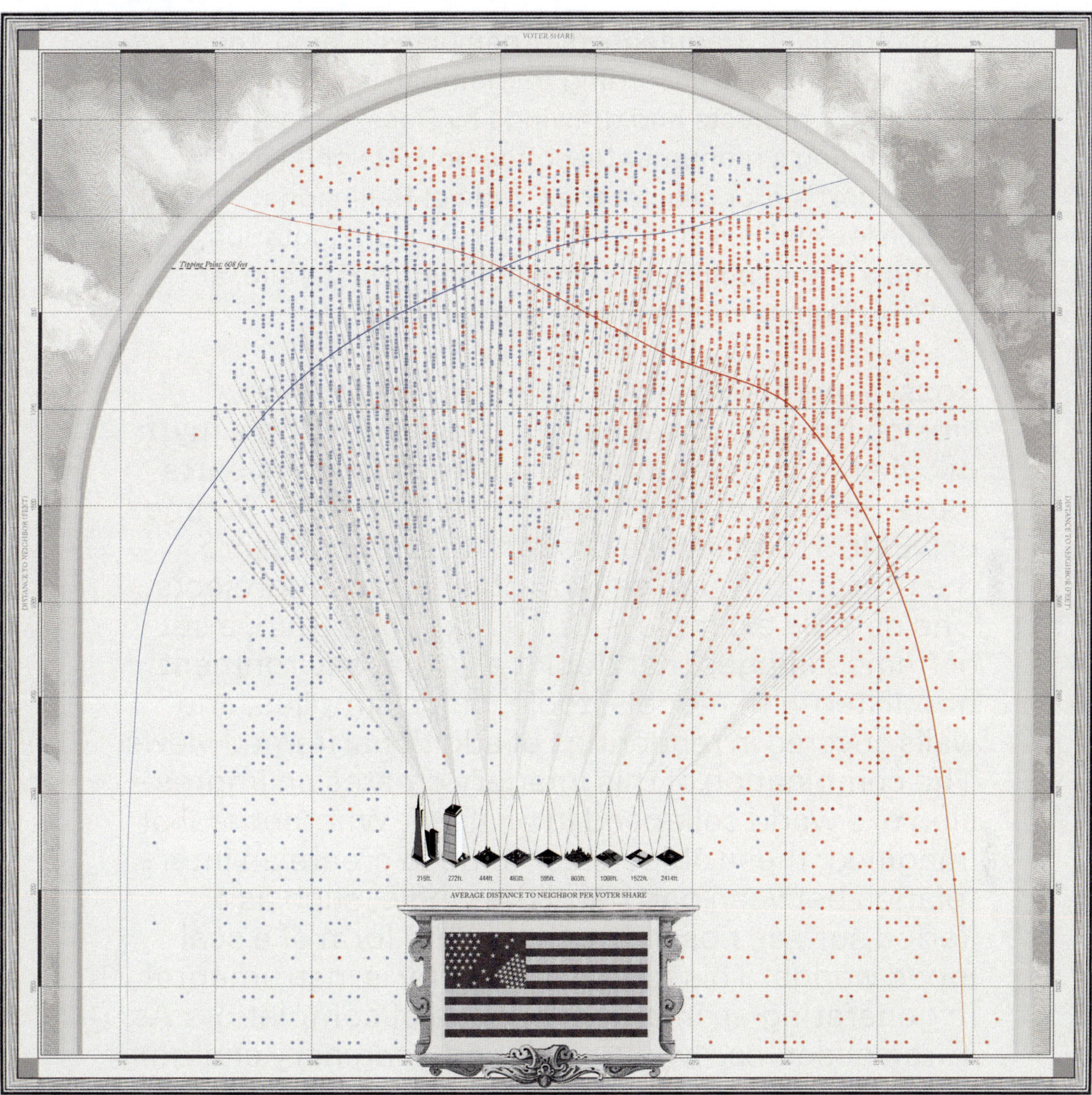
VOTER SHARE
Tipping Point: 608 feet
DISTANCE TO NEIGHBOR (FEET)
DISTANCE TO NEIGHBOR (FEET)
215ft.
272ft.
444ft.
483ft.
595ft.
803ft.
1086ft.
1522ft.
2414ft.
AVERAGE DISTANCE TO NEIGHBOR PER VOTER SHARE

> photocopies: fragments of urban plans (Como, the city of Vitruvius according to Giambattista Caporali, in 1536), projects and drawings by Rossi himself (including a monumental coffee pot), Reichlin and Reinhart's proposal for the Castle of Bellinzona, hillside and lakeside views, a Piranesian quotation, and a finger-pointing figure by Tanzio da Varallo, a 17th-century Lombardian painter.[1]

Rossi's method marks a shift from dispensing illusion through false realism to constructing a myth of coherence by superimposing incongruous parts into a unified whole. Neyran Turan and Mete Sonmez of NEMESTUDIO have brought this practice into the present through several of their recent projects. One notable example is *Our Junk, Their Ruin*, a set of framed images that depict a virtual environment populated with models, tools, office supplies, and walls covered in renderings of additional framed views. The combination of this imagery creates an impression of a world collapsed in on itself. Whether real or imagined, these objects combine to create an interrelation between parts and the whole, such as a kerfed surface possibly echoing the form of a scalloped wedge. This formal familiarity is instrumental in generating an imaginary sense of completion. As Turan observes, "while depicting imaginary characteristics, one of the main features of capriccio painting was its interest in verisimilitude or slight (in) familiarity." A similar approach is rooted in their contemporary work. While the installation may not be a complete capriccio in fullness, it plays with the line of generating reality and falsehood simultaneously through the construction of an artificial context.[2]

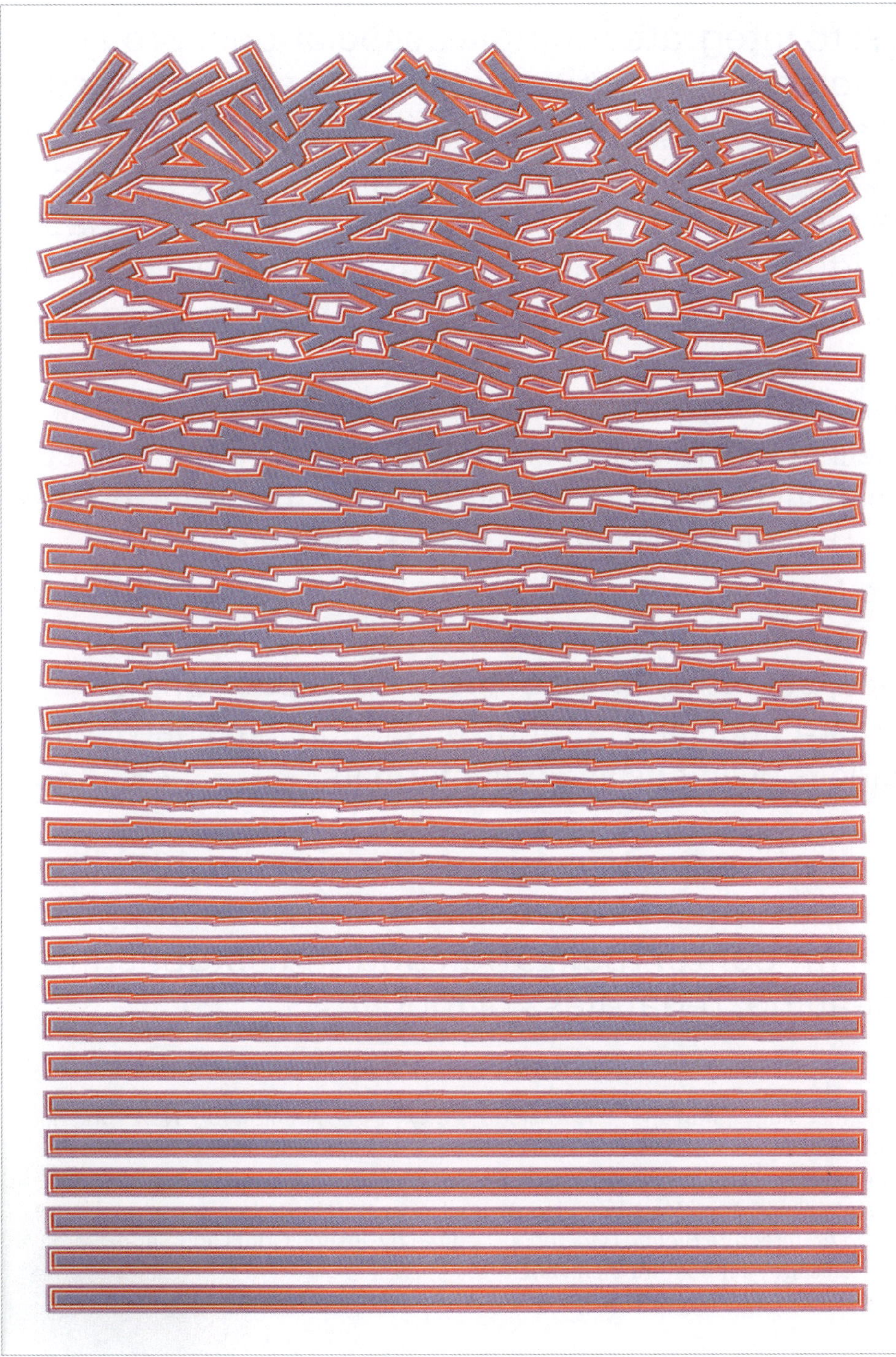

This drawing is comprised of thirty-two striped, offset colored bars arranged horizontally. Initially stable and orderly, by the seventh, a subtle vibration disrupts the sequence. By the twentieth, the bars have dissolved into eighteen rectangles, aligned along a central axis and rotated. By the final row, the rectangles swing freely, untethered from one another. This transition from structured stripes to fragmented rectangles suggests a formal evolution from stability to instability. The color scheme enhances the part-to-whole relationship, with the concentric patterns indicating interrelations between elements. As the composition gradually becomes more abstract, the rules of transformation remain unclear. Is the arrangement randomized, or is it governed by a hidden logic? Despite the ambiguity, the precise progression reflects a meticulous approach to constructing a dynamic, shifting visual system.

Outpost Office

Rossi to integrate multiple associations, projects, and objects. His work creates an analogous document that stitches together the buildings with their influences, alongside real and imagined urban contexts. This method of collection relies on the interrelated individual projects within Rossi's oeuvre to enhance their significance. As Michael Meredith wrote:

> The ongoing cultivation of a body of work counters the instant amnesia of media by constructing collective relationships within and across time, between formats and buildings. Unlike a 'project,' the body of work focuses not on the dialectic between text and building, or the implementation of an ideology or an a priori idea, but rather on an ethos of production and the construction and curation of relationships between various buildings and other formats.[4]

The continued relevance of this practice highlights the importance of the easily disposable image as a tool for contextualization and the establishment of meaning, regardless of motive.

Notes

1. Nicolin, Pierluigi. "Tafuri and 'The Analogous City.'" *ANY: Architecture New York*, no. 25/26 (2000): 16–20.
2. Turan, Neyran. "Can Images Implode?" *Room One Thousand*, no. 5 (Timeless): 188–98.
3. Johnston, Sharon, and Mark Lee. "House Is a House Is a House Is a House Is a House." In *Chicago Architecture Biennial Guidebook*, edited by Joseph Grima and Sarah Herda, 44. Chicago: Chicago Architecture Biennial, 2015.
4. Meredith, Michael. "Toward the Body of Work." *LOG*, no. 35 (2015): 11–14.

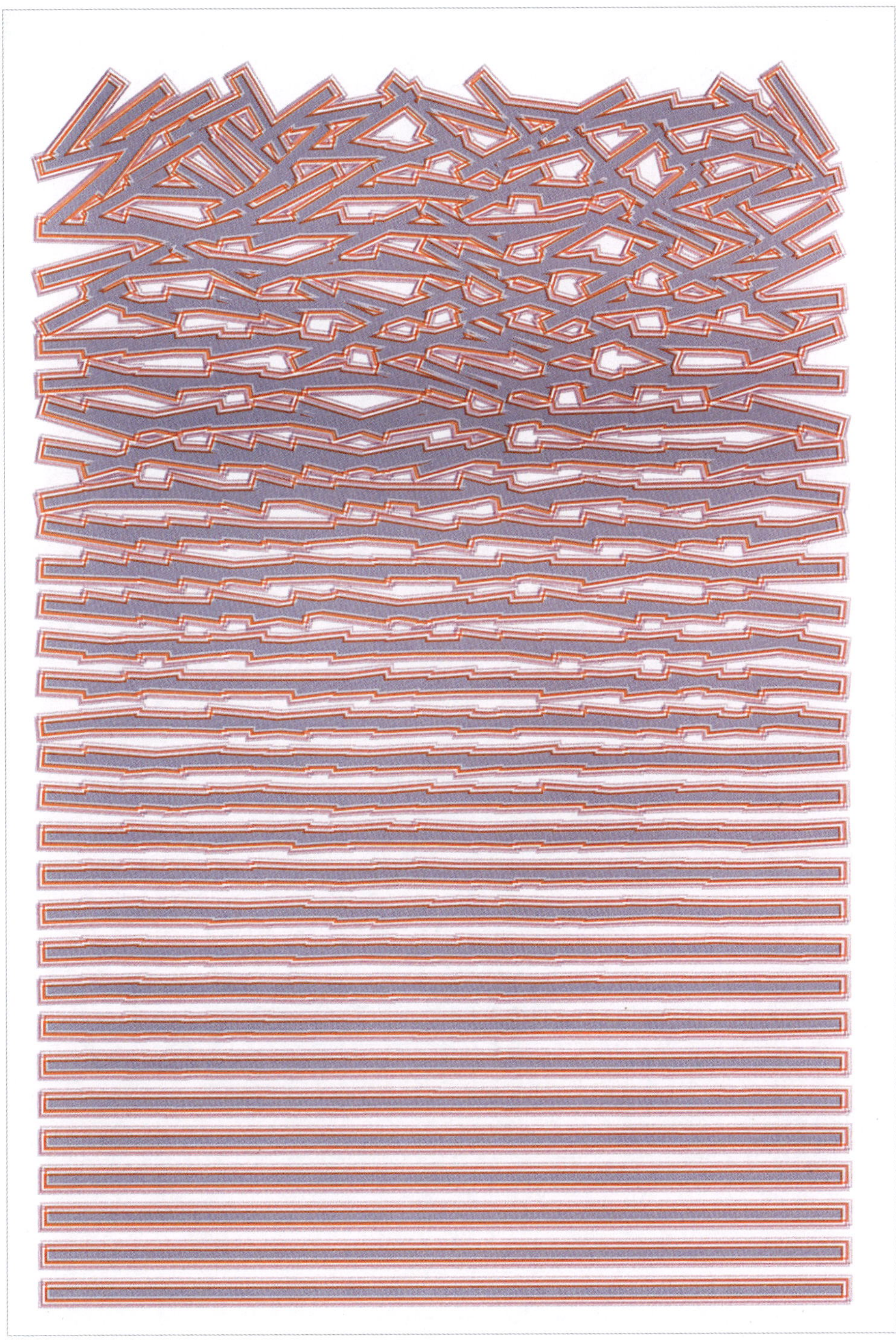

The second drawing in this series presents a fragmented version of the original figures, breaking them into misaligned, drifting bands. Upon closer examination, three key discrepancies emerge: the misalignment stems from the use of two different printheads, the figures are divided into six distinct fills rather than three, and the colors shift into varying shades and hues. These visual artifacts suggest both a breakdown in the system of reproduction and an unintentional complexity born from the printing process. The misalignment, likely caused by the difficulty in aligning printheads across two machines, gives the impression of translucency and movement. This blurring effect not only creates a sense of jitter or motion but also points to a joyful complexity, inviting interpretations that move toward abstraction and spatial exploration, suggesting that a simple setup can lead to rich and unexpected visual outcomes.

Outpost Office

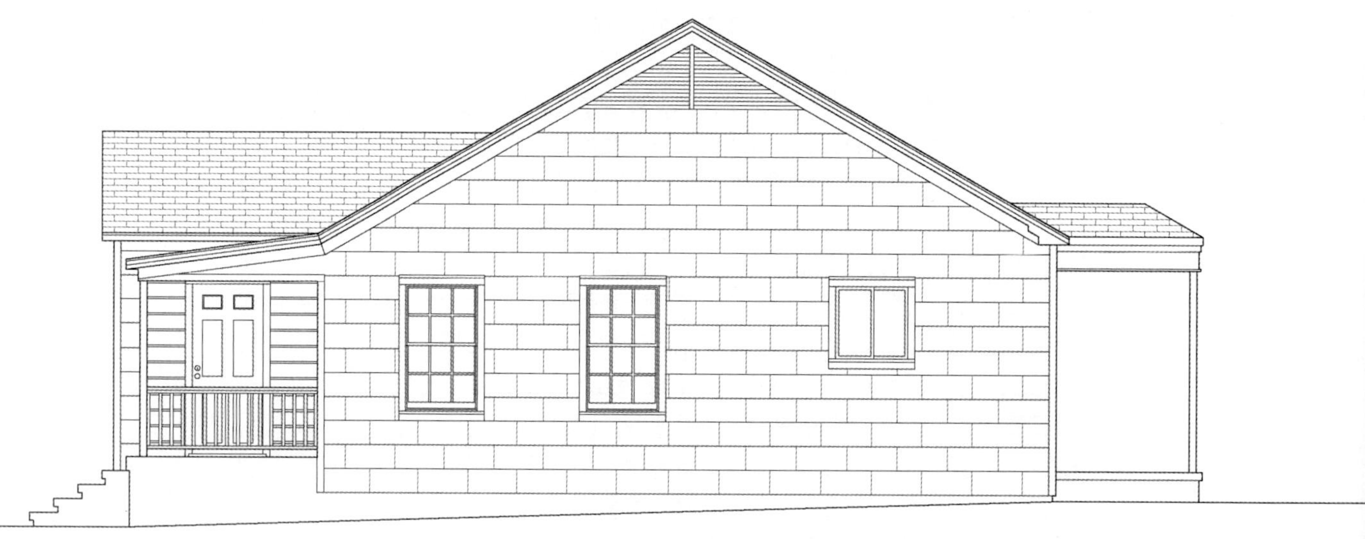

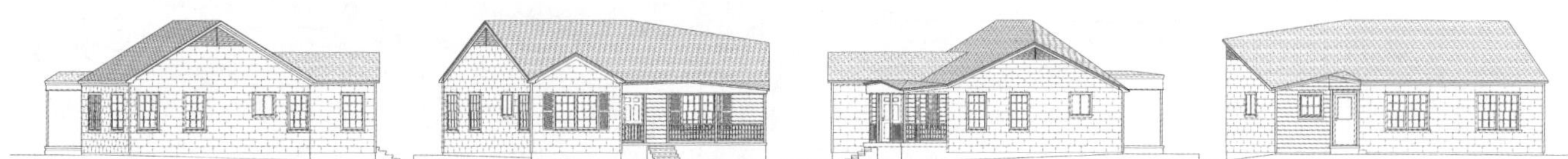

This second set of four elevation drawings shows the proposed alterations to the house. There's a clever playfulness in the design, as the elevations lean into the inherent flatness of the form, subtly transforming the familiar into something both recognizable and strange. Through this technical yet mischievous manipulation, the design both adheres to and transcends architectural conventions, challenging how we read and interpret flat representations of buildings. Rooflines are merged and recalibrated into a building in a less fluid manner than is typical in an ordinary orthographic projection. The roof's form exhibits an arrhythmia implying that perhaps a seismic event has occurred.

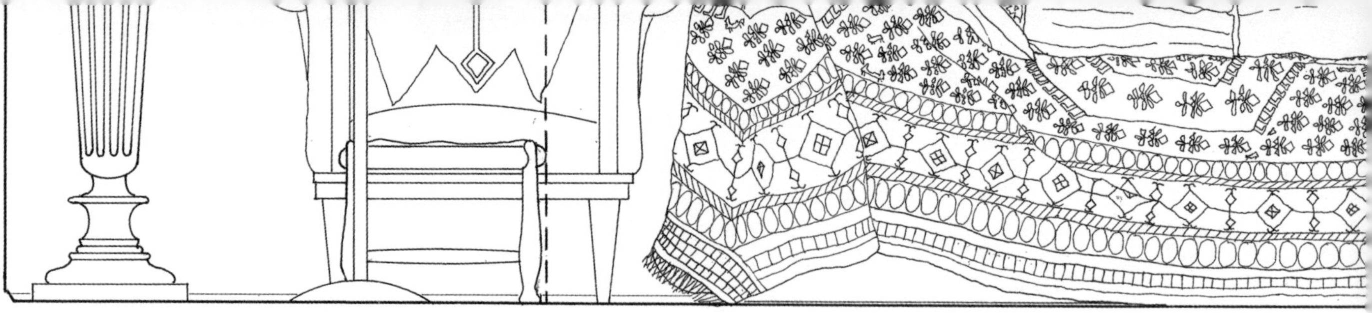

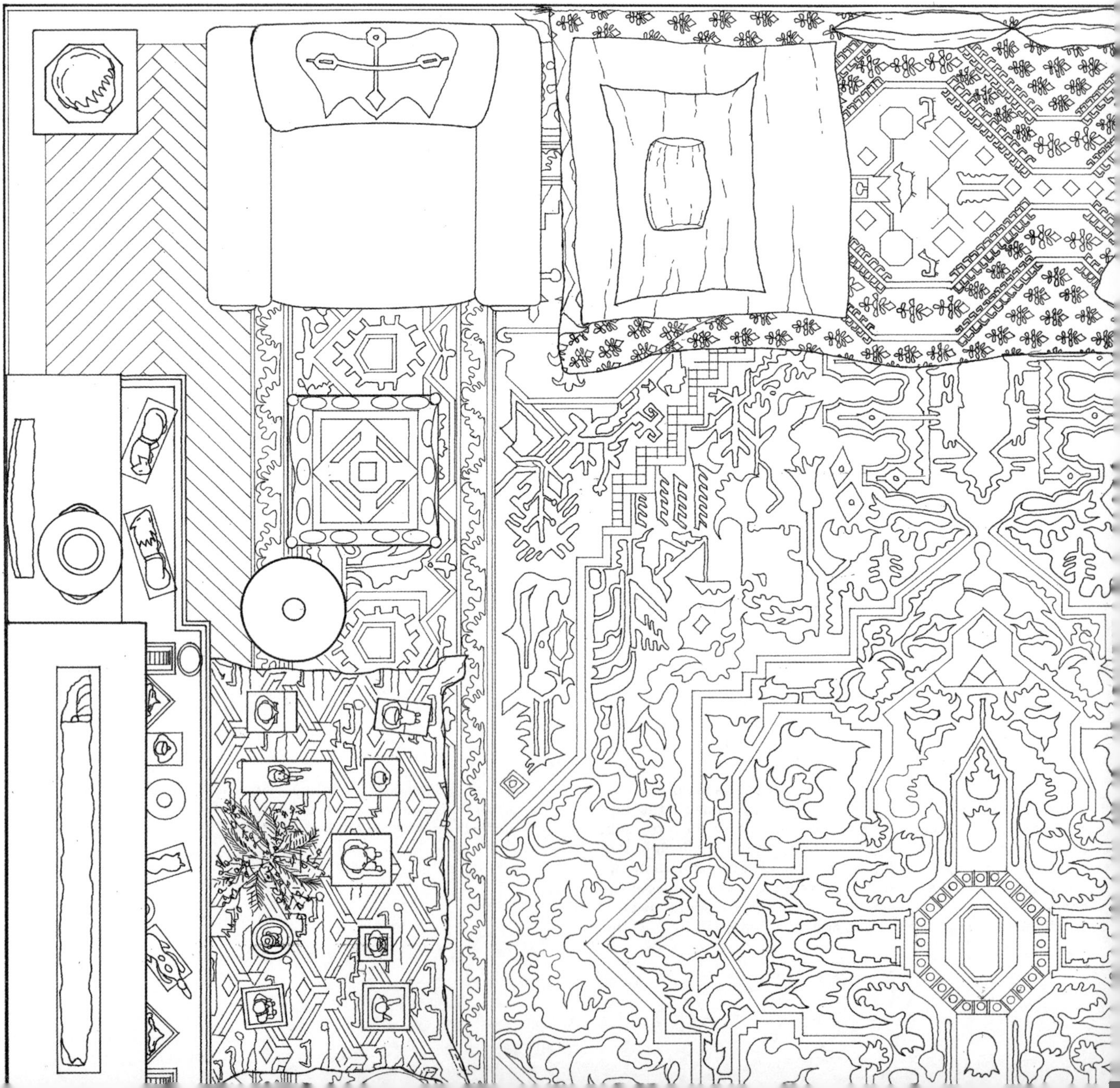

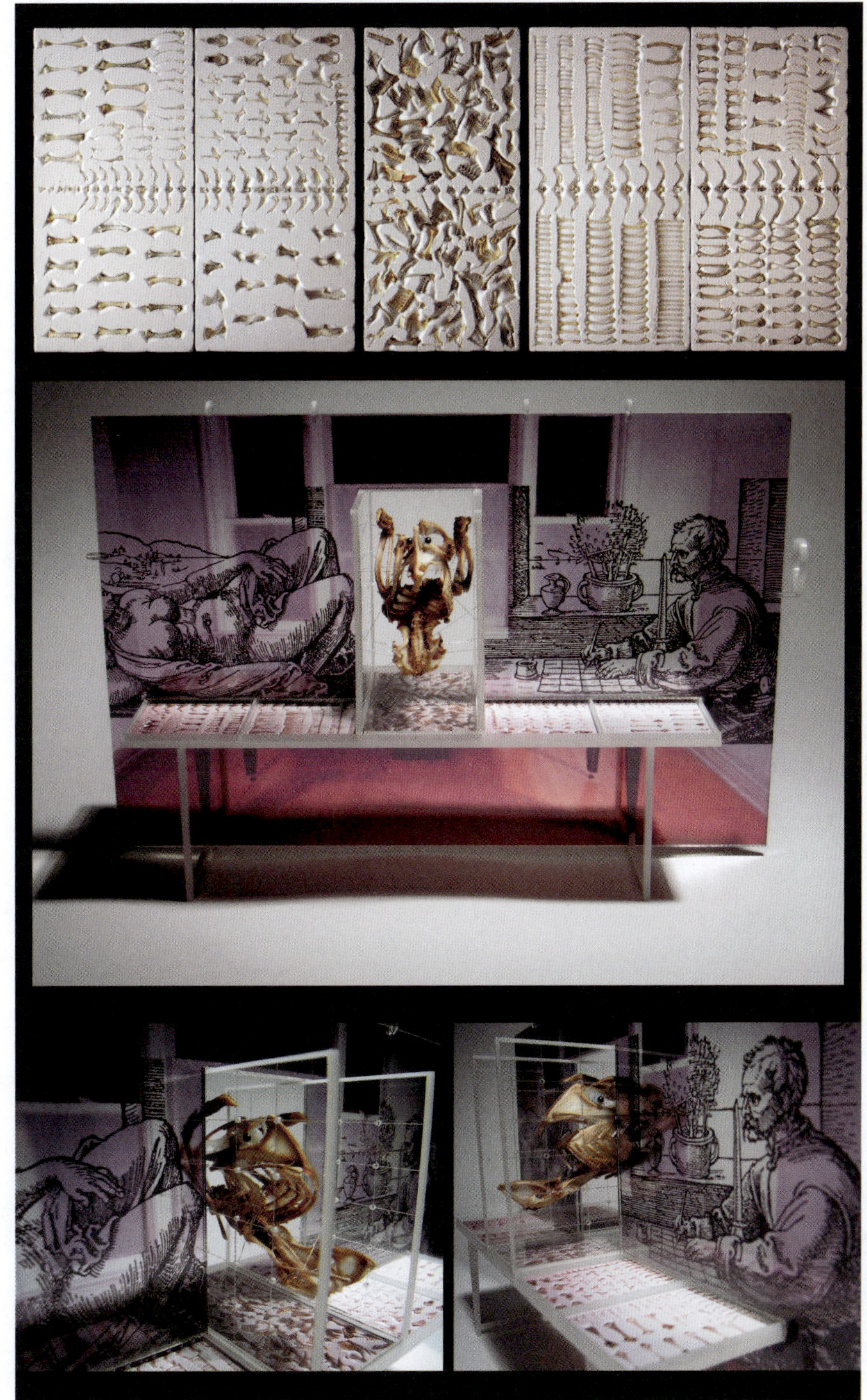

These photographs clearly fall outside the conventional boundaries of drawing, yet that's precisely what makes the submission both mischievous and compelling. The photographs, featuring chicken bones from a series of family dinners, serve as a lament and memorial for the bird, elevating it to a pedestal in recognition of its role in feeding a family. The superimposition of Dürer's work adds a layer of connection between the chicken's evisceration and the artist's experience as a woman navigating the world, consuming and consumed, always subject to the male gaze.

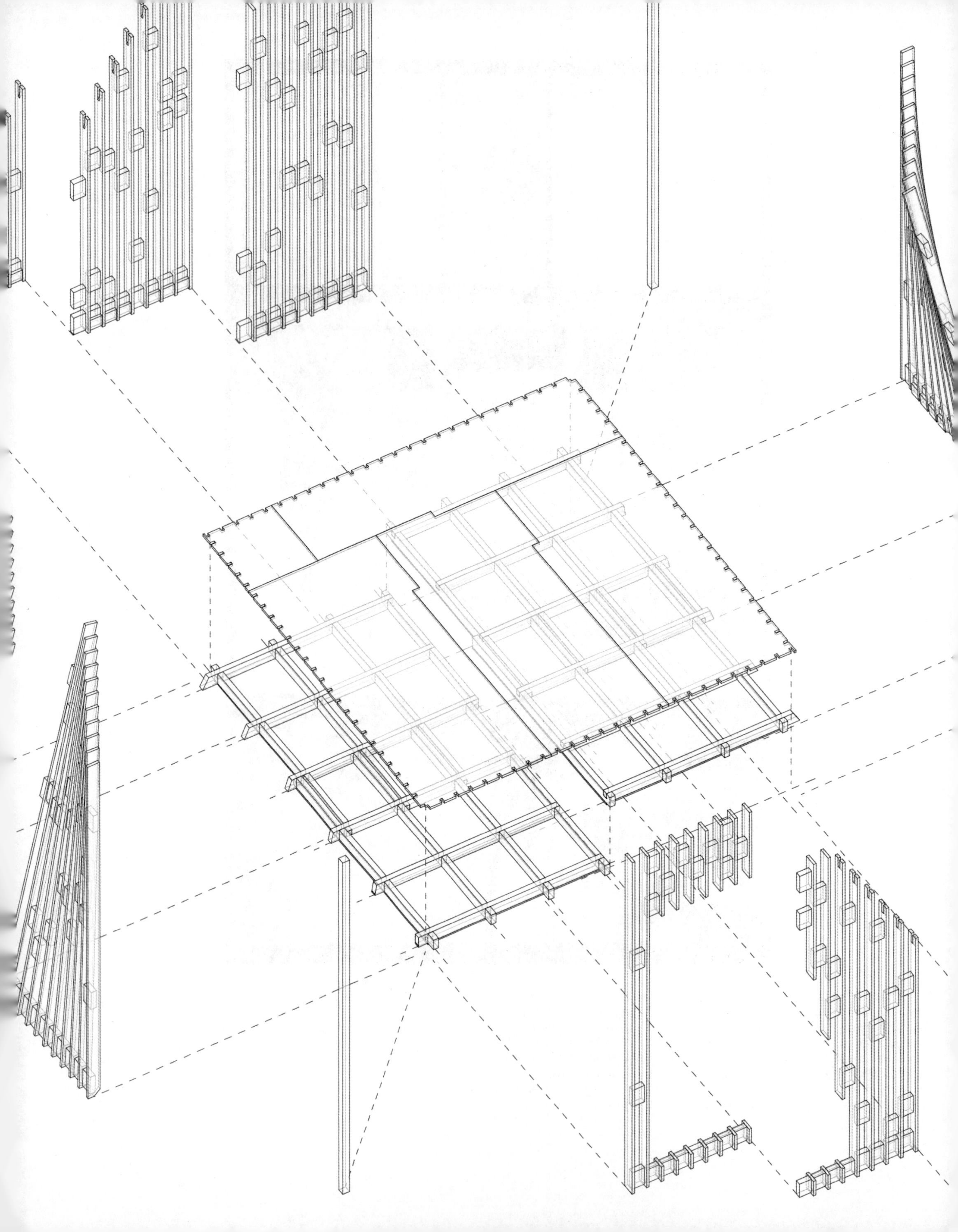

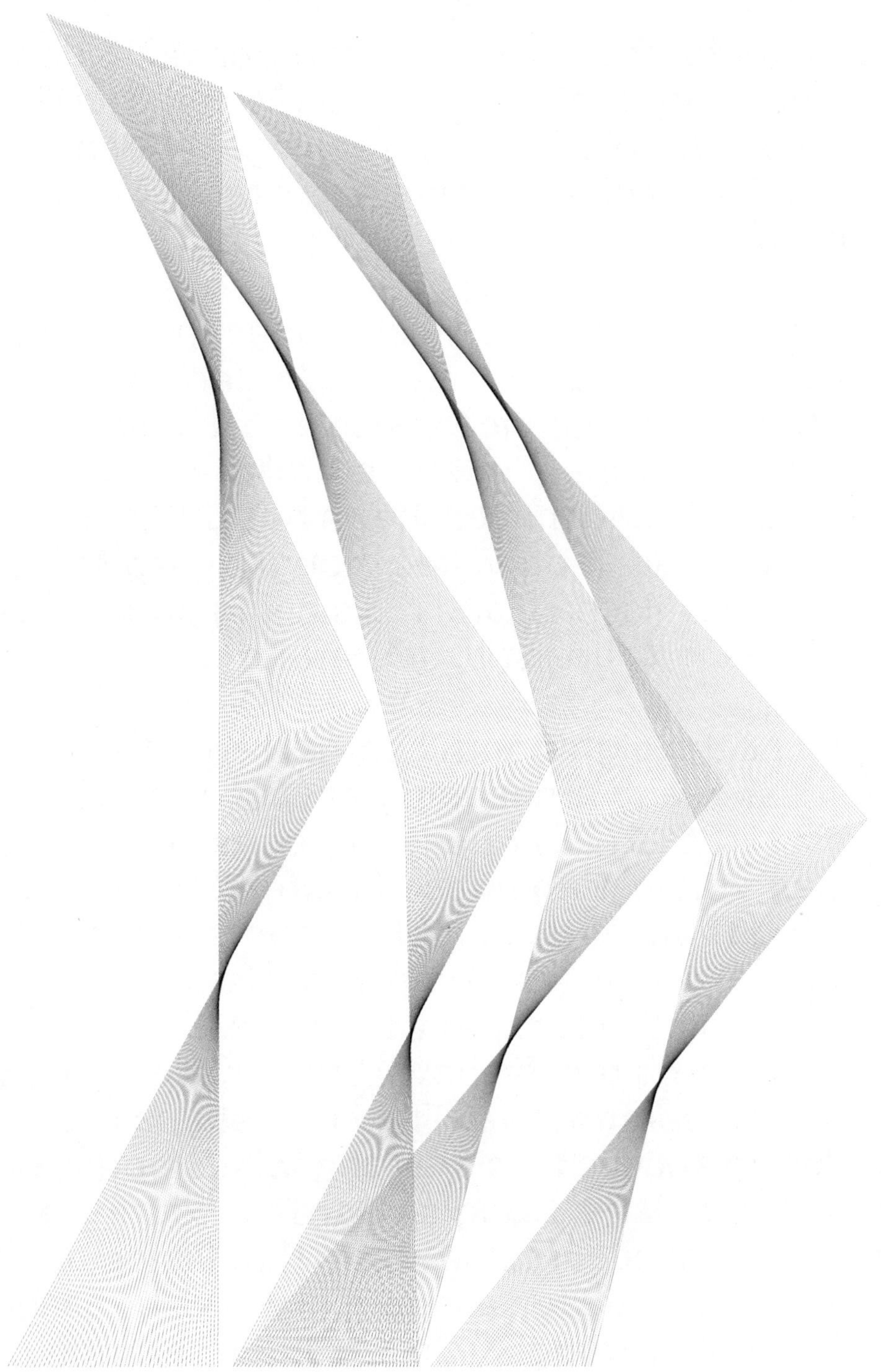

This drawing presents a technical guide for assembling a large string installation created for a museum, with overlapping lines that trace the informal sequence of string deployment within the space. These lines not only capture the method and flow of the installation process but also evoke a subtle Joseph Albers-like quality, oscillating between flatness and spatial depth. This dynamic blurring between two-dimensional representation and three-dimensional form is heightened by the lack of contextual markers, encouraging the viewer to experience the lines as optical effects. The drawing's precision and ambiguity convey both the technical aspects of assembly and the spatial perception of the installation itself, making one wonder whether the viewer's attention is drawn more to the intricate process of construction or the final immersive effect of the space created by these simple strings.

Our prompt for the *Drawing Im/proper* exhibition and symposium, which opened on March 6, 2020 at University of Colorado Denver College of Architecture and Planning, was: *A mischievous drawing and a dutiful drawing.*

One might claim that the most proper and dutiful task of an architectural drawing is to facilitate the translation of an imagined space into a built environment. The "improper" architectural drawing, one might argue, is one that eschews this utilitarian purpose. Instead, it provokes thought, inspires speculation, sows mischief, and risks being pronounced self-indulgent, solipsistic, or gratuitous.

As early as the eighteenth century, architect, stonemason, and archaeologist Giovanni Battista Piranesi (1720–1778) refused to construct actual buildings, dedicating himself instead to dutifully producing thousands of meticulously rendered antiquarian etchings of Rome. His infamous *Carceri* prints, which have led many to qualify him as the first "paper architect," subvert the conventions of constructed perspective. They present us with bewildering spaces that are otherwise impossible to realize. Similarly, Douglas Darden, "during a shameless, unaccountable storm that lasted nearly nine years," crafted ten allegorical works he called "condemned buildings." Constructed through drawing and storytelling, these buildings "are a turning-over" of persisting ideologies about the (dutiful) role of architecture.[6] For Soviet architects Alexander Brodsky and Ilya Utkin drawing was a form of imaginative resilience and political dissent.

Their stark, witty, and dystopian collection of etchings served as a form of creative resistance during the Cold War, a time when the Soviet Union imposed severe propaganda-driven sanctions on art and architecture.[7] Under Alvin Boyarsky's leadership of the Architectural Association, drawing practices were cultivated as a form of critical architectural inquiry. This approach nurtured a whole generation of influential architects, including Zaha Hadid, John Hejduk, Daniel Libeskind, and Bernard Tschumi, among others.[8] This is but a small sampling of memorable drawing practices that, together with the im/proper collection presented here, demonstrate that, in the realm of architectural drawing, dutifulness and mischievousness intertwine to create a productive friction.

Architectural drawings serve to envision future possibilities, present potential realities, sustain creative world-making, and explore new opportunities for existing in the world. Both drawings and architecture can fulfill these functions. In the practice of architecture, drawing can act as a "motive force," when focused on the process of speculation, and discovery.[9] A drawing thus oriented can operate as a play-space for imaginative inquiry and as *a site* for drawing out emergent possibilities. As such, to probe at (im)propriety in architectural drawing practices is to call out the multifarious roles that drawing plays within the discipline.

In the following excerpts, four contributors to the *Drawing Im/proper* exhibit—Nat Chard, Perry Kulper, Natalija (Nada) Subotincic, and Mark West—reflect

Imagine a world where architecture and artifact are as restless as verbs. Within this world Perry Kulper thrives as a dutiful sleuth. While scrupulously peering through the mounting translucent layers of mylar with the determination of a detective archivist, he chases shifting trajectories with his scalpel and pen.

Bound to the surface and compressed into a pictorial horizon, these atmospheres defy capture by covertly seeking strategic horizons. Incidents of logic briefly surface around drawing, not about the drawing content. Within this terrain of coincidence, ALL lies in a latent relational duration that is continuously arresting itself only to immediately be released—a pseudo disguise sanctioning a profound ambivalence between the pictorial and strategic. Moments of resistance become what they need to, by seizing tangents serendipitously lying in-wait within their proximity. Escaping detection seems unavoidable as defensible notations revise the multiple densities found within these depths.

Yet depth is defied once this world rises-up from the waning surface, interminably building upon itself, whilst rotating about in a spectral display. The punitive nature of the surfaces and frames, now long gone, is faintly recalled through the presence of disquieting shadows emerging just beyond where they once held sway. Nothing is settled within Kulper's mischievous ambient entourages.

With a few loose screws,

— Natalija Subotincic

When studying the man who contextualized the psyche of others by making a sense of their social and cultural engagement with others, how do you grasp the agency of the place in which he formed his ideas? Nada Subotincic's forensic scholarship into Sigmund Freud's drawings, descriptions and naming (mostly from his letters) of the realms in which he worked and lived is played against her drawn archaeology of his possessions and home. Meticulous studies of his belongings in London are re-located on her drawn survey of his apartment in Vienna based on Edmund Engelman's photographs of Freud's home at Berggasse 19, just before he left for England in 1938. These drawings are more than maps of territory, charged with the implications of relationships between the artifacts, furniture and their possible inhabitation (and of possible relationships). As with archaeological drawings that resist comment or prejudgement, this cartography is spare, analytical and drawn without hierarchy. The care and respect with which not just the objects or rooms but also the stitches in the rugs are drawn sets out a relational structure where we are compelled to form our own psycho-spatial analysis. While Freud was mostly coy about his relationship with his surroundings, Subotincic lays her resonance with the world out for you. When invited for dinner, underneath your plate her table teases you with a display of the bones of every animal she ate during a stage of her life. Laid out dispassionately as if specimens from the archive of a natural history museum, as with her drawings they tickle as much as tell.

— Nat Chard

in scale. These structures simultaneously coexist in a decontextualized setting, creating an atmosphere of congested activation through their asynchronous proximity to one another. Like an over-packed family group photo, distant cousins stand on their toes to get into the frame. The image is washed with a sepia tone, obliterating materiality and allowing the parts to gather into a coherent whole.

The effect captivates, not merely as a visual catalog of architecture, but more for its possibilities of adjacency and contradiction. Cockerell has created an urban scene that foretells the sort of competitive monumental urbanity that the twenty-first century confronts as a normative condition, where layers of overlapping monumental buildings create vertiginous negative space between them. In rendering the individual buildings as a field of self-similar objects, Cockerell positions himself as the editing author of all that is depicted. His choice to portray them as a single, overlapping composition allows the observer to read the piece as a uniform, monolithic construct. As David Watkin, Cockerell's biographer, wrote:

> This strange romance, these pyramids, porticoes, and domes, is surely the idea, years before its time, of Banister Fletcher's celebrated *History of Architecture on the Comparative Method*. One can only envy Cockerell for having lived before the invention of stylistic labels by architectural historians. Thus, unhampered by considerations of whether a particular building was 'Baroque' or 'Neo-Classical' he could dart from one period, place, or person to another.[1]

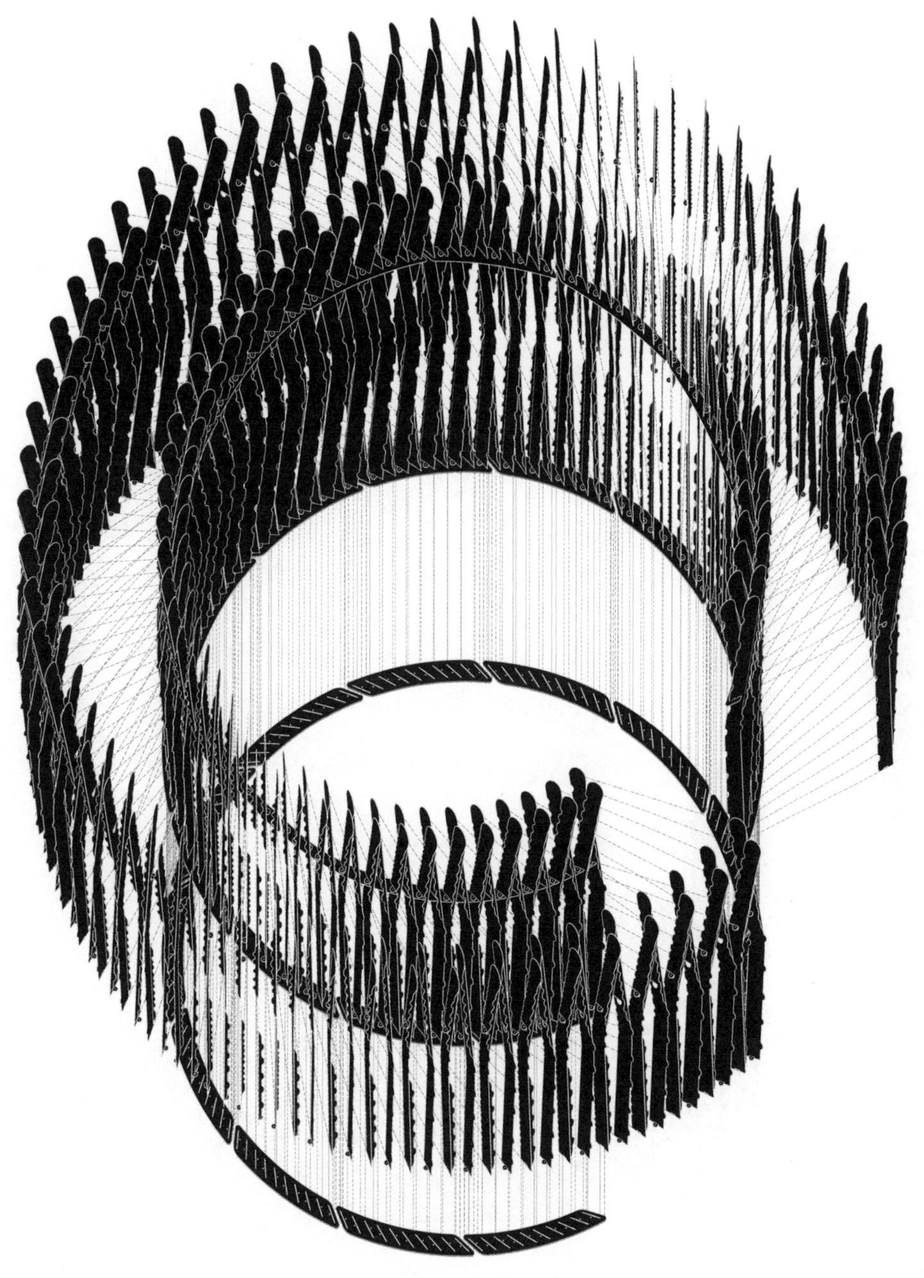

This drawing presents a radial array of components depicted from an oblique projection. The black-filled components, outlined in white, allow for clear relief and figuration, emphasizing their impossibly thin profiles. The assembly consists of three distinct steps: a base, a set of arching and bending spines, and a collar. Each component appears frozen in a moment of transformation, suggesting a dynamic choreography that unfolds over time. While the radial composition hints at symmetry, the irregular densities of the black forms break the expected order. The technical precision of the drawing engages with the fourth dimension—implying movement beyond the static view, reminiscent of a zoetrope. Though clearly a technical diagram, the drawing evokes a sculptural quality, where the delicate thinness of the fins gives a sense of fragility and impermanence, further amplifying the interplay between materiality and abstraction.

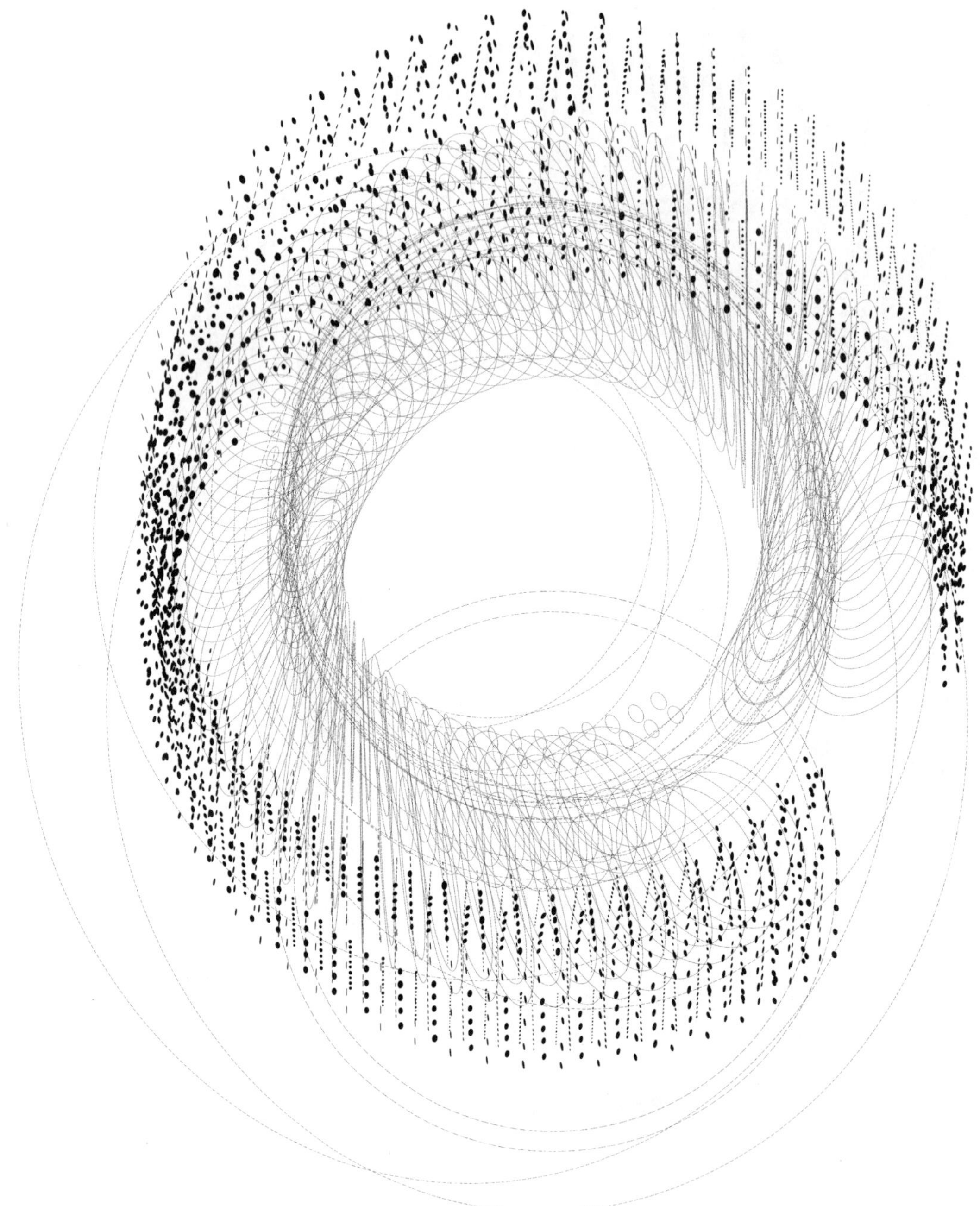

The second drawing deepens both the clarity and complexity of its predecessor, expanding on the abstract geometry through two distinct sets of graphic information. Dark spots, now seen as oblique ellipses, shift in scale and position, suggesting deeper calibration and potential points of fixation to stabilize the twisting and revolving elements. Overlaid onto this composition is a dramatic series of dashed ellipses, further complicating the movement and suggesting a more dynamic relationship between the forms. The abstract dance seen in the earlier drawing evolves into a celestial arrangement, resembling an astronomy of geometric figures. This descriptive and interpretative drawing captures the structural essence through its declarative circles and elliptical gradients, offering a visual exploration of curvature and control that transforms geometry into a kind of poetic motion.

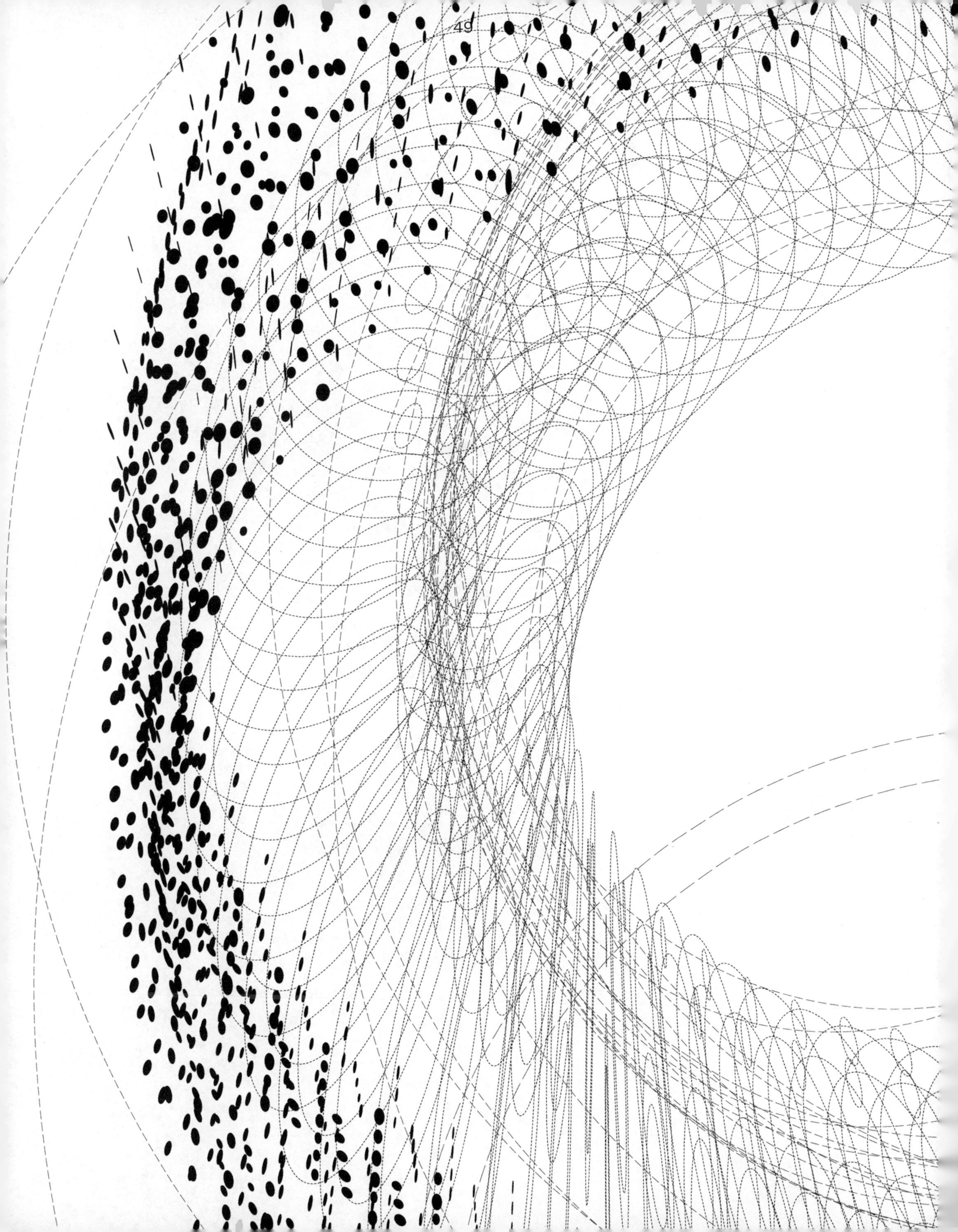

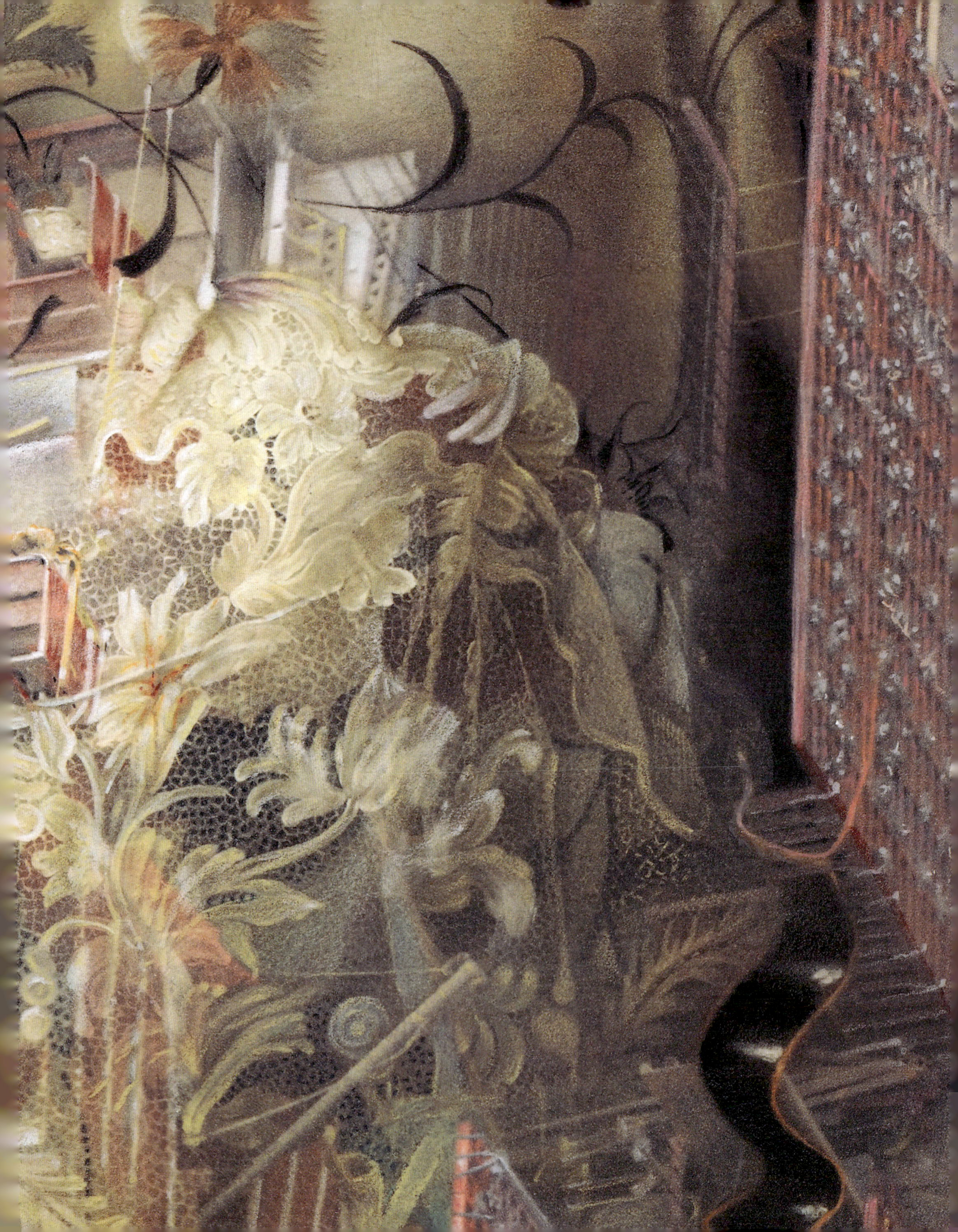

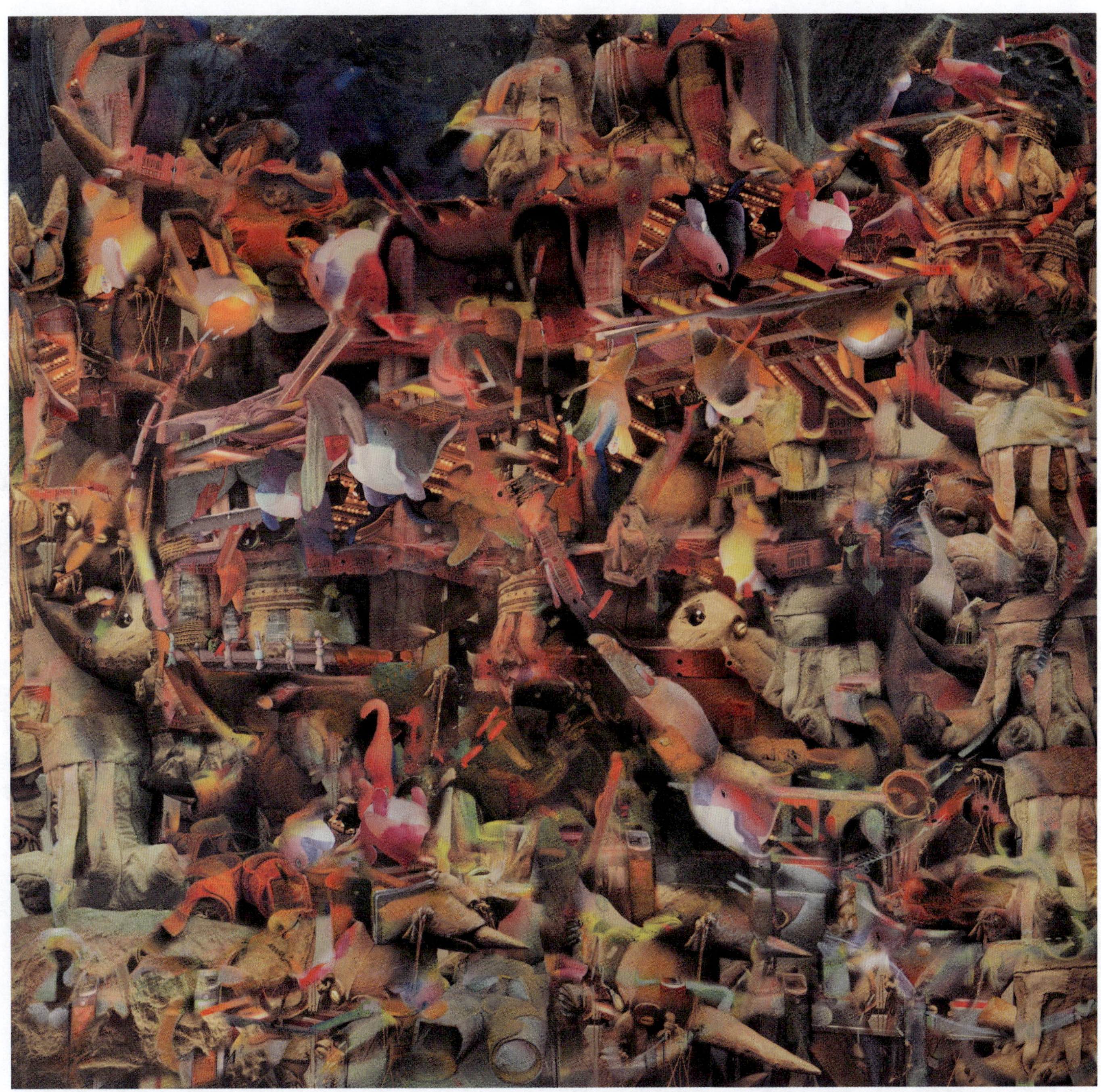

This drawing presents a seemingly limitless clash of form, color, and figure, suspended without an apparent ground or clear vantage point. Elements from various scales and contexts—such as a bird's eye, a soffit filled with lights, and a barcoded ticket string—emerge in the abstraction, providing fleeting glimpses of the familiar. Yet, the image remains unsettled, deliberately refusing any cohesive interpretation. Lines and shadows weave through the scene, offering hints of continuity, but ambiguity prevails. The composition recalls the intricate, fragmented quality of a Hieronymus Bosch painting, where one can observe details endlessly without ever fully grasping the whole. Objects like stuffed animals appear in isolation, further complicating any clear sense of scale or narrative. Despite its abstraction, the drawing remains undeniably spatial, inviting the viewer into an expansive, open-ended exploration reminiscent of a "seek and find" puzzle a child might play in search of a certain figure in the cacophony of forms.

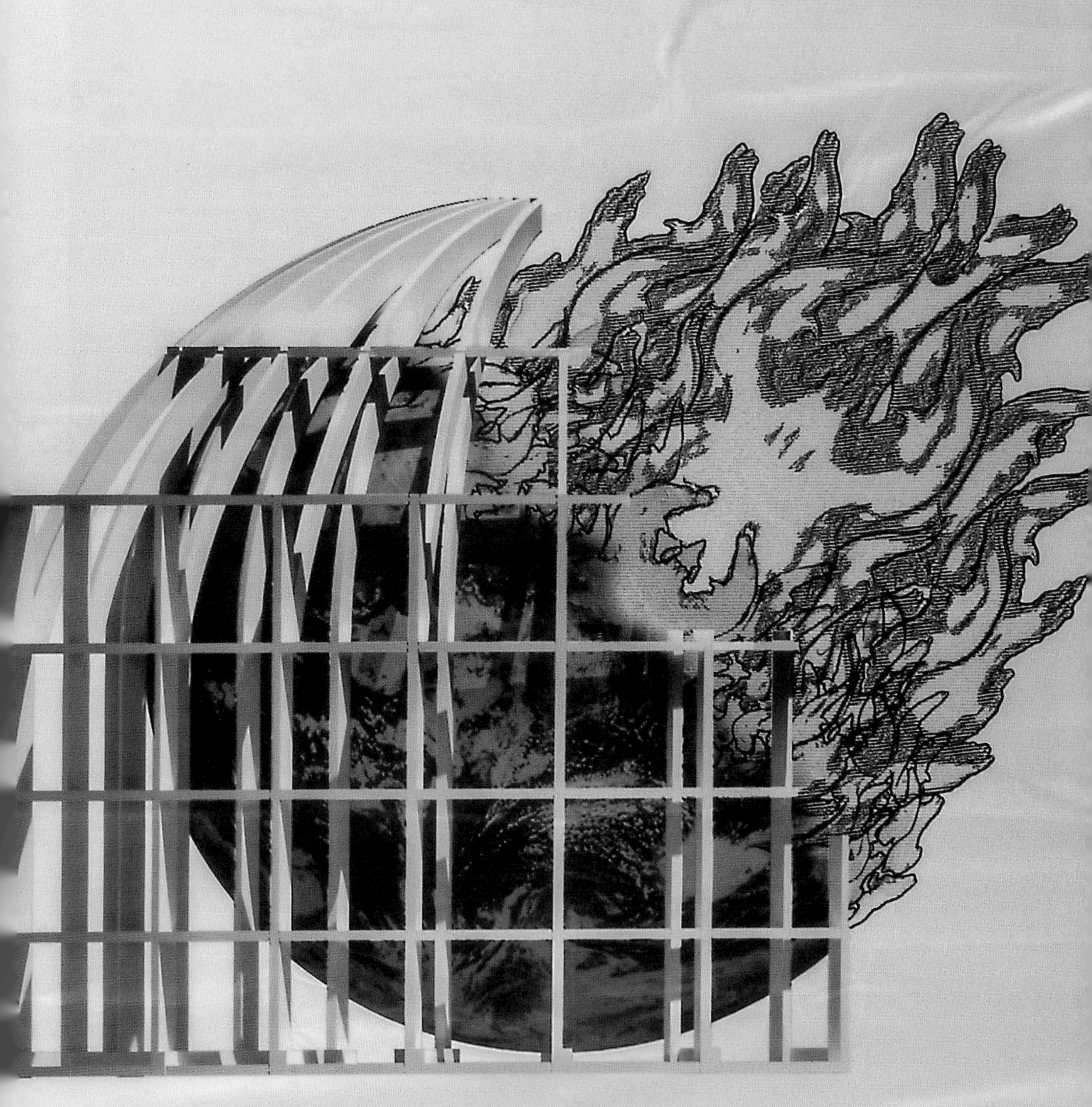

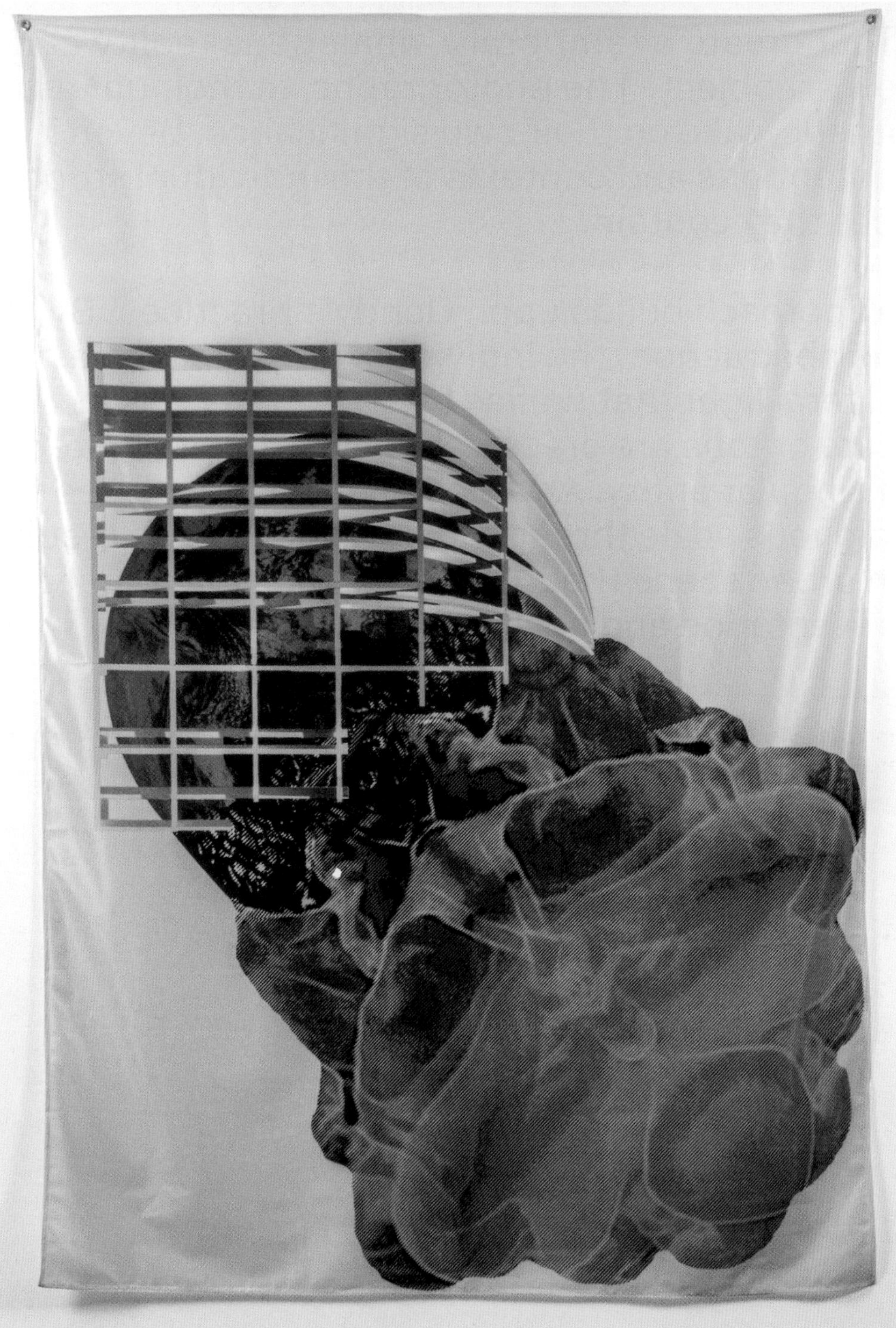

In this second image, the flames have turned to smoke, introducing a temporal dimension that suggests we are witnessing the later stages of Earth's conflagration. Yet, the image retains a sense of hope, hinting that there might still be time to reverse the damage. It serves as a call to reconsider architecture's role in the climate crisis, urging a shift from being passive contributors to becoming active stewards of the environment. The smoke filling the dome illustrates the consequences of human activity choking the planet, but the enclosure could also represent a protective container—an apparatus for potential restoration. This duality challenges us to see architecture not only as a discipline with environmental impact but also as holding the capacity for renewal and repair.

DeTour create a temporary, analogous reality and a new art object. The photographs, in their unique aesthetic, take on their own significance, beyond the intentions and contexts of the individual student pieces they contain.

The approach builds upon Gandy's practices. By using abstraction, the individual projects are cast in a literal light that unifies them. Differences in texture or tone are erased as they are represented as a singular entity. Additionally, they are placed in ambiguous scale through juxtaposition. The result is an urban scene that hovers between deliberate representation and accidental discovery.

Note

1. Bonner, Jennifer, Michelle Benoit, and Patrick Herron, eds. *Still Life: Platform 9*. New York: Harvard Graduate School of Design / Actar Publishing, 2016, pp. 8–9.

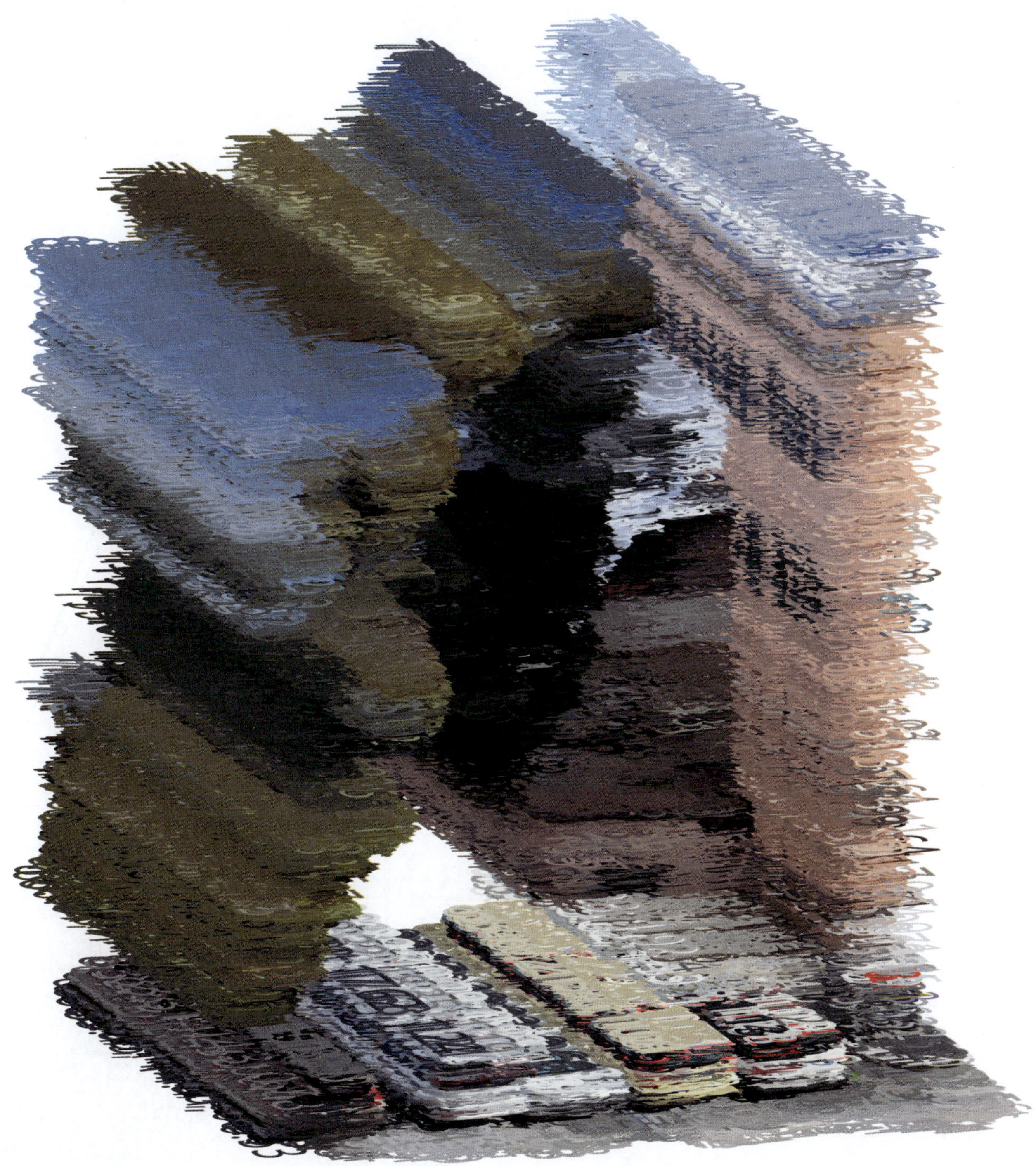

This image is a three-dimensional projection, reproduced photographically, of numbers densely packed atop one another, forming a billowing cloud of colorful data. Scanned surfaces are revealed not in typical flatness, but as gradients of muddy tones. Amid this abstract data, fragments of form emerge: cars, window openings, a slice of asphalt. The image is a notional cast of a scanned artifact, capturing the incomplete reproduction of precise surfaces. Point cloud data is transformed into a new type of notation. The fuzziness of this transformation blurs the boundary between image and data, representation and abstraction.

A/P Practice

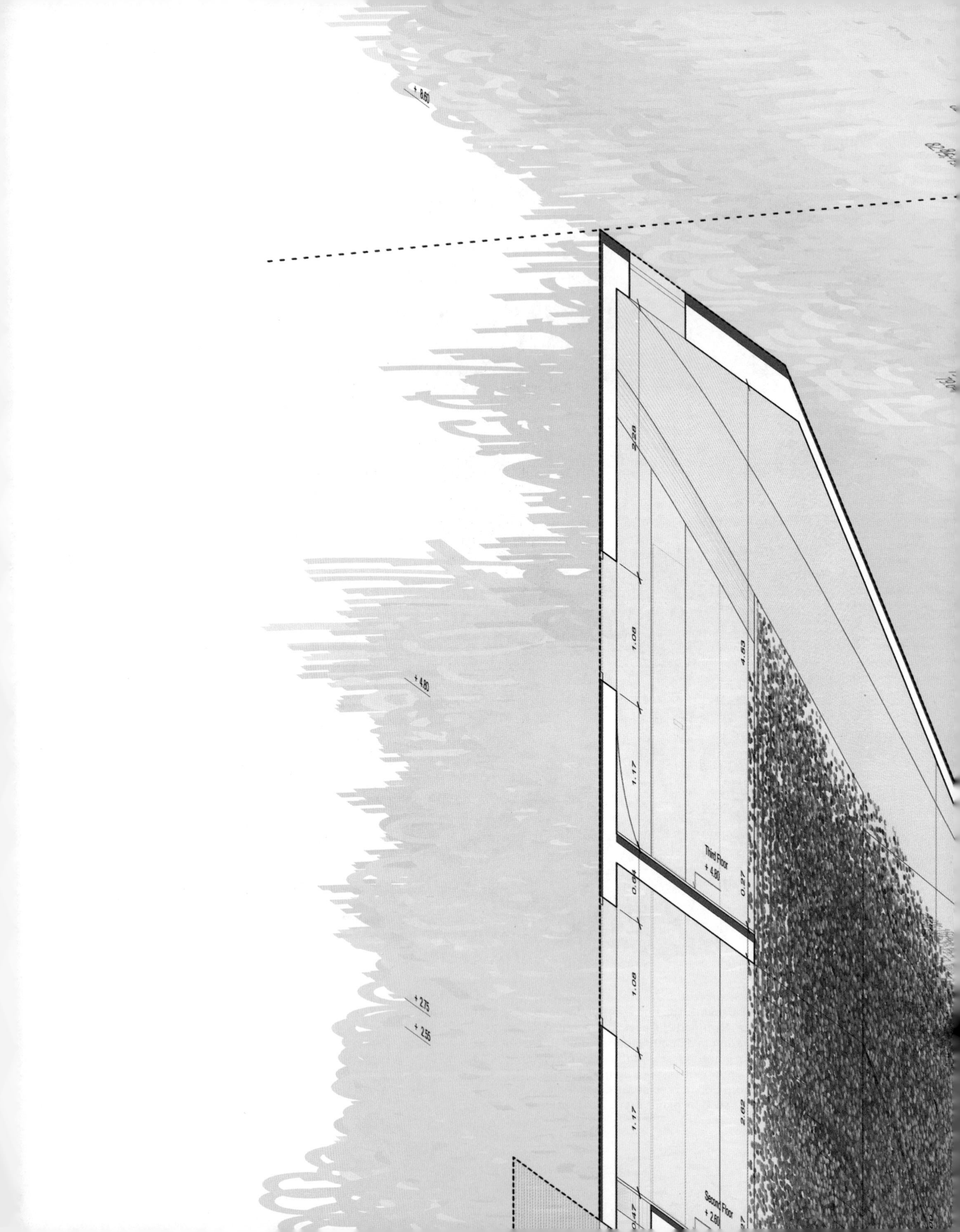

+ 8.60

+ 4.80

+ 2.75

+ 2.55

Third Floor
+ 4.80

Second Floor
+ 2.60

2.28

1.08

1.17

0.64

1.08

1.17

4.53

0.27

2.62

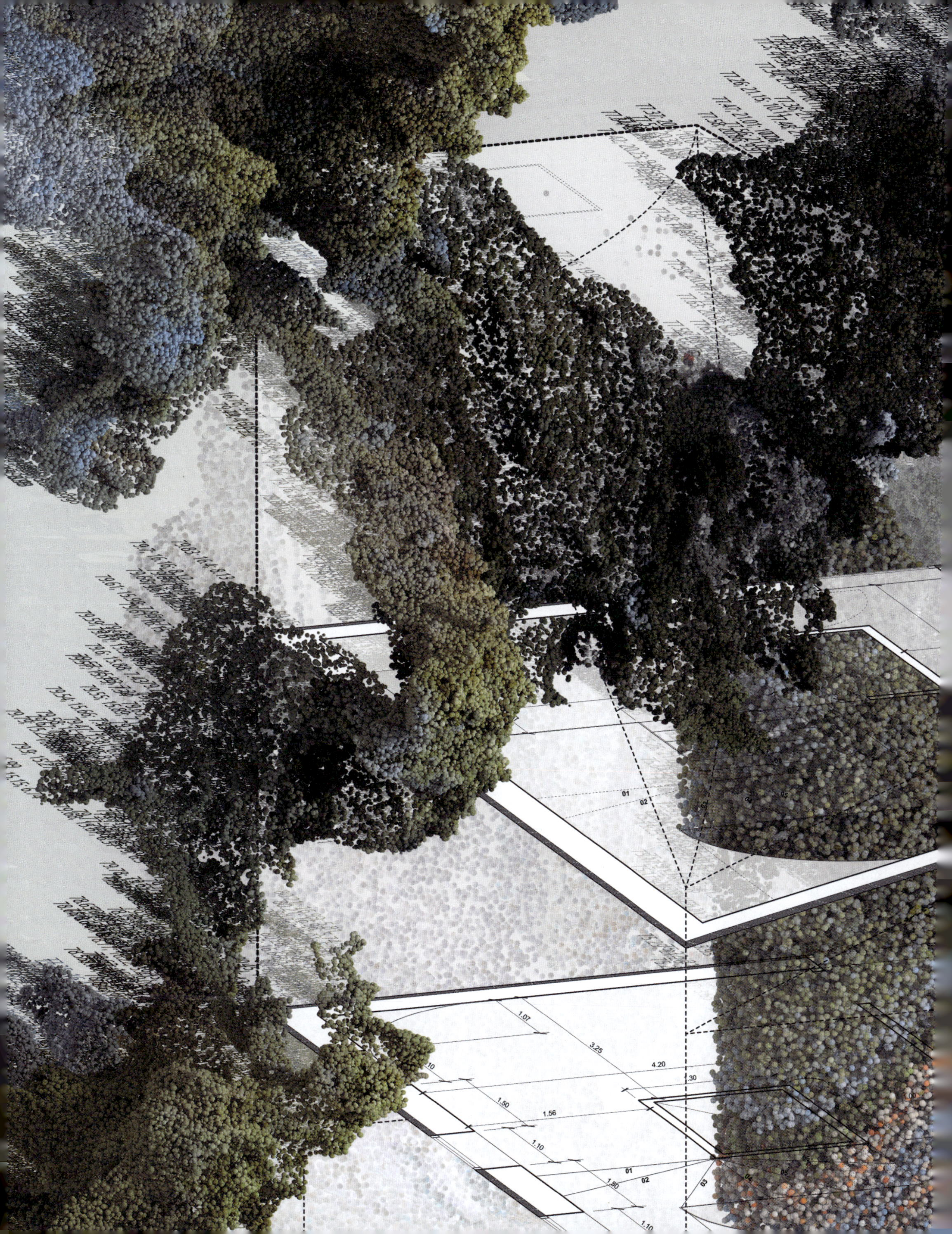

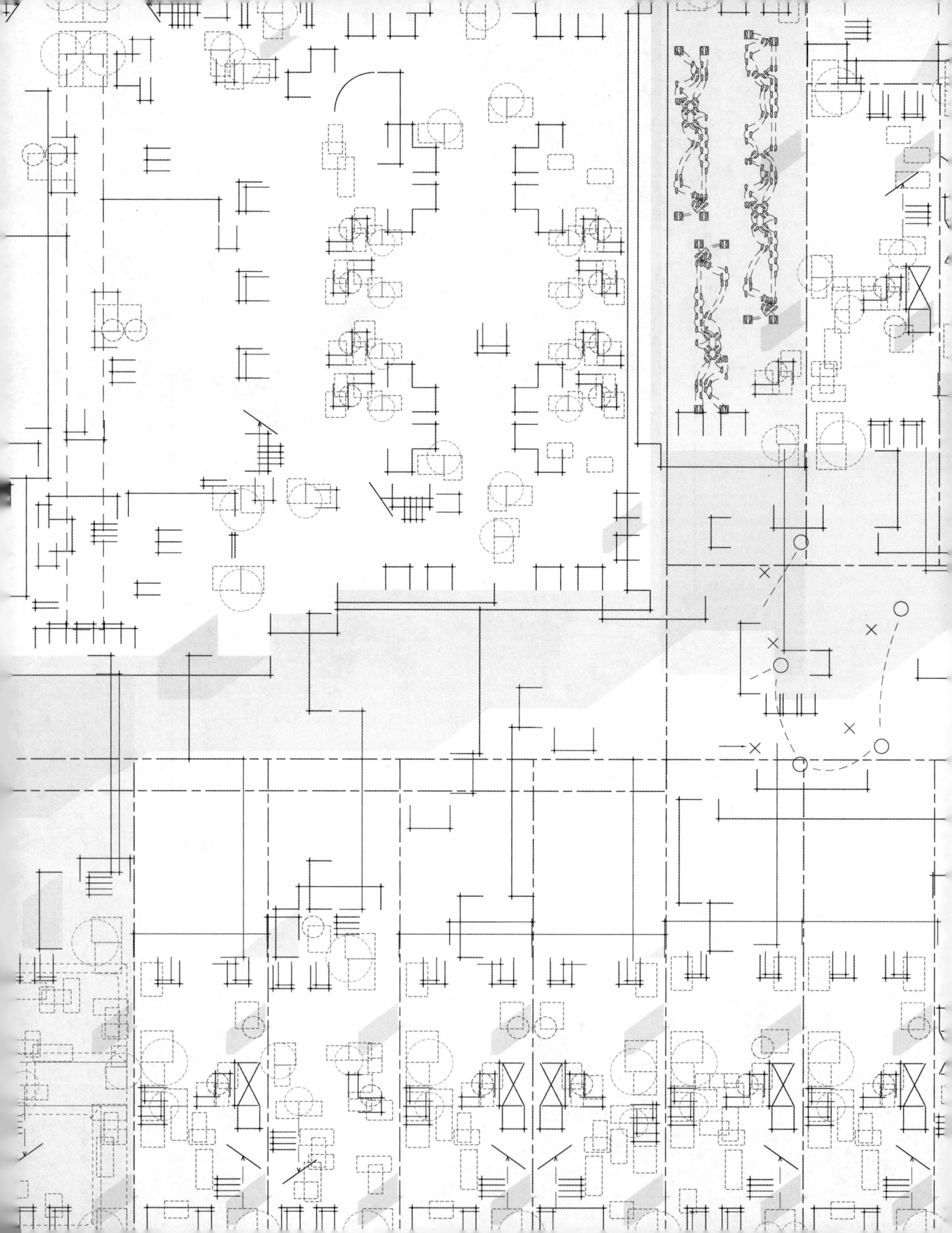

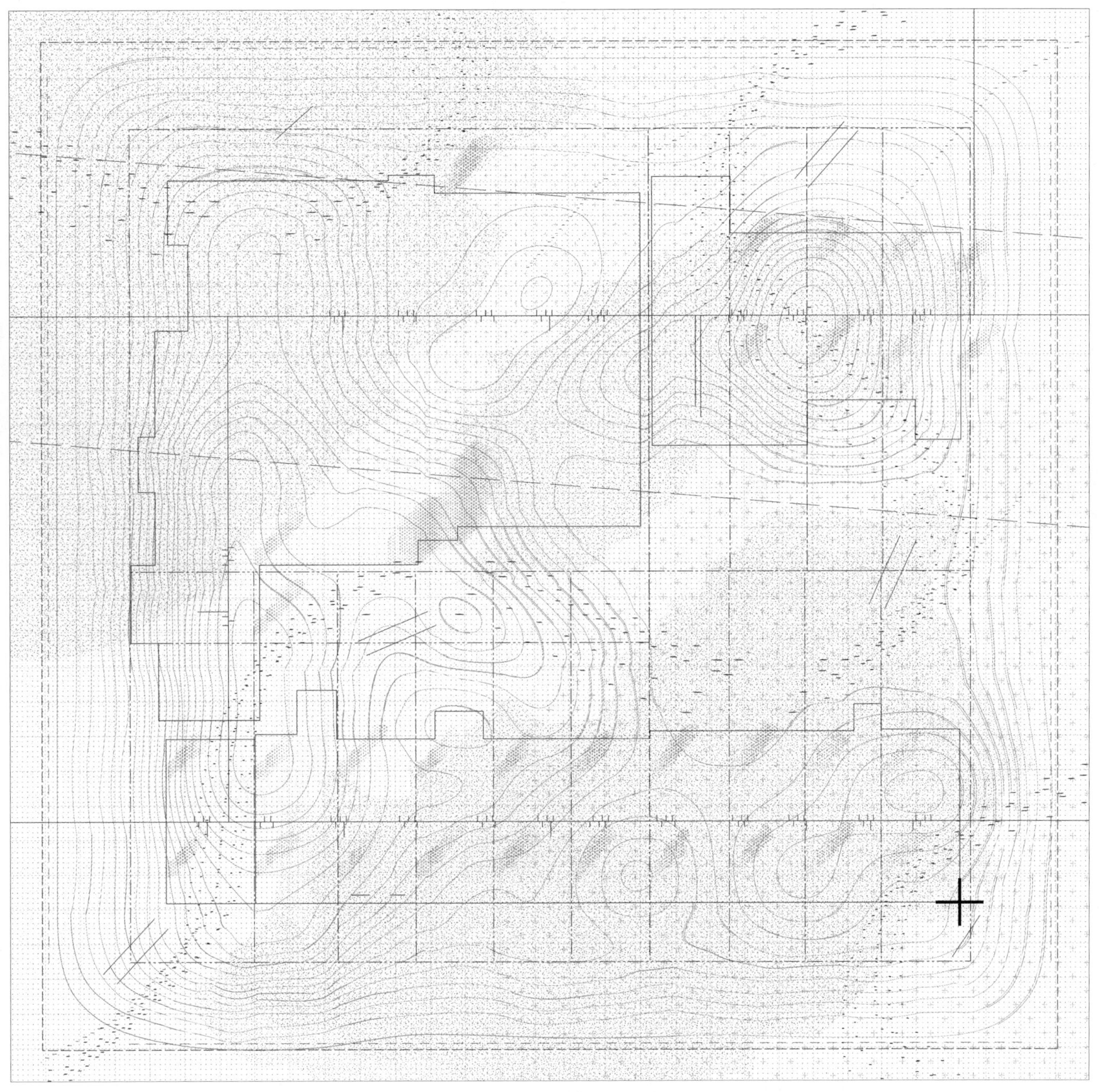

The construction of the second drawing immediately raises questions. While the reiteration of the base point and the clear property line notations provide a recognizable orientation in relation to the first drawing, much remains uncertain. The lines of topography, surface hatching, pattern overlays, and overhead clearance markings obscure a definitive reading. Are these lines representing a hilly wetland before construction begins, or do they depict a site returned to its natural state after the erasure of built forms? The ambiguity presents the viewer with a scene where only the disregarded traces of former occupations and property boundaries remain. The drawing seems to straddle a space between the technical and the illustrative, suggesting a mischievous engagment with time and absence. Architecture's acts of construction and destruction are suggested through the quiet resonance of what is missing, like the works from NEMESTUDIO, where temporal ambiguity similarly is invoked.

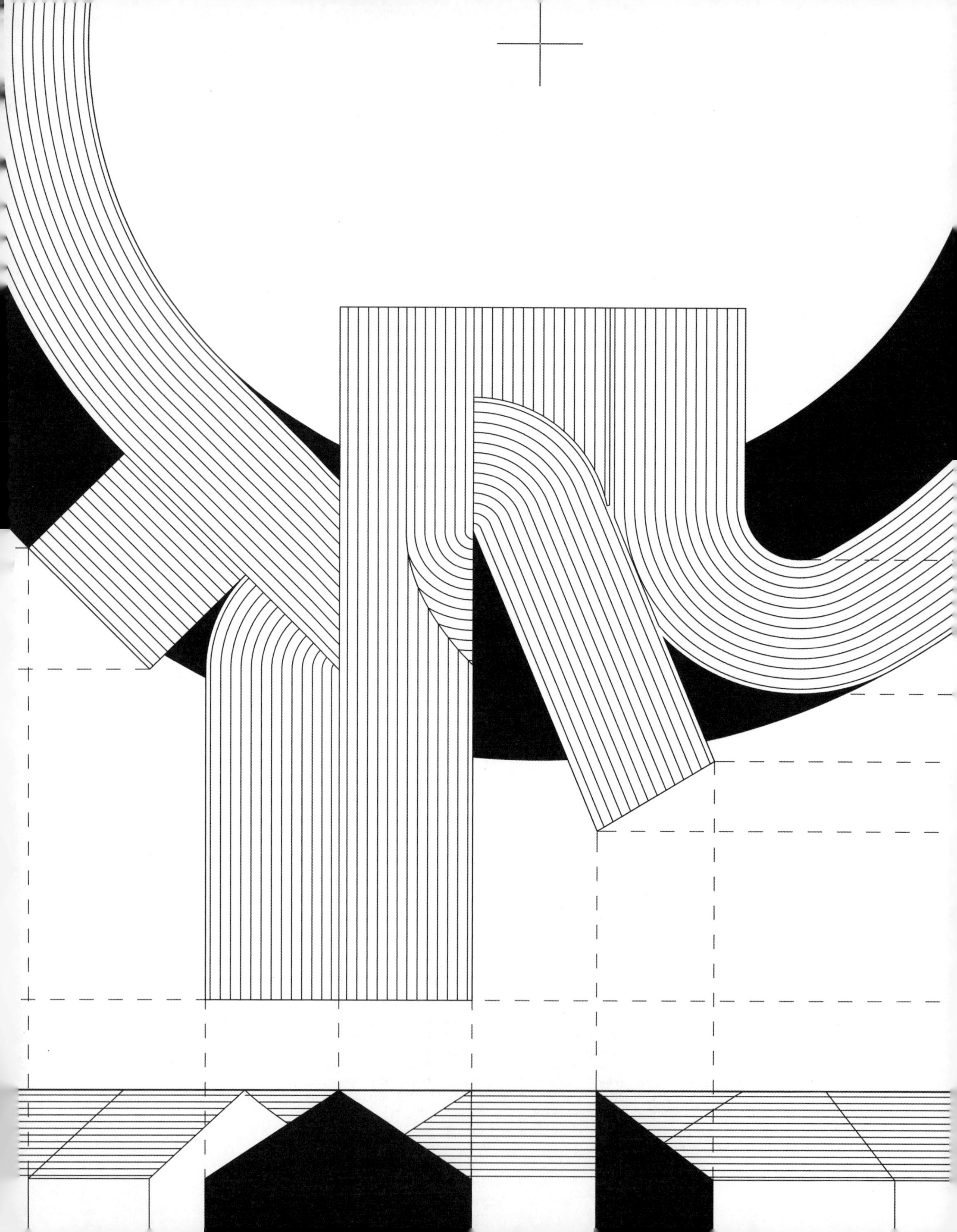

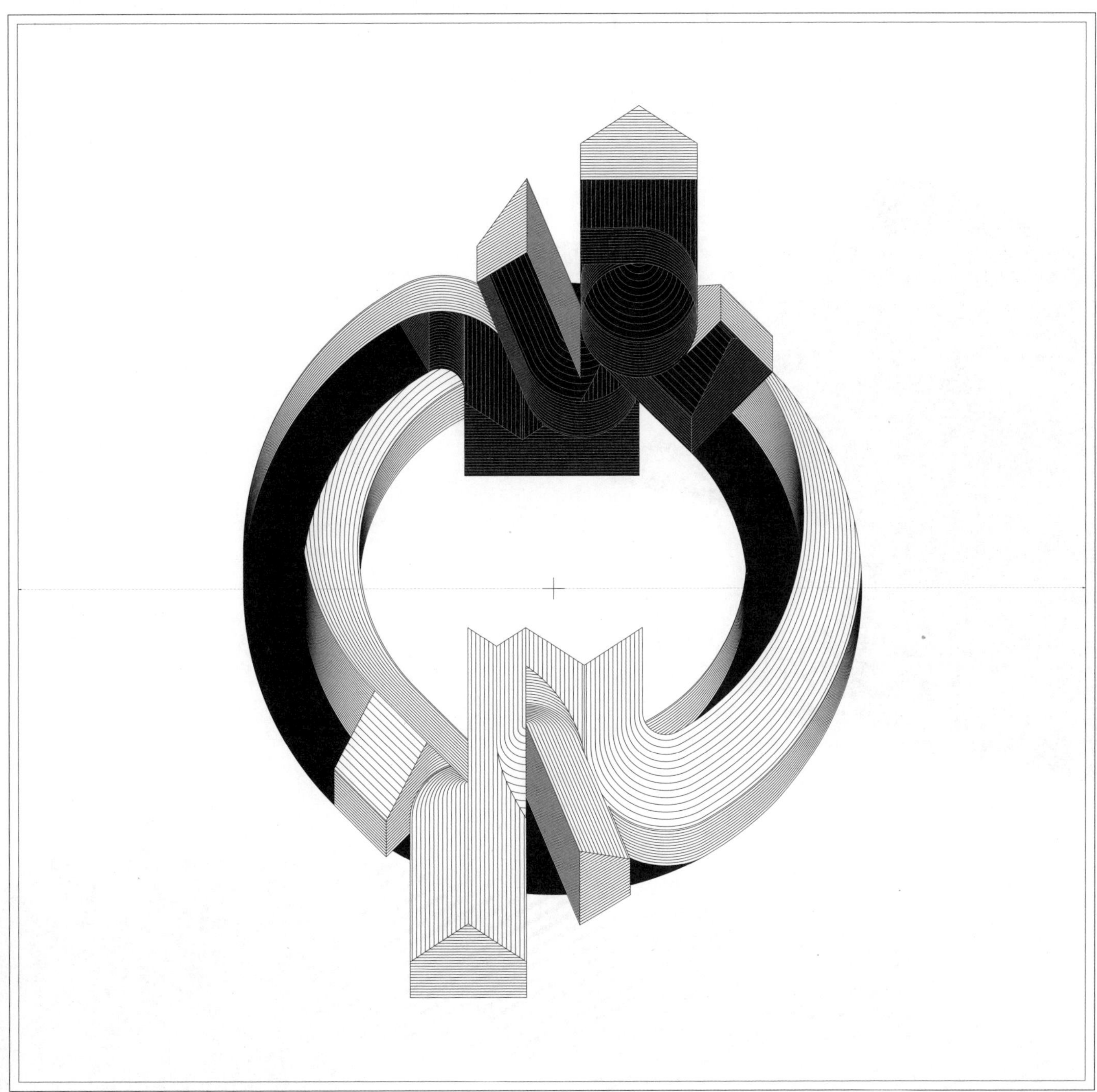

This drawing, a three-dimensional parallel projection, presents a complex, abstracted structure with striking black figuration balanced by ordered striation. While house-like in appearance, it defies conventional notions of scale, adornment, and order. The thinness of the surfaces suggests that this is not a fully realized house but rather an exploration of geometric abstraction. The worm's-eye view begins to reveal the interaction of gabled forms, highlighting how they clash and converge. A central dividing line on the page flips the viewpoint from a top-down isometric view to a worm's-eye projection, creating an ambiguous sense of depth reminiscent of M.C. Escher's work. The intentional abstraction and spatial ambiguity enhance its capacity for expression, inviting idealization. The stark contrast between figure and ground reinforces its conceptual nature.

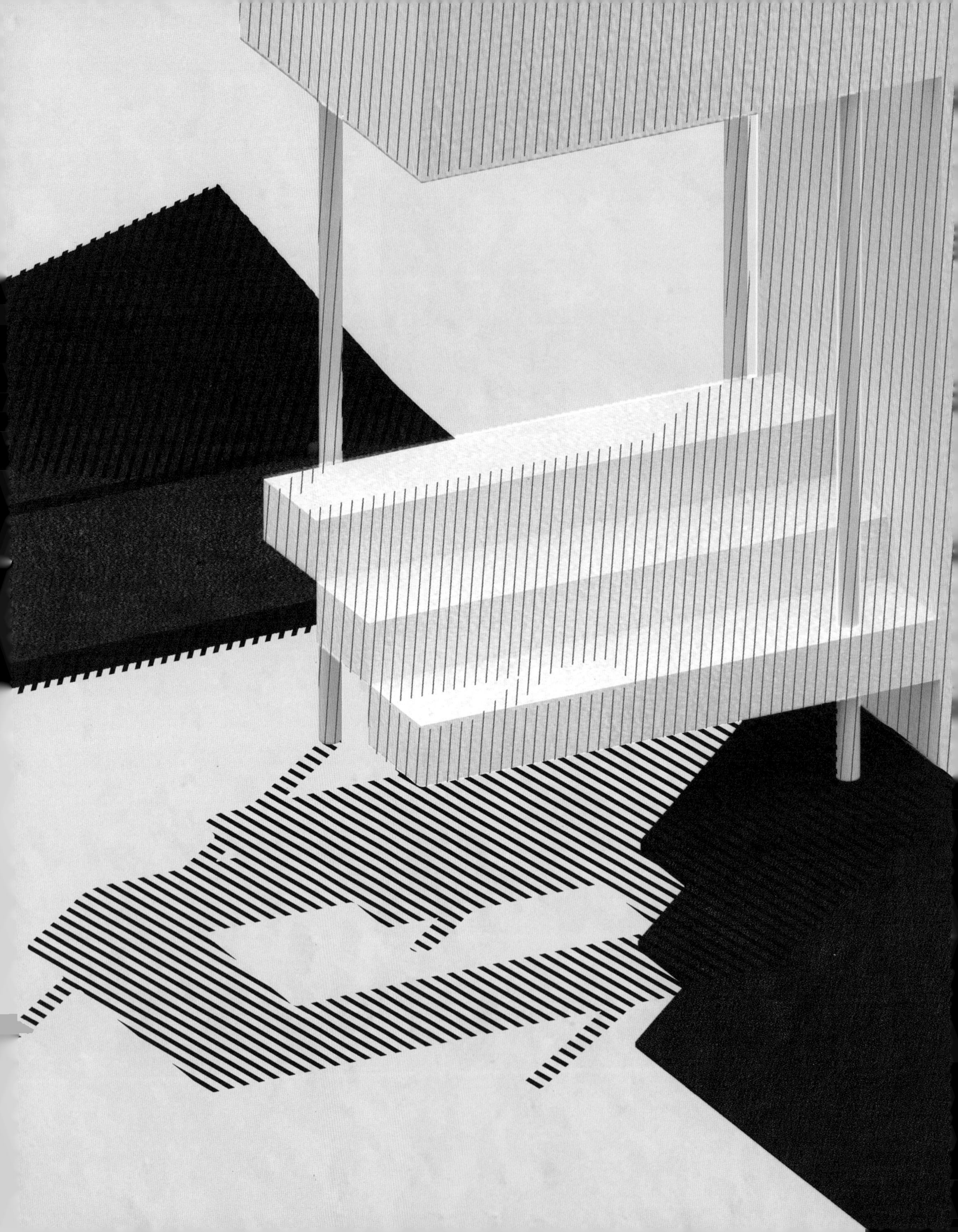

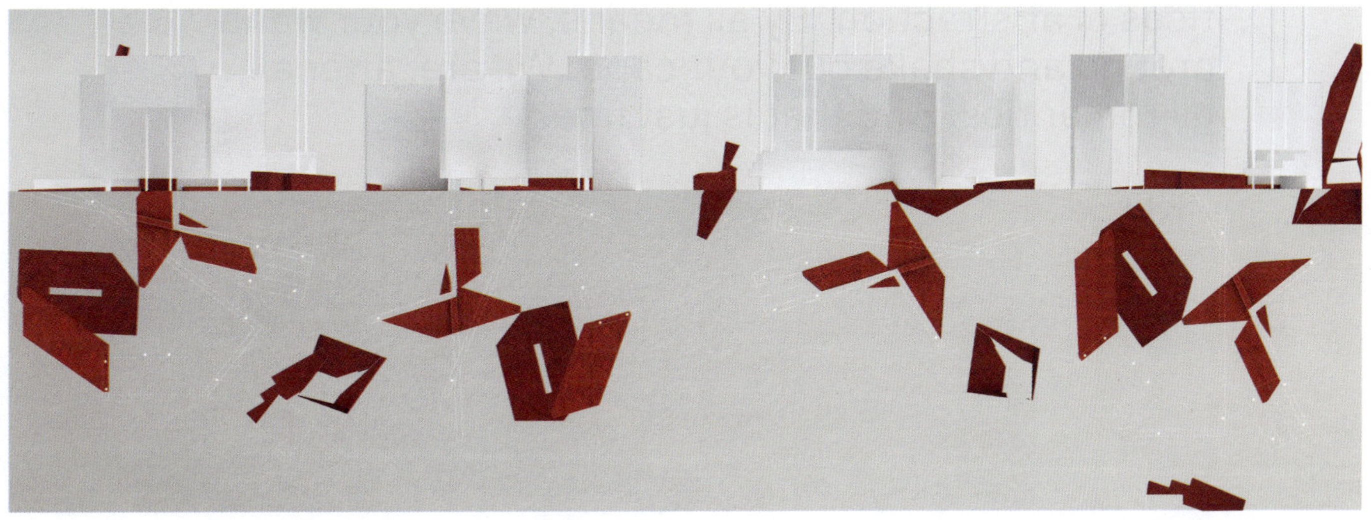

In the second drawing, the format shifts from isometric to a composite of elevation and plan. The structure features repeating architectural elements—posts, stairs, walls, and surfaces—suspended in air and superimposed with careful precision. Dominating the composition is a mat of crimson surfaces, cut and layered, suggesting figures projected onto the ground with a potential correlation to the geometry of these floating objects. The drawing playfully blurs boundaries by presenting both elevation and plan simultaneously, while figures defy convention by crossing the ground plane and drifting into the plan view. This could imply a cut in the plan corresponding to the section or elevation, though it remains ambiguous. The tension between clarity and uncertainty invites speculation: are we witnessing a new interpretation of domestic space, or a more abstract exploration of form and projection? This duality between architecture and abstraction gives the drawing its mischievous edge.

These reflections intentionally suggest a connection to the romantics of the eighteenth and nineteenth centuries. However, I do not intend to imply any form of temporal categorization. Rather, I hope to draw parallels between contemporary image-making practices and a time when architects embraced a touch of fabulism and an inclination to reorient reality through the mischievous, slightly dishonest, practices of abstraction. By all means, wave your wand around and shake out your cape. We are, after all, all romantics. And that is just fine.

–KH

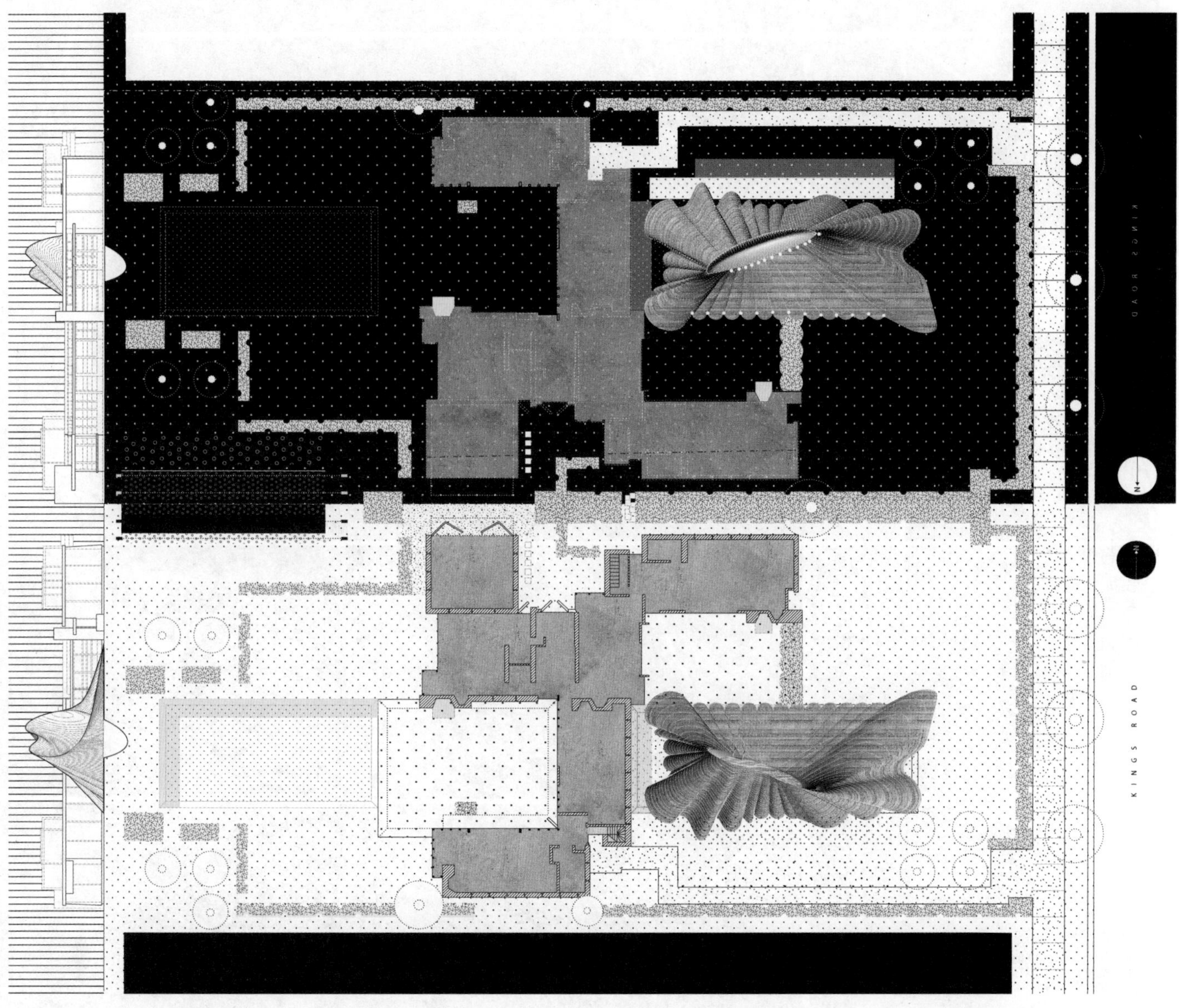

This drawing, split into two parts, presents a complex play on orthographic projection and architectural conventions. On the right margin, the text “Kings Road” appears twice—once in black on a white field and once in reverse, white on black—signaling a deliberate manipulation of conventions. The lower half features a conventional plan and section of a pavilion nestled into the swale at R. M. Schindler's iconic Kings Road House. Above, a mirrored, inverted projection on the black field seems to show a plan looking up into the floor of the pavilion, yet ambiguity prevails. The pavilion's projections do not adhere strictly to conventional rules; instead, they offer an interpretation that blends upright and inverted views, challenging spatial logic. The use of hatching and texture enhances the aesthetic quality, while the design, sharply contrasting with Schindler’s original work, feels sculptural and abstract, aligning more with the land's contours than the house’s formal language.

BairBalliet

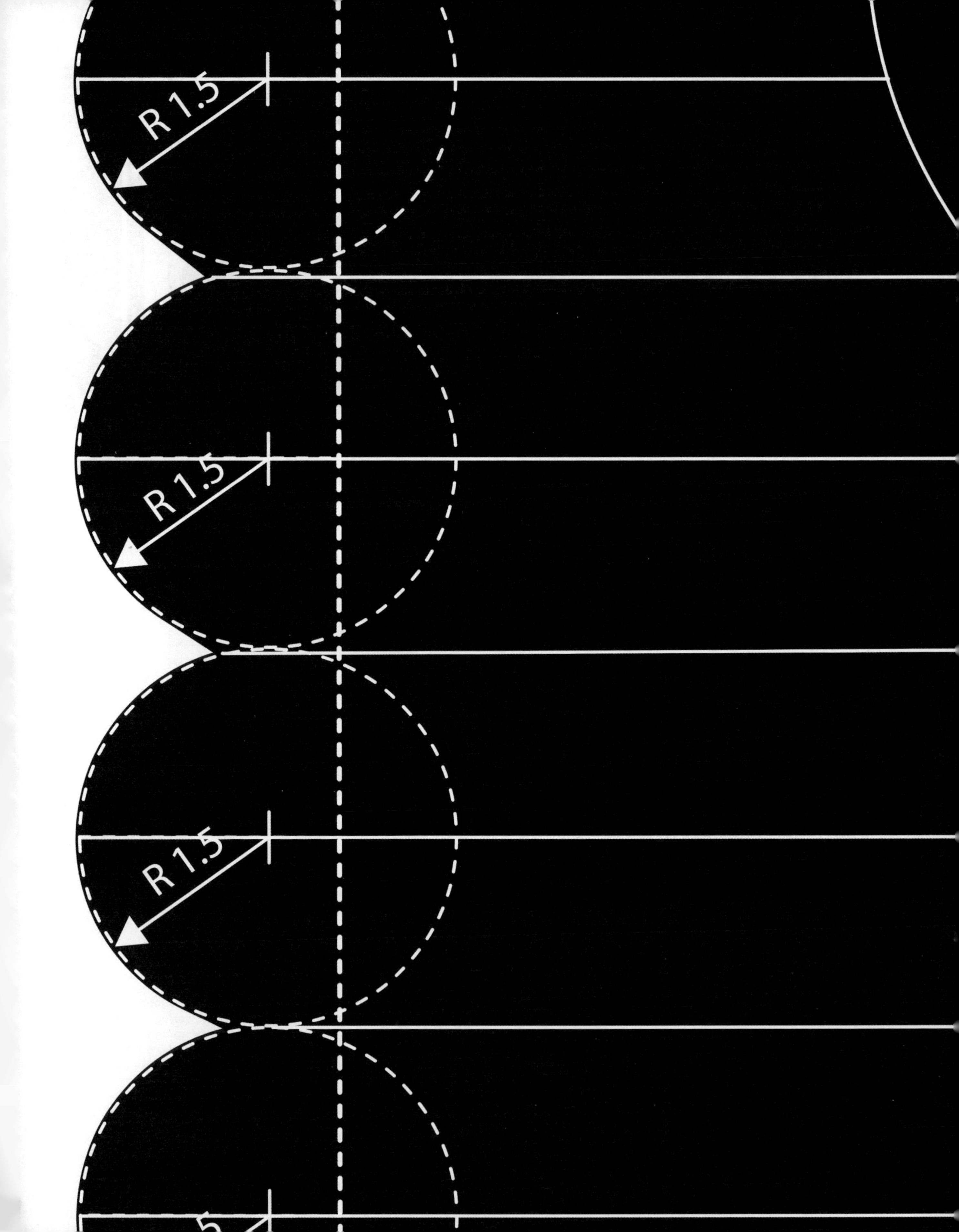
R 1.5
R 1.5
R 1.5

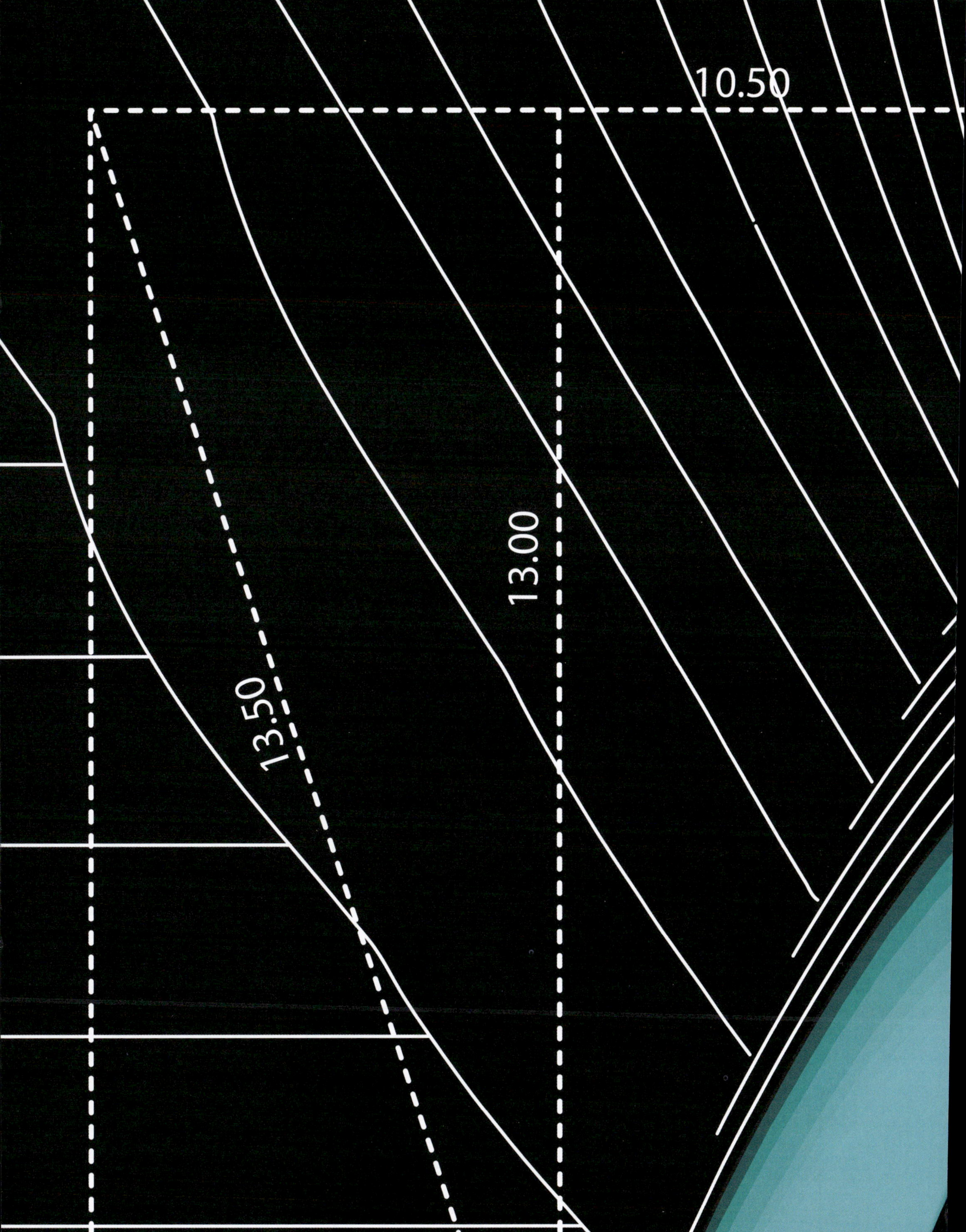
10.50
13.00
13.50

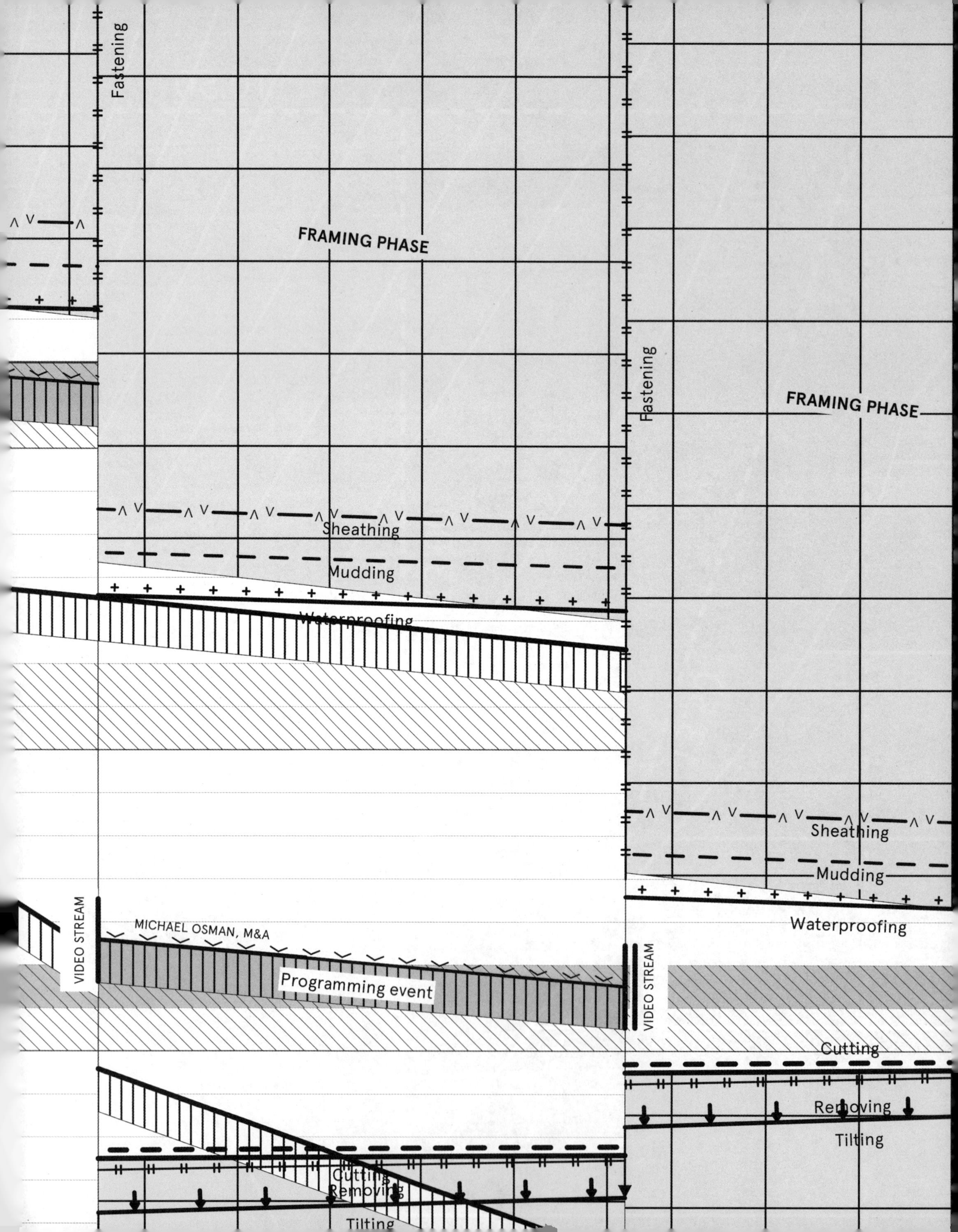

Fastening
FRAMING PHASE
Sheathing
Mudding
Waterproofing
VIDEO STREAM
MICHAEL OSMAN, M&A
Programming event
Cutting
Removing
Tilting
VIDEO STREAM
Fastening
FRAMING PHASE
Sheathing
Mudding
Waterproofing
Cutting
Removing
Tilting

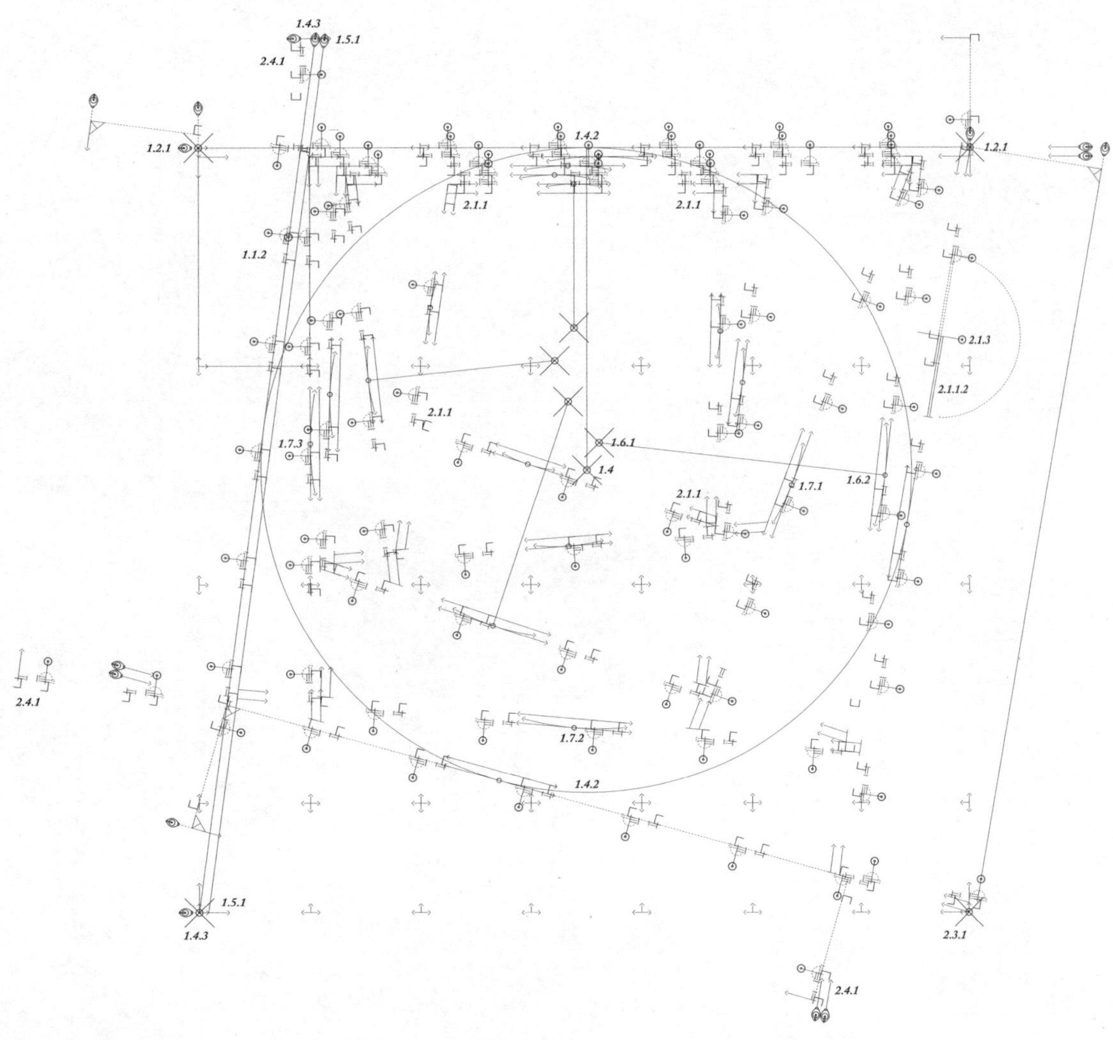

This drawing, related to the same temporary installation described earlier, introduces ambiguity by abandoning traditional anchor points, a defined Cartesian grid, or a clear index of notations. Instead, it layers time within a single image, creating a simultaneous representation of all stages of the walls being constructed and deconstructed. The drawing reimagines space as inseparable from the dimension of time, blurring the boundaries between fixed architectural elements and their temporal transformation. Overlapping coordinates suggest either a flattening of multiple datums into one comprehensive image or the layering of various moments into a continuous sequence. The result is evocative of dance notation, a choreography of architectural movement, where framing plans shift and overlap. Through this technique, the drawing invites viewers to perceive architectural space not as static but as fluid and dynamic, capturing moments of both creation and decay in one unified composition.

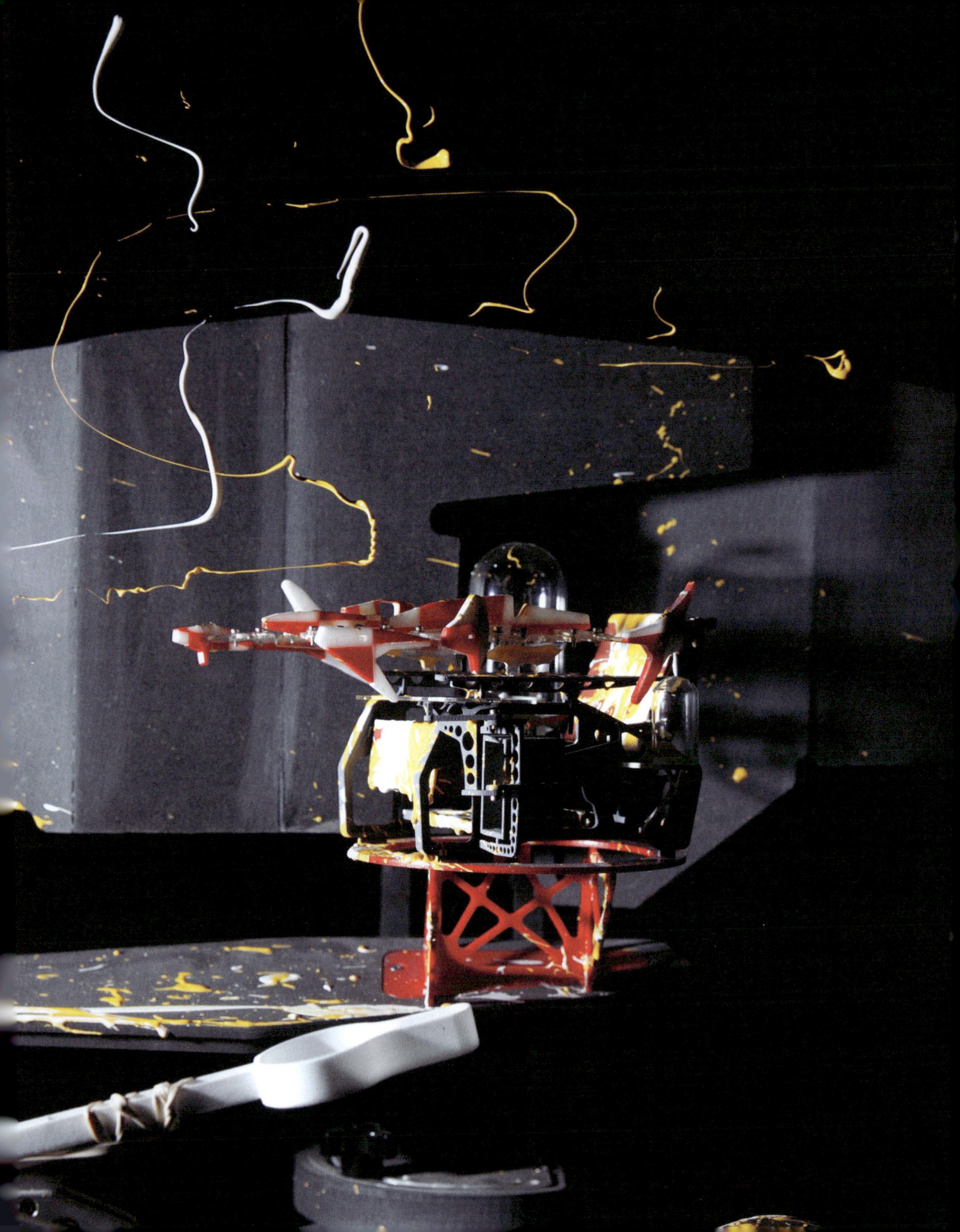

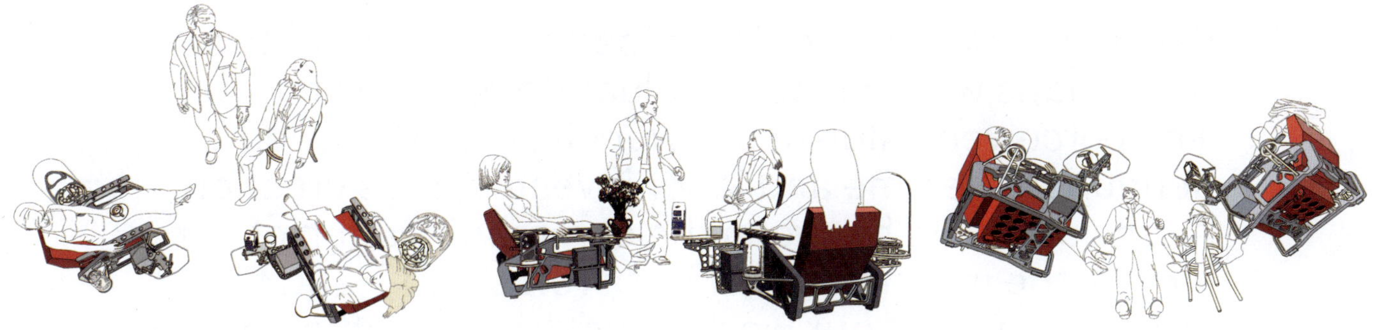

The ambiguous apparatus atop the device in the previous image is now clarified to be a chair depicted in this drawing, shown from three vantage points. The chair links these two images into a narrative about scale, purpose, and perception. Its meticulous design and carefully selected colors evoke the precision and functionality typical of medical or industrial equipment. The new perspectives encourage a reading that is less about experimentation and more about intention, as the same objects seen in the first image's splattering of paint now appear almost therapeutic, with a palliative, reflective quality. The calm, stable arrangement of figures seated and standing contrasts sharply with the dynamic motion captured previously, suggesting a duality in how objects function and are perceived. This scene prompts reflection on how shifting contexts reveal different facets of design, inviting viewers to consider not just the purpose of the chairs but the deeper interplay between the crafted object and its environment.

decades. The drive for increased efficiency exists at direct odds with the self-evaluation of our own work. The perceived value of our work is, in part, dependent upon the time and labor invested in its creation. A tension exists between the commodification of our labor—the mechanism of our profession—and the intrinsic value of our work. This drive for efficiency often clashes with how we assess our own work. Personally, my sketches have never felt complete even after a few dozen, or hundred, or even thousand hours of further exploration. This way of working has the quality of a magic trick—your audience is led to believe that the laws of physics have been defied, while you've simply hidden the rabbit at the bottom of your hat. The trick's value is entirely derived from its novelty, virtuosity, and deception.

Now consider a drawing that was difficult to produce but appears simple. Here is a trick of a different sort. At first glance, the work seems unassuming, perhaps even ordinary. Its casual familiarity may lead its audience initially to dismiss it. Here the trick lies in the irreproducibility of the effect: the more familiar the effect, the more striking the realization of its difficulty, resulting in greater impact. In some ways, this mode of production values a mastery of the tools of production, creating a singular and complex flow of work while allowing for unpredictable or variable outcomes. The greater the variability in workflow, the more unpredictable and irreproducible the results become. In this case, the audience sees the rabbit and recognizes it but has no idea from where it came. Rather than being stashed away, it is gradually revealed. The longer one contemplates

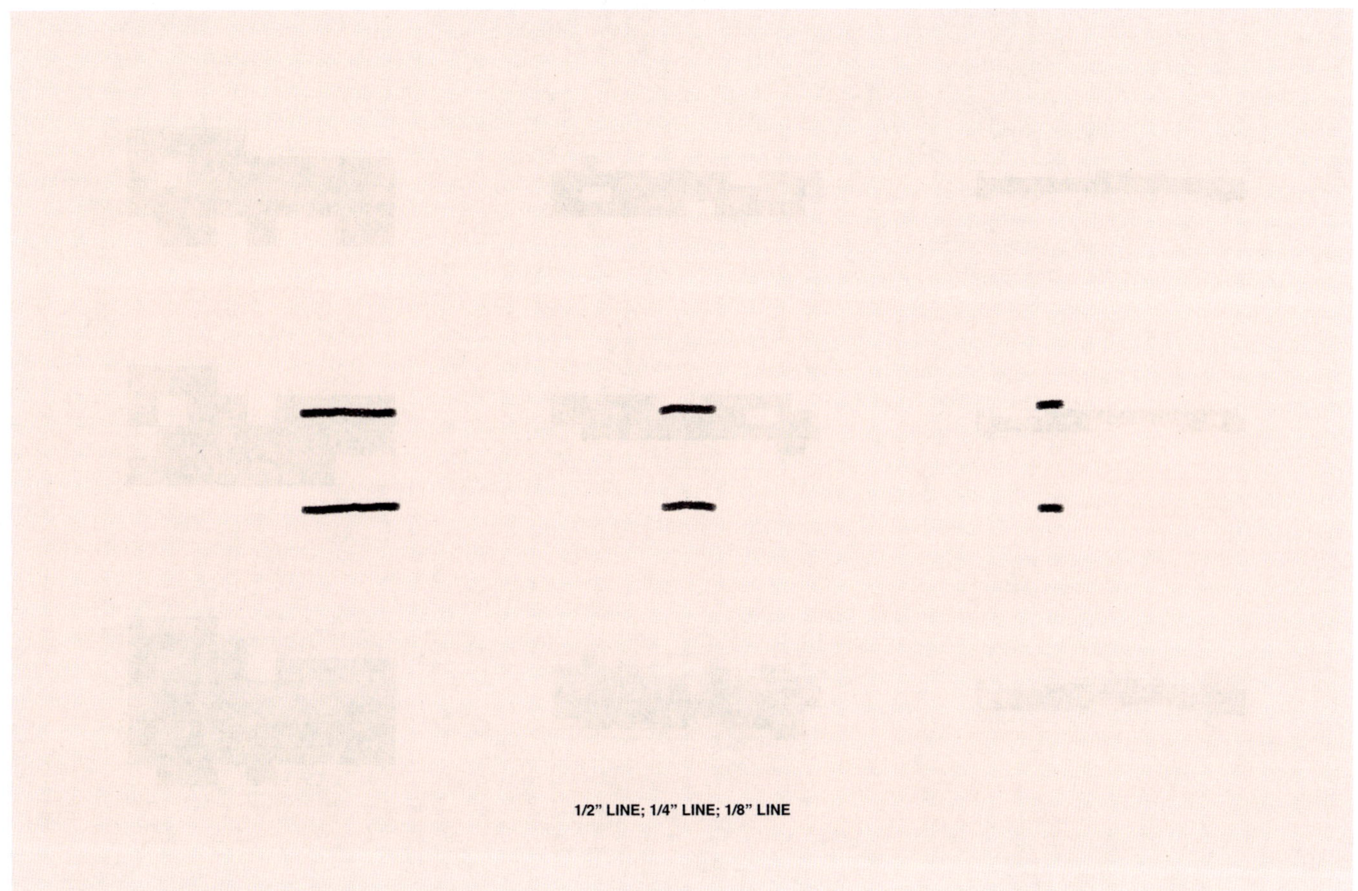

Six seemingly hand-drawn lines appear on a small sheet of peach-colored paper, arranged in three pairs of varying lengths. Below each pair, a title indicates its precise length, though a closer look reveals slight variations between the lines, hinting at their human origin. The drawing feels like a rapid sketch, perhaps intended to capture an idea with minimal effort, much like an architect's initial musings on a cocktail napkin. The piece suggests expediency, as if the drafter aimed to convey proportional relationships with the fewest strokes possible. Yet, the measured captions beneath the lines give the impression of intentionality and precision, turning what might seem casual into a clever commentary on the preciousness of hand-drawn work. This piece nods subtly to the value of time and efficiency in design, embodying a playful balance between speed and exactitude.

Medium Office

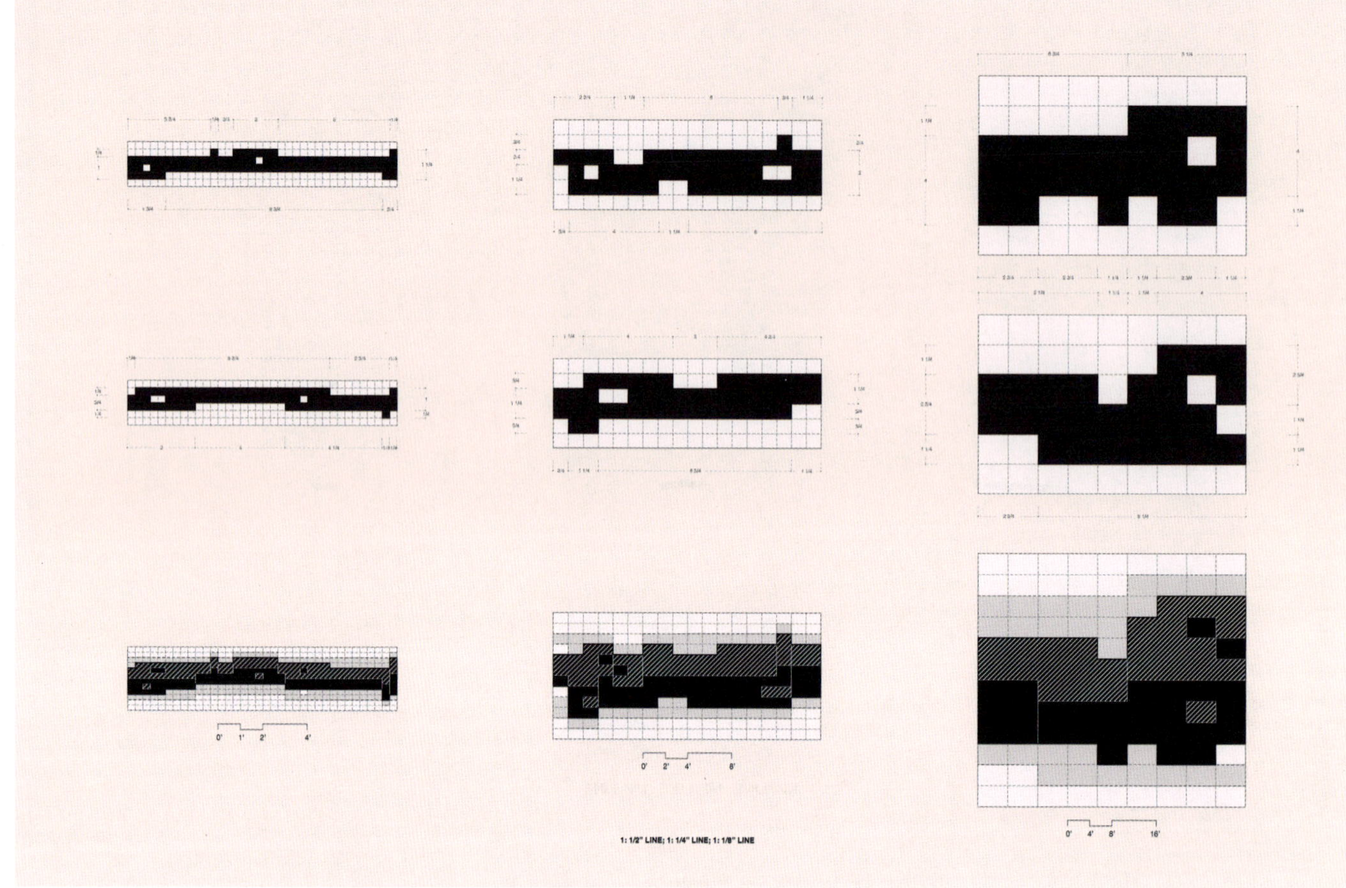

This drawing presents three rows of black figures—each a "line" drawn in low resolution and situated on a scaled grid that shifts across rows. Titles, a scale bar, and dimensions are included, yet their relationship remains elusive. The top row reads as an elevation, the middle as a plan, and the bottom as an oblique orthographic projection view. The scaling shifts across each grid, altering the resolution of the figures, though it's unclear if this variation is due to the figures' own change in scale or to inconsistencies within the grid itself. Dimensions are rounded, distorting any straightforward interpretation of scale; while the figures are all the same physical size, their dimensions fail to align. This ambiguity plays with perception, inviting the viewer into a game of interpretation, as the resolution and scale seem to defy a coherent reading.

Medium Office

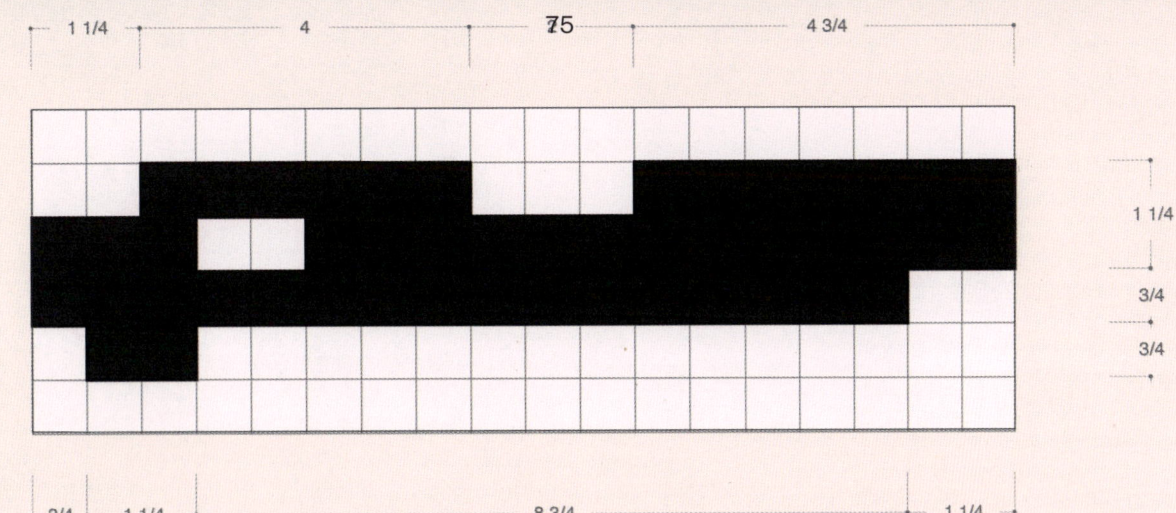

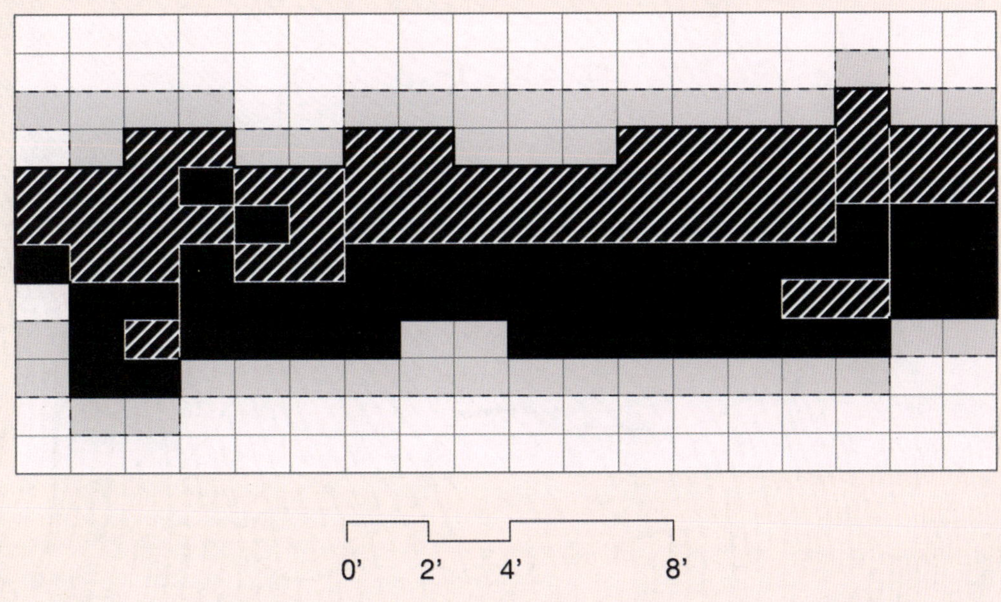

1: 1/2" LINE; 1: 1/4" LINE; 1: 1/8" LINE

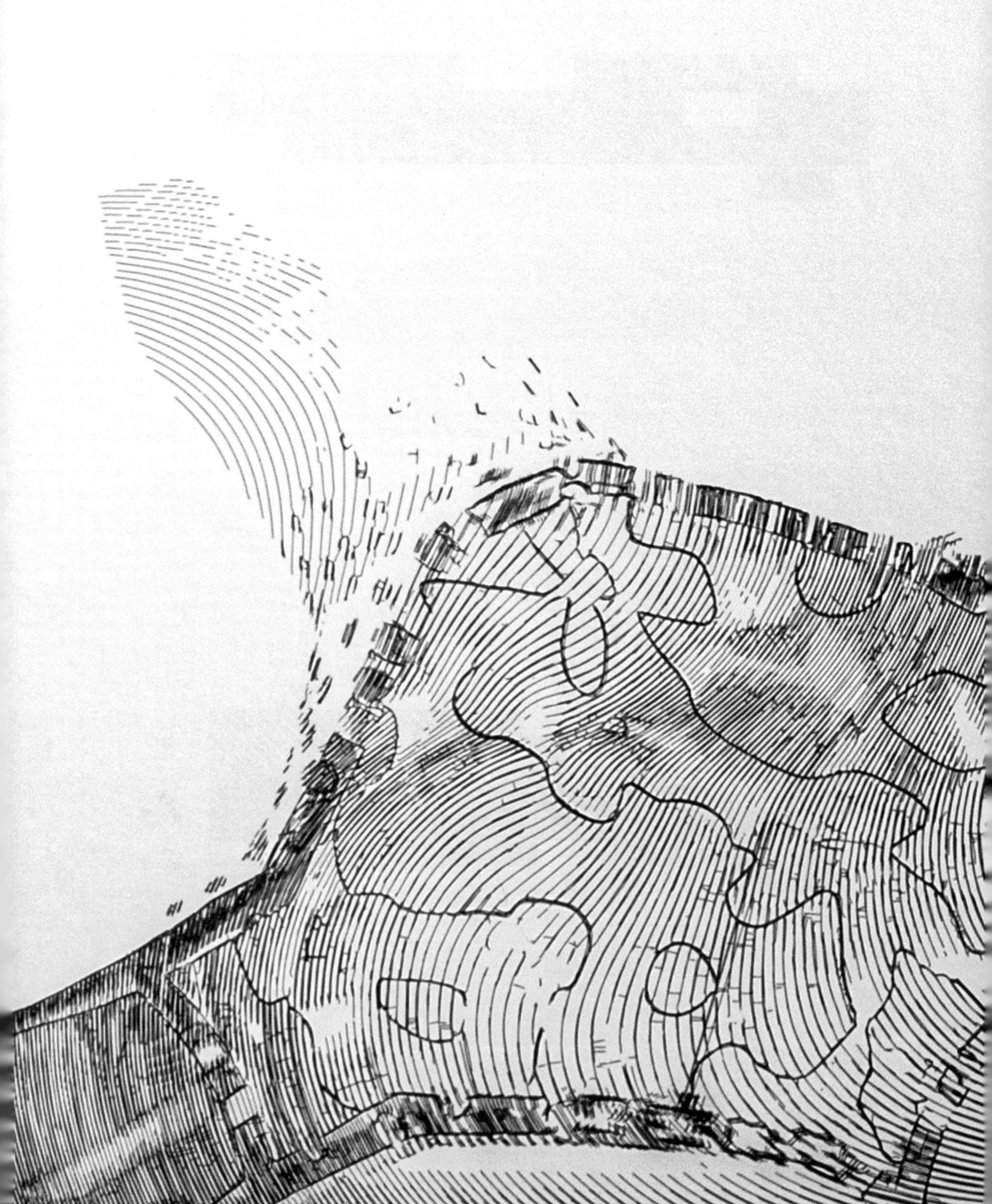

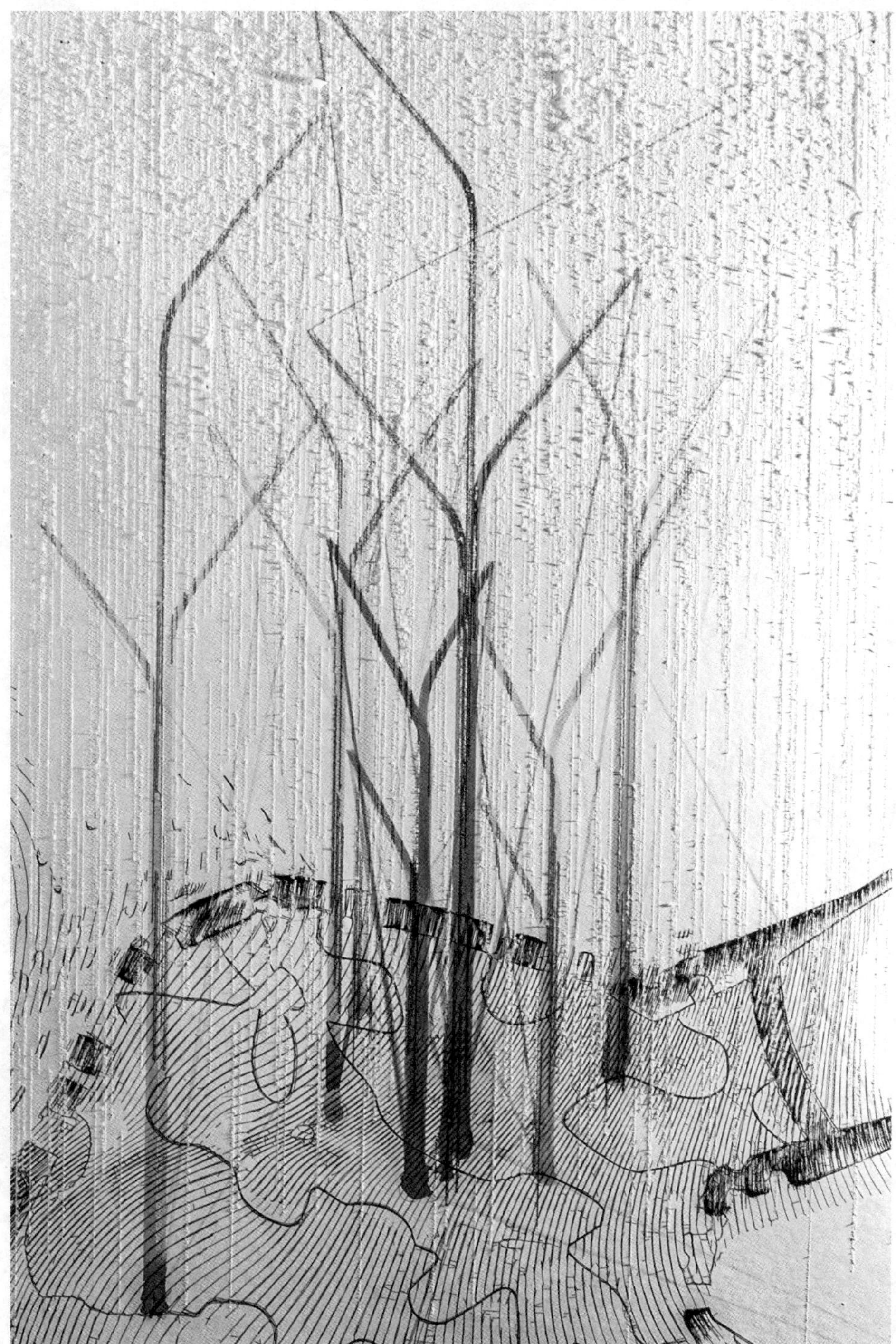

This pen-and-ink drawing, a close-up detail of the previous image, incorporates two disruptive elements. First, the cardstock has been vertically scored and scraped from bottom to top, creating deep imprints. Second, a field of drifting vertical lines emerges from the core of the geode-like section, fading as they rise across the page. Though these treatments might initially seem to be hand-applied, their geometric precision hints again at a potentially machinic process. The juxtaposition of manual and mechanical elements echoes the themes of ambiguity and evolution within the drawing, where something is seen growing out of the original form. The organic lines emphasize a vertical thrust and evoke a sense of transformation: trees have emerged from the original form.

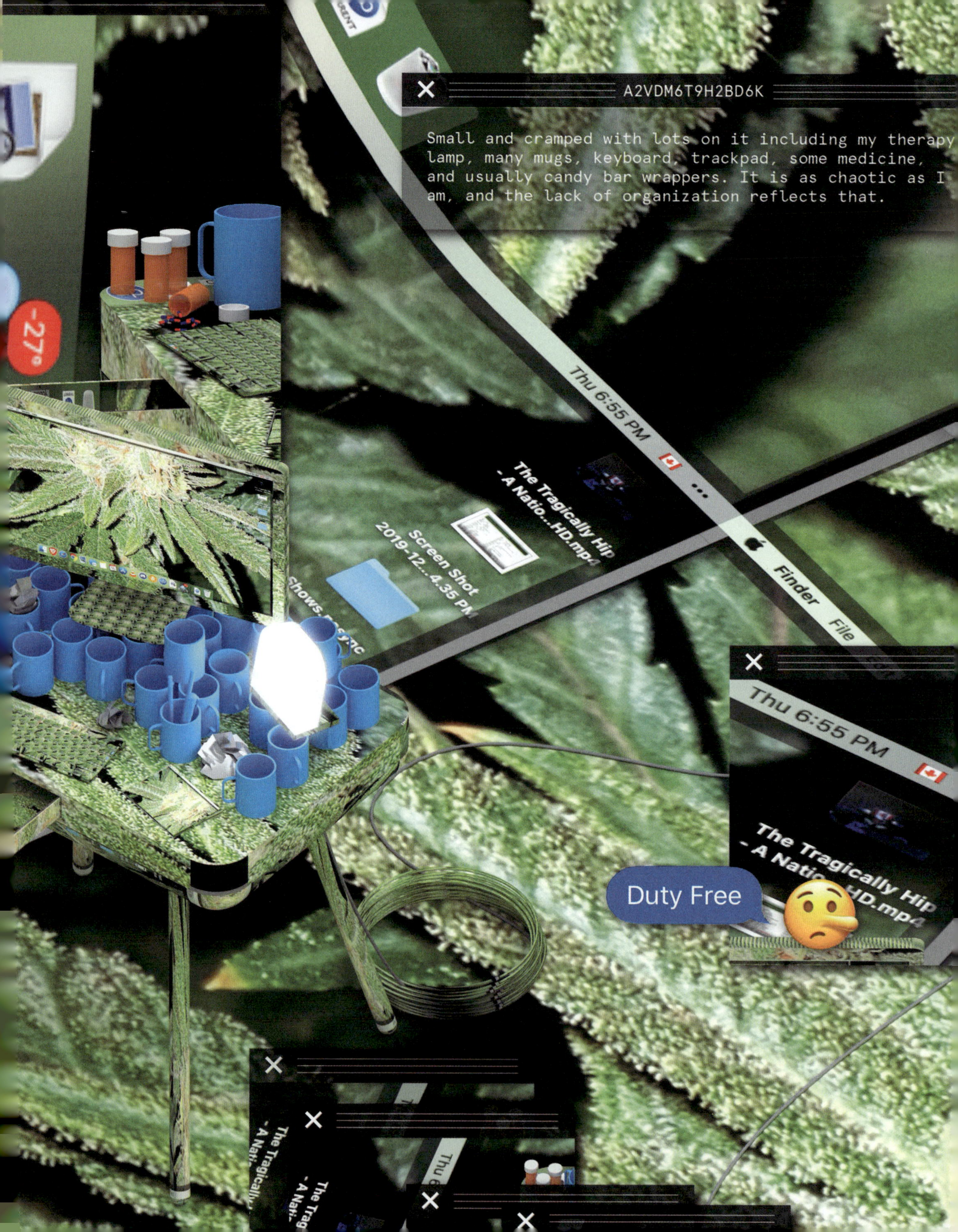
A2VDM6T9H2BD6K
Small and cramped with lots on it including my therapy lamp, many mugs, keyboard, trackpad, some medicine, and usually candy bar wrappers. It is as chaotic as I am, and the lack of organization reflects that.
-27°
Thu 6:55 PM
The Tragically Hip
- A Natio...HD.mp4
Screen Shot
2019-12...4.35 PM
Finder
File
Thu 6:55 PM
The Tragically Hip
Duty Free

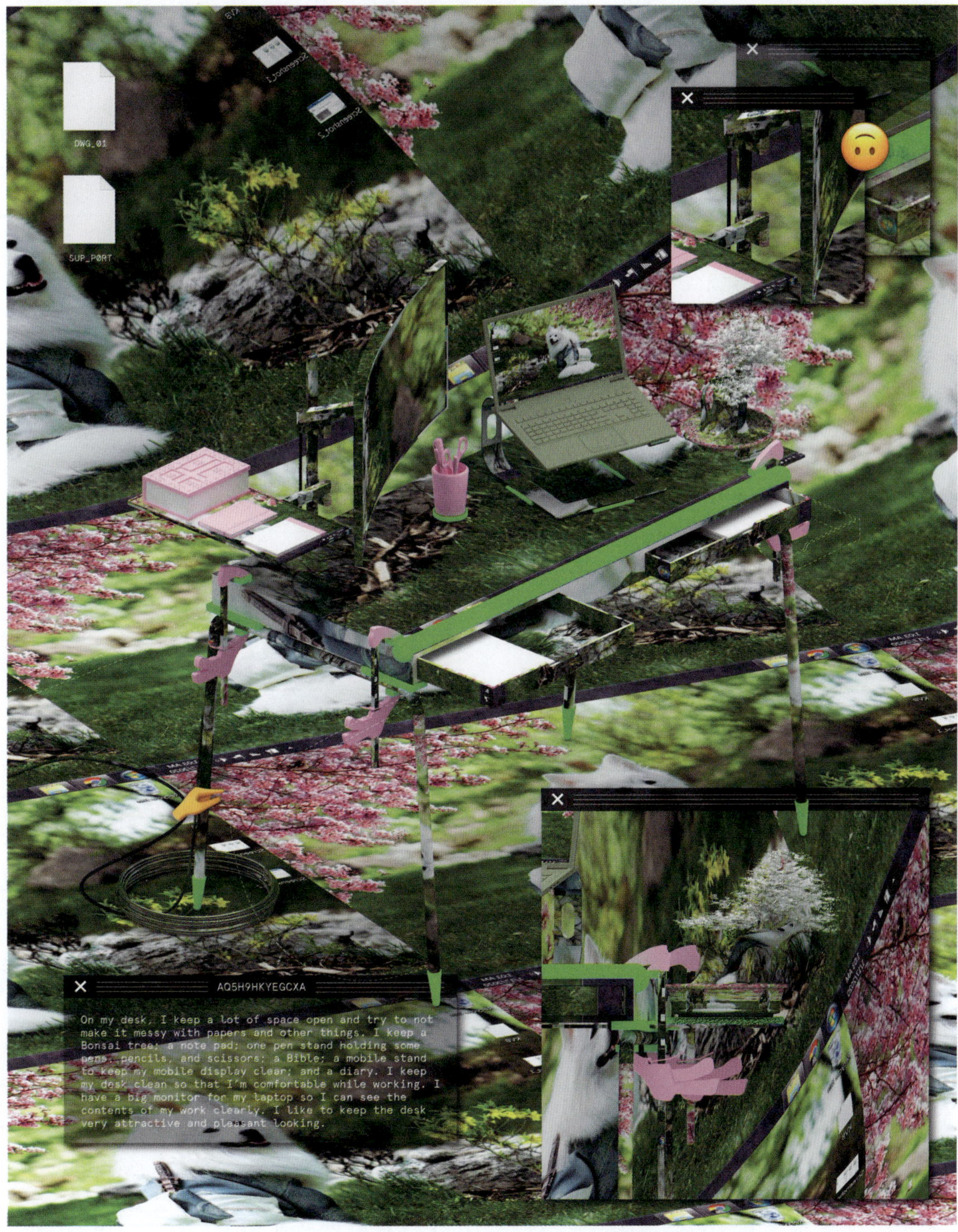

The previous scene of chaotic clutter is replaced by a rendering of calm and order: pens and scissors sit neatly in their designated places, while a pad, a Bible, and a notebook are carefully arranged. The backdrop for the desktop, and for the overall image, is a photo of a dog resting under cherry blossoms. A text file declares, with serene clarity, "I like to keep the desk very attractive and pleasant looking." This glimpse into a creative mind suggests studiousness and responsible virtue. While playful and idealized, this scene, paired with its companion image, perhaps offers a slightly sinister vision of a working life fully engulfed in the realm of the digital.

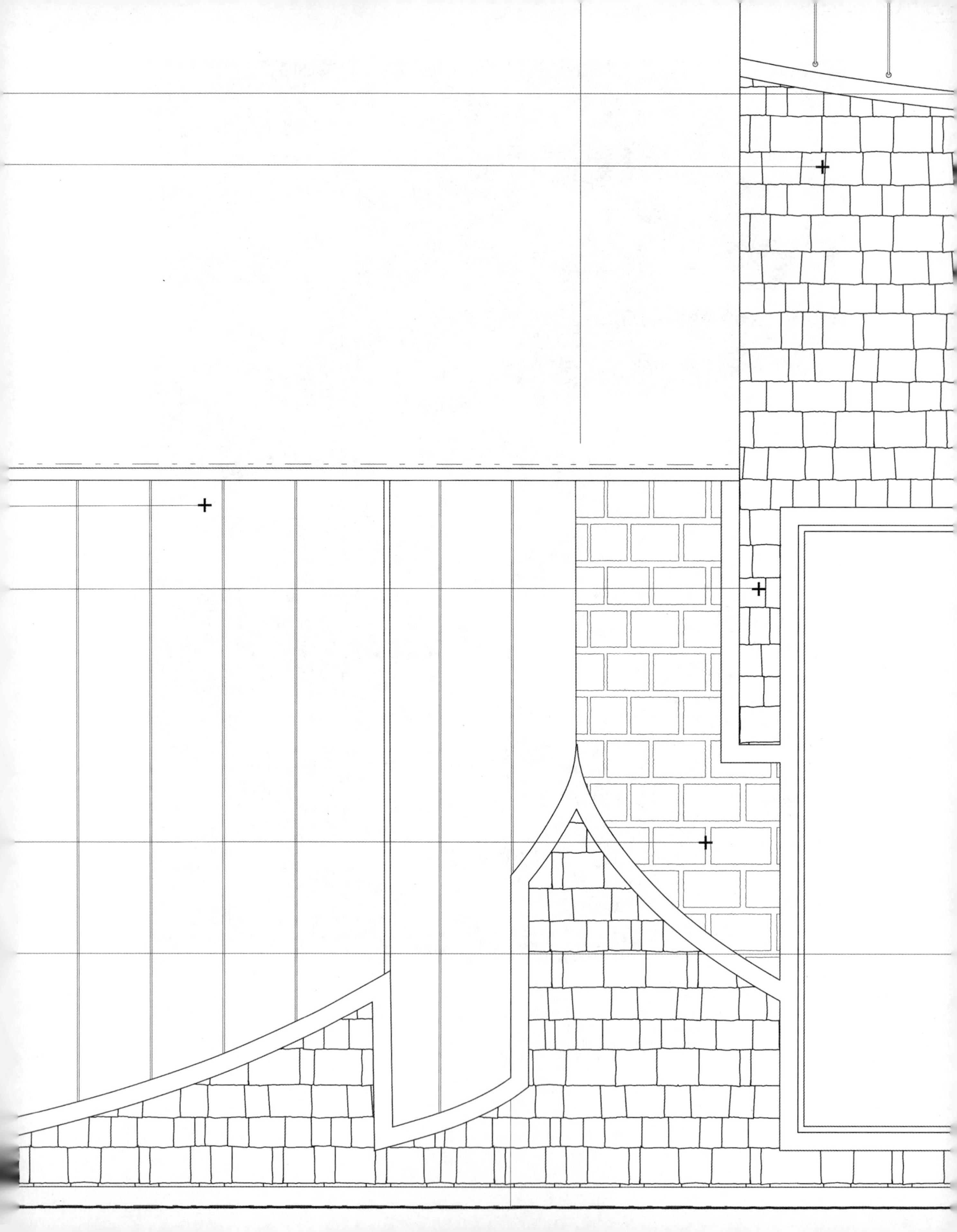

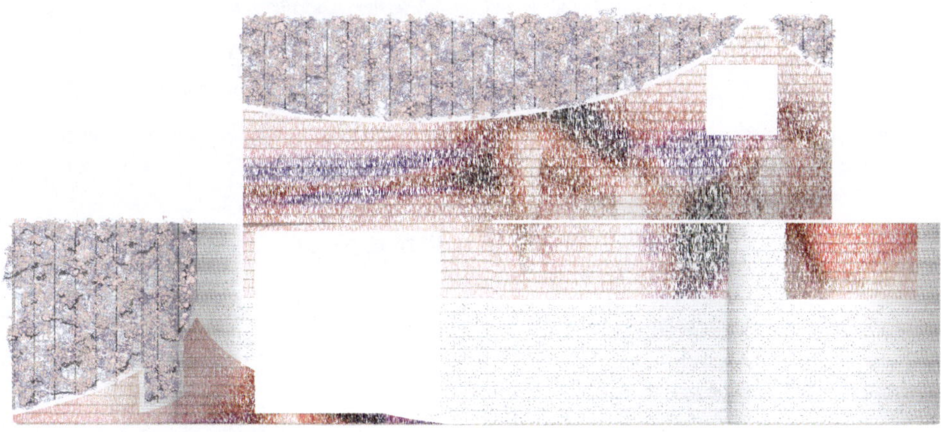

This elevation transforms a conventional construction drawing into a richly layered and textured depiction of life overtaking structure. The upper portion of the wall is adorned with thousands of delicate pink and purple leaves and flowers, overwhelming the orderly confines of architectural drafting. Waves of blue, mauve, tan, and purple sweep across the façade, subtly revealing the underlying shingles through faint horizontal hatch lines. The concrete masonry units are rendered in a smoky, shadowed effect, softening the material's typically stark appearance. Despite the layers of natural and abstract interpretation, the windows remain curiously blank, leaving us to wonder what is being withheld from view. The flatness and sterility usually associated with construction drawings dissolve here, replaced by a sense of depth, volume, and vibrancy. This drawing blurs the line between building and nature, embodying a desire for architecture to become a living, breathing vessel for organic matter.

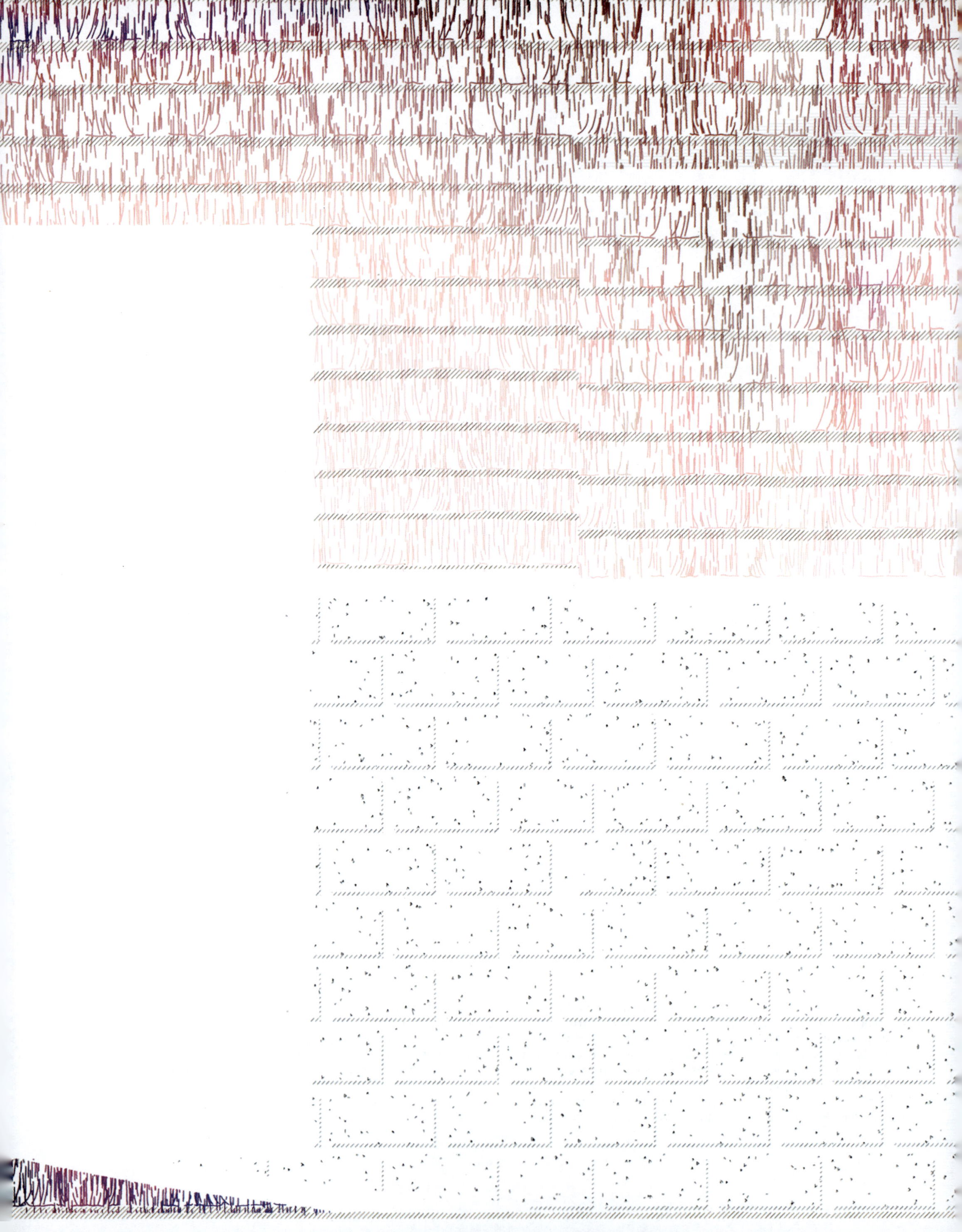

I recently had a conversation with a friend who was perplexed, perhaps to the point of denial, by the miasmic qualities of architecture culture today. With no clear movement to adhere to or push back against, and a general sense that we can all pull references or significance from wherever we please, this friend felt there was nothing projective to tap into or move toward or away from. We are, in short, stuck in the mud. I don't particularly agree with this assessment. On the contrary, this hyper-individuation is, in many ways, exactly the promise that our discipline always gave. It has gelatinized the creative landscape. This is, in my view, a perfect moment to play. To feel unfettered by a clear demarcation of acceptable discourse is to feel the ability to do just about whatever you want. Be improper. Be precarious. Do things incorrectly and know that there never was a correct way to do things to begin with. Drawing is always meant to work this way. A line on a sheet of paper can be whatever you want it to be and whatever you say it is. It is just a line, after all.

Have fun.

All the best,

KH

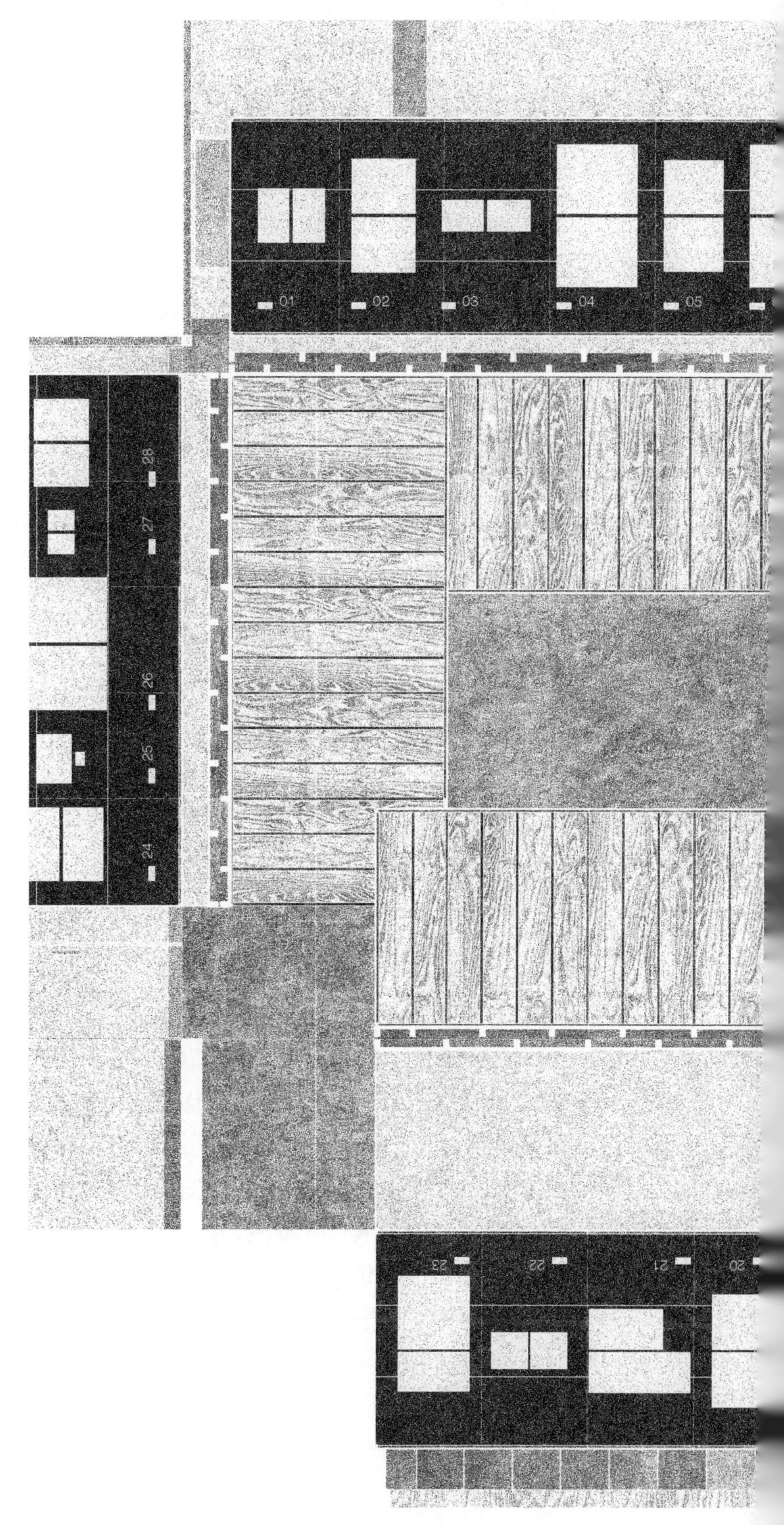
01
02
03
04
05
28
27
26
25
24
23
22
21
20

more indoctrination, more vocational training, imposing a debt which traps students, young people, into a life of conformity."

Perhaps drawing can uniquely position architecture students, to learn independently over their lifetimes and think for themselves. Through drawing, students may ask questions, see things in new ways, challenge dominant forms of production, and resist capitalistic, hegemonic, and entrenched approaches to catalyze new practice models. In this sense, drawing might serve as an antidote to the prevailing sentiment that a college education's purpose is to indoctrinate students into a particular way of doing things, fostering a blind devotion to the mechanistic, profit-driven industry of architecture.

I regularly debate—just last week, in fact, with a fellow academic—whether our role in education is to teach vocational skills (such as using building information modeling (BIM) software, conducting building code research, or writing construction document specifications) or to teach thinking skills. When put this way—vocational versus thinking—virtually everyone says, "Of course, we need to teach students how to think." However, most then qualify this concession by stating: ". . . at the same time, *some* BIM software training, *some* exposure to code analysis, and *some* knowledge of spec writing is important if students want to get a job when they graduate." In other words, while thinking skills are nice, the priority is to produce employable students. We need to begin this indoctrination process, and preferably sooner rather than later.

The antidote to this immense pressure on architectural education may be found in the act of drawing, but not just in its proper, accepted forms. We must privilege drawing in its improper forms—drawing as an act of mischief, resistance, protest, and analysis. The prevailing culture of architectural practice which perpetuates homogeneity in all its forms, will never change if we forget that the real role of education is to teach students to think.

The forms of drawing featured in the original exhibition and now in this book, point to a way out of the rut in which we find ourselves. It won't be easy—resistance never is—but it is precisely in its role as provocateur that education will remain valuable. If education is meant merely to train workers, architecture firms can accomplish this faster, cheaper, and more effectively.

The work here effectively models how the act of drawing can, on one hand, communicate, serve, and produce (the proper drawing in each pairing). On the other hand, it models how drawing can push against a prevailing culture, productively dislodge and discomfort our thinking, offer manifold interpretations and readings of what architecture can mean for humanity, for marginalized voices, for those who typically are not part of the conversation (the improper drawing in each pairing). These drawings emerge from a process that embraces slowness and resists conformity. They are uncomfortable, messy, uncertain, purposefully inefficient, refreshingly unclear, open to interpretation, and decidedly not designed to sell anyone on an idea. Above all, they

BairBalliet is the Los Angeles- and Chicago-based architectural design practice led by Kelly Bair and Kristy Balliet. Kelly is an associate professor at the University of Illinois Chicago. Kristy is on the design faculty at the Southern California Institute for Architecture.

JAJA Co is the Boston-based architectural design practice led by Michelle Chang. Michelle is an assistant professor at Harvard University.

Nat Chard is a Professor of Architecture at The Bartlett School of Architecture.

Medium Office was a Los Angeles- and New York-based architectural design practice led by Alfie Koetter and Emmett Zeifman. Emmett now leads the Palo Alto-based architectural design practice NOUNS and is a member of the faculty at Stanford University. Alfie now leads the Los Angeles-based architectural design practice Loaf.

HouMinn is the Denver- and Vancouver-based architectural design and research practice led by Marc Swackhamer and Blair Satterfield. Marc is a professor at the University of Colorado Denver. Blair is an associate professor at the University of British Columbia.

EXTENTS is the Ann Arbor-based architectural design practice led by Cyrus Peñarroyo and McClain Clutter. Cyrus is an assistant professor at the University of Michigan. McClain is an Associate Professor at the University of Michigan.

Hume Architecture is the Brooklyn-based architectural design practice led by Nathan Hume. Nathan is an associate professor of Practice at the University of Pennsylvania.

Acknowledgments

There are many to thank for helping to bring this book to the world.

My deepest thanks, of course, must go to those who contributed their work, forming the book's content. This book would not have been possible without their thoughtful response to a dutiful and mischievous prompt. Thank you to the many contributors to the book. Without your hard work, this project would of course never been possible.

I want to offer my greatest thanks to Marc Swackhamer for sponsoring this project from its inception, for serving as a sounding board throughout the realization of the book, and for his thoughtful words of encouragement. This book wouldn't have happened without his boundless and consistent support.

Thank you to Anca Matyiku for collaborating with me on the exhibition, which resulted in this cross-section of incredible and diverse work. Your contributions to this book, in many ways, galvanized it. Thank you to Amir Ameri, Sarah Hearne, José Ibarra, Will Koning, Leyuan Li, Alex Yueyan Li, Matt Shea, and Rick Sommerfeld for encouraging me and providing advice in the hallways of the funny old building where we spend so many of our days.

Many thanks to Luke Bulman, for his optimism and efforts to push this project toward completion through many exciting challenges.

I would also offer a profound thanks to Ashley Simone for seeing the promise of this book and shepherding me and it through the publication process. It would not be what it is without your support and clarity in our many conversations.

Thank you to Toby Gardner for being a true partner in editing and clarifying my words and thoughts. I will always enjoy the memories of our many deep and profound conversations. I'll look forward to our future collaborations.

Thank you to Stephanie Santorico, Nan Ellin, Stephanie Kelly, Leo Darnell, and Matt Gines from the University of Colorado, Denver, for helping to facilitate this project.

Thank you to Carolyn Wilson for the late nights, early mornings, and insightful conversations.